THE RISE OF
RADICAL EGALITARIANISM

Aaron Wildavsky

THE AMERICAN UNIVERSITY PRESS

Copyright © 1991 by Aaron Wildavsky
The American University Press
4400 Massachusetts Avenue, N.W.
Anderson Lower Level
Washington, D.C. 20016

Distributed by arrangement with
National Book Network
4720 Boston Way
Lanham, MD 20706

3 Henrietta Street
London WC2E 8LU England

Library of Congress Cataloging-in-Publication Data
Wildavsky, Aaron B.
The rise of radical egalitarianism / Aaron Wildavsky.
p.   cm.
Includes bibliographical references and index.
1. Equality—United States.   2. Individualism—United States.
3. Political culture—United States.   I. Title.
JC575.W55   1991   320.5'3—dc20   91-21893 CIP

ISBN 1-879383-00-4 (pbk., alk. paper)
ISBN 1-879383-01-2 (cloth, alk. paper)

The paper used in this publication meets the minimum requirements of
American National Standard for Information Sciences—Permanence
of Paper for Printed Library Materials, ANSI Z39.48–1984.

Contents

Tables and Figures   vii

Acknowledgments   ix

Preface: The Search for the Oppressed   xi

Introduction: Why Worry?   xxvii

I   Then and Now

1   Who Wants What and Why? A Cultural Theory   3

2   Resolved, That Individualism and Egalitarianism Be Made Compatible in America: Political Cultural Roots of Exceptionalism   29

3   The Internal Transformation of the Major Political Parties: Democratic Activists Are Increasingly Egalitarian, Republicans Individualist and Hierarchical   49

4   Is Egalitarianism Really on the Rise?
with Brendon Swedlow   63

II   The Culture Wars

5   The Three Cultures: Explaining Anomalies in the American Welfare State   101

6   The Media's American Egalitarians   115

7   Theories of Risk Perception: Who Fears
    What and Why?
    with Karl Dake   133

8   The Turtle Theory, Or Why Has the Democratic Party
    Lost Five Out of the Last Six Presidential Elections,
    Yet Retained Strong Control of the House, Won
    Majorities in the Senate, and Kept Three-fifths of
    State Houses and Most Governorships?   151

III   Contra Egalitarianism

9   The Reverse Sequence in Civil Liberties   169

10 A Review of *The New American Dilemma: Liberal
    Democracy and School Desegregation*   181

11 The Crime of Inequality: The Bork Nomination   193

12 Groucho's Law, Or If Anything Americans Can
    Accomplish Isn't Worth Doing, Why Bother Trying to
    Remedy Problems of Race or Poverty or Aging or . . .   213

13 If Inequality Is an Abomination in the Sight of God,
    Why Should There Be Bishops or a Pope?   227

14 The Rise of Radical Egalitarianism and the Fall of
    Academic Standards   233

Notes   243

Index   261

Tables and Figures

TABLES

P.1   Oppressed Minorities in the United States, 1972   xii

3.1   Democratic Delegates to the Left of Rank and File
       and the Public at Large, 1984   59

3.2   Ideology and Policy Preferences, 1984, for Partisan
       Activists and Rank-and-file Party Followers   60

4.1   Differences between Members of Local-intervenor
       and Direct-action Antinuclear Groups   78

4.2   Differences between Styles of Antinuclear Groups   79

6.1   Change in Problem Importance before and after
       Viewing Experimental Newscast   129

FIGURES

P.1   The Growth of the Oppression Gap   xiii

2.1   Model of Cultures in Context   33

3.1   Interparty Differences on Issue Positions among
       Convention Delegates, 1972–1980   51

3.2   Interparty Differences on Group Evaluations among
       Convention Delegates, 1972–1980   52

3.3   Policy Preferences among National Convention
       Delegates, 1984   54

3.4   Preferred Budgetary Allocations among National
       Convention Delegates, 1984   56

3.5   Delegates' Decline in Party Support, 1972–1984   57

6.1   Stages of Media Power   131

10.1   Degrees of Consensus on Busing   189

12.1   Are Institutions Biased?   225

Acknowledgments

This book originated in a series of public lectures I gave at the School of Public Affairs at American University in the winter of 1990. When American University Press asked me to turn these lectures into a book, it became evident that they needed supporting data and concepts. Thus I added both old essays and new ones to undergird and round out the arguments about the rise of radical egalitarianism and its consequences. I wish to thank the dean, Cornelius Kerwin, for his splendid hospitality, the students in my seminar on political cultures for their stimulation, and the audiences at the lectures for their excellent questions.

Preface:

The Search for the Oppressed

My satiric intent should not fool anyone. Life has a way of outperforming our intentions. I begin this book with "The Search for the Oppressed" because it contains my earliest observations and reflections on cultural change. I saw equality rising but I had yet to understand egalitarianism. Now that I understand more, though not enough, I am not so sure it is so funny.

Los Angeles

Presidents of the 19 California state universities and colleges were asked yesterday to be a little more tactful when turning down white male job applicants because of their race and sex. . . .

To prove his point that some applicants are now being badly handled, Keene [Dr. Mansell Keene, vice-chancellor for faculty and staff affairs] enclosed copies of two letters—one from a rejected applicant, the second from a personnel officer on one of the campuses.

The personnel officer wrote, saying that although the department head "saw you as our top candidate, I will not be able to make you an offer. . . ." The letter explained that the affirmative action program seeks employees from "recognized oppressed minority groups."

"Although the department initially viewed your ancestry as satisfying the requirements of affirmative action (he was from the Middle East),

This chapter appeared as an article in *Freedom at Issue,* no. 16 (November/December 1972), pp. 5–16.

consultation with our institutional advisers indicated to us that your
ancestry does not qualify you as an oppressed minority." . . .

He might very well have felt like a member of an oppressed minority
once he got the letter, Keene acknowledged.

San Francisco Chronicle, May 6, 1972, p. 2

Why are there now 374 percent of minorities in the United States of
America? To say that minorities cannot be majorities reveals a woeful
misunderstanding of contemporary American arithmetic. Start with
100 percent consumers, 52 percent women, 20 percent youth, and 20
percent black, Chicanos, Puerto Ricans, and so forth, and you already
have 192 percent. Since it would be tedious to mention all the other
minorities, they are listed in the Table P.1, though it should be recognized that the numbers and percentages are rising so they are likely
soon to be out of date.

The theory explaining and predicting this extraordinary rise in
minorities is both powerful and simple; it belongs in the general class
of economic theories of which it may be said that demand creates its
own supply. The dynamic behind this theory depends on the mutual
reinforcement of twin propellants: The proportion of privileged elites
(defined as people of high formal education and income) has been
increasing at a geometric rate, while the proportion of oppressed

Table P.1   Oppressed Minorities in the United States, 1972

Percentage of the Population	*Minority*
100	Consumers
52	Women
20	Youth
20	Blacks, Chicanos, Puerto Ricans, Indians, etc.
15	Physically, cosmetically handicapped, including obese
6	The unemployed
30	White ethnics (Poles, Italians, Greeks, Irish, etc.)
17	The poor
15	Commuters (they lead lives of quiet desperation)
75	The middle classes (cf. Alinsky)
8	Deviants (homosexuals, lesbians, the happily married)
6	Prisoners
6	Recipients of welfare
4	Other
374	GRAND TOTAL

minorities for them to lead has been decreasing at an arithmetic rate. This "oppression gap"—the constantly decreasing ratio between privileged elites and oppressed minorities—is responsible, as I shall explain presently, for the vast inflation in the value of oppressed minorities that accounts for one of the characteristic conditions of our time: the Oppression Gap.

Figure P.1, a graph showing "The Growth of the Oppression Gap," puts some empirical flesh on the bones of this theory. Though straight lines are rarely found in nature, the exponential growth of available students in places of higher education from 5 percent in 1930 to 20 percent in 1950 to more than 50 percent in 1970 comes as close to a straight line as anyone has a right to expect. The proportions of people

Figure P.1   The Growth of The Oppression Gap

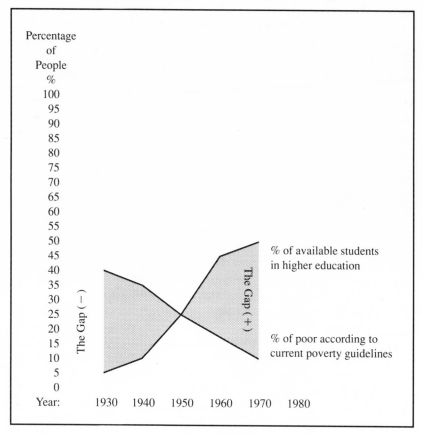

in poverty, using today's official governmental standard of $3,840 for a family of four in constant 1960 dollars, shows a less spectacular yet steady decline from 40 percent in 1930 to 26 percent in 1950 to 17 percent in 1970. The shaded areas between the two lines constitute the Oppression Gap.

Everyone knows that the politics of noblesse oblige has become the preeminent status symbol of our time. No one who is anyone, who wishes to be thought well of by his fellows, can fail to make his contribution. All he needs is an oppressed minority willing to let him help it. This, however, is where the Oppression Gap has caused trouble: As the supply of oppressed minorities was decreasing, the demand for them was increasing. Thus the country was faced with a situation in which oppressed minorities would not have been available for aspiring elites at virtually any price. In economic terms this would be considered a catastrophe; there would be no way to clear the market, thus destroying the economy of elite leadership.

How, then, could supply be increased? Here we must return to the doctrine that demand creates its own supply. The elites creating this demand may be characterized by their high intellectual capacities, their unceasing energy, and their ambition. In a word, they are inventive. Accordingly, through repeated attacks on the problem in the past decade, they have discovered that it is possible to increase the supply by changing the informal rules governing who is entitled to be considered a member of an oppressed minority.

Certification as an Oppressed Minority

It used to be that an oppressed minority was a group that suffered discrimination. Jews, Negroes, and—in an earlier period—the Irish were evident candidates. Under these general rules, it would have been extremely difficult to get the proportion of minorities much beyond the one-third of the nation that Franklin D. Roosevelt described as ill-clothed, ill-fed, and ill-housed. Ingenious demanders have since found a way to increase the supply.

The basic change has been to stop considering each individual as a whole and instead to allow facets of the person to be parceled out among various aspects of oppression. Once that is done it is not difficult to discover that everyone suffers abuse in one way or another. At the same time the idea of oppression has been expanded to include both psychic damage and failure to achieve a hypothetical potential.

The Japanese, who as an ethnic group have the highest income in the nation, may still be said to receive less than they would if they were not discriminated against. The otherwise privileged can be considered a minority to the extent that they are victims of an overall oppressive system. The ultimate in these rule changes is found in the ability of radicals to convince themselves that, despite every conceivable worldly advantage, they suffer worse psychic abuse than anyone.

How much we take all this for granted was brought home to me when, without quite realizing where I was headed, I began thinking about ways in which I personally had been oppressed. Soon, following ineluctably along this train of thought, I discovered myself to be a member of three hitherto undiscovered oppressed minorities. I am, to begin with, a left-handed person who has suffered from this condition—over which I have no control—many times in my life. Left-handed people have more trouble writing clearly and hence have difficulty in making themselves understood when they fill out applications or otherwise try to communicate to others. Brilliant ideas may be lost because others claim they cannot read their writing. Everyone knows that certain jobs in industries are denied to left-handed people. One need only think of the inescapable fact that no left-handed person can become a shortstop or third baseman, and few indeed are fortunate enough to become catchers. Besides, left-handed children are often forced to write and eat and do other things right-handed, which simultaneously oppresses and confuses them. No wonder we lefties are stigmitized as peculiar.

More subtle, perhaps, but oppressive nonetheless is the fact that my name begins with W, which puts me among those unfortunates whose final initials are among the last four in the alphabet. Of us it can be truthfully said that we are the last to be seated in school and the first to suffer from the withholding of books, pencils, and erasers. Many a time I have watched the classroom seats give out before they reached me or have failed to receive a critical piece of supply that, for all I know, may have substantially affected my life chances. Compensatory remedies in the form of policies that distribute benefits from Z to A— rather than the other way around, as is now done in our alphabetically chauvinistic society—are clearly available, but the vested interests of the vast majority have prevented these policies from even being considered by responsible decision makers.

The last form of oppression I experience is the most insidious and also, alas, the most personally painful. It arises from a cultural stereotype so deeply rooted in the American character that no one heretofore

has been able to verbalize it (though a significant minority have daily
been abused by it). There is a virtually ineradicable bias in American
life against talkative people. Heroes in the movies—one notices—are
always strong, silent types. Their virtue is equated with how little they
say compared to how much they do. The man* who trades on words,
however, is always suspected of being a hypocrite or, worse still, a
weakling whose words belie (or are an anemic substitute for) his deeds.
Still waters run deep, they say. From this we know that shallow waters
burble incessantly. There is a growing awareness in America that
females have been discriminated against by the fact that they have had
to repress their true natures in order not to appear smarter than the
boys they wished to date. How much more true this is (and how little
recognized) of those of us who love to talk and must constantly squelch
the very nature of our innermost beings lest we be thought of as weak
and insubstantial and (perish the thought) wordy.

I can document the existence of all these minorities by mentioning a
speech in which Ronald Dellums, the congressman for Berkeley,
California, verbalized his own growing realization of them thusly:
"There are black niggers, brown niggers, red niggers, yellow niggers,
women niggers, long-haired niggers, old niggers. The overwhelming
majority of the people in America today are niggers [defined as] anyone
who is not part of the power structure of the nation and faces discrimination of any type" (Oakland *Tribune,* March 19, 1972, p. 1).

Now I do not mean to suggest that there is a conspiracy afoot to
increase unfairly the proportion of oppressed minorities beyond all
reasonable bounds. Quite the contrary. There is absolutely no central
direction, no guiding hand, no hierarchical authority issuing orders
that are obeyed. The situation is very much like the decentralized
decision making described by Michael Polanyi in his seminal work on
science. Motivated by an insatiable desire to gain new knowledge and
to be rewarded by publishing it first, scientists around the world are
busy trying to make discoveries. By reading journals and from informal
contacts they come to guess the fields that are most fruitful and which
endeavors will receive the most praise. No one tells them what to do;
yet they coordinate their efforts—that is, take each other into account—because it is in their mutual interest to know what others are
doing and to act accordingly. Similarly, there are innumerable Americans with elite characteristics who, in our day, believe that status
stems from the ability to improve the lot of those they define as

---

*[This was before one had to say "person."]

underprivileged. This can be done only by discovering an underprivileged group that will allow the elite member to do something for it. But the old-time minorities are well populated with elites who have established a claim to have done (or who are trying to do) something for them. The best, the most efficient, the cheapest way of gaining reward, therefore, is to find a hitherto undiscovered oppressed minority and do something for (or to) it before anyone else does.

The casual, almost incidental, manner through which members of the privileged elite coordinate their activities emerges nicely from a recent account of the move toward social criticism among those who write for the famous *New Yorker* magazine. Headlined "NEW POLITICS NEW *NEW YORKER*," the report (*Time* [May 1, 1972], pp. 34–35) observed that the magazine, which had long "seemed almost immune to dramatic change," now "vibrates in tones of tough liberalism and occasionally radical outrage," and "that the *New Yorker* is today one of the most socially activist and politically polemical among major magazines." Although "the change coincided with some of the roughest [financial] weather the *New Yorker* had ever encountered" and "outsiders naturally assumed that [editor William] Shawn's response to adversity was new politics for the *New Yorker*—an impression strengthened by an advertising campaign that emphasized the stinging prose . . . Shawn and his staff insist that there was no connection. They felt no pressure." They agree that "the real reason for the *New Yorker*'s political preoccupation lies in the subtle relation between them"—that is, Shawn and his staff. The magazine has hardly any "hierarchical structure." While the editor approves everything that is published, seldom does he tell anyone what to write about or when to write it. Rather, he picks and chooses among the items suggested or submitted by the staff writers. The pieces come out with the same critical political slant not by direction from on high, but by opinion way below—opinion that just happens to be compatible with those above. "The altered tone and emphasis have come" (*Time* concludes with a quote, apparently from Shawn) "not because of a deliberate or calculated change in policy, but simply because certain authors responding to the heightened sense of trouble at the end of the 60's and since . . . have become interested in saying certain things, and we, the editors, are sympathetic."*

---

*Illustrations are taken from whatever I happened to be reading when this essay was written—proof, I trust, of the ubiquity of the evidence presented herein. Any theory of society should be tested by reading the next day's newspapers.

If the market for one's services could be described precisely as a "sense of trouble" then one might just have an interest in heightening it to increase business. There is no need for outside pressure because enough comes from inside. Nor would a personal interest necessarily appear in naked form when all one's friends feel the same way and they appear to have their moral clothes on. Creating the demand to supply your own product—a nice literary equivalent of the protection racket—has an ancient lineage in the history of humankind. The ancient warning was also there, but no one remembered: "Once you pay the Danegeld, you never get rid of the Dane."

It stands to reason that oppressed minorities do not proliferate in a just society. To justify its aspirations for leadership, therefore, the privileged elite has a vested interest in crying (that society is) foul. The need to rationalize the position explains an otherwise incredible phenomenon: Injustice in America grows apparently in direct proportion to efforts to alleviate it—an insight more appropriate to conservative market theorists (however disguised) like Jay Forrester and Edward Banfield than to radical social critics. The direct implication of this line of argument, after all, is that citizens should urge government to stop tampering with economic and social forces. Unless, of course, one is suggesting revival of the ancient heresy known as "sinning to increase virtue" by generating more evil for good men to overcome. In favor of the general proposition, it may be said that there is a sense in which every act to remedy past injustice creates future injustices for those who do not get special treatment.

By this time the reader should have taken the hint: There may be no theoretical limit on the number of minorities who are deemed oppressed—that is, treated unequally. "Equality" has been called the graveyard of political theorists. One of the many meanings of that infinitely elusive term is that people should be treated as they deserve. Our friends deserve special treatment by virtue of the fact that they stand in a closer relationship to us. Equal treatment to all those standing equally close to us therefore requires unequal treatment in more general terms and is in that context incompatible with another version of equality. It is difficult to imagine any set of conditions in which people could be considered equal in *all* respects. Thus the most deeply rooted ideas can be turned upside down with a little imagination. In my youth, for example, the idea of quotas for employment or for admission to universities was anathema. Nothing seemed more discriminatory than taking in or rejecting people on the basis of who they were rather than on what they could do. Now quotas have become the way in which governments and private organizations attempt to compensate for past injustices. Equality of opportunity conflicts with the desire to achieve equality of result. Thus we arrive at the point where people must be treated unequally in order to achieve "equality."

The Making of Minorityness

There is no social equivalent to the physical expression "half-life" when it comes to minorities; the quantity of "minorityness" never decays, being possibly the only known instance of perpetual motion—unless it may be more properly compared to breeder reactors, which produce more fuel than they consume. The beauty of the search for the oppressed is that it generates its own growth: The more minorities one finds, the more there turn out to be, for the discovery of oppressed-minorities (the two words uttered in the same breath, linked as if they were one) is invariably followed by efforts to compensate the victims in the form of special treatment. By multiplying the disadvantaged advantaged until they outnumber the advantaged disadvantaged, the formerly privileged (the advantaged disadvantaged) approach the status of the presently underprivileged (the disadvantaged advantaged), thereby becoming yet another oppressed-minority.

This is one way to get to the stage, as when "AGITATOR ALINSKY ADVISES MIDDLE CLASS TO ORGANIZE" (San Francisco *Chronicle,* April 25, 1972, p. 6). Speaking on "the middle class revolt" at the posh Jack Tar Hotel, the late Saul Alinsky* correctly noted that around three-quarters of the people in America are middle class, "not only economically, but in terms of life styles, ways of thinking and goals." Among these, Alinsky found the lower middle class ("the guys making under $10,000 or $11,000 a year") to be "disenfranchised" the most. "They feel absolutely lost, defeated and frustrated. They're the ones paying the taxes for advantages they don't enjoy themselves. They hoped to retire on Social Security, but inflation has wiped out its value. Everything they believed in is being wiped out. On top of it all they're being stigmatized as the racists, bigots and ignoramuses of our society." Organization is essential for the middle classes, Alinsky concluded, because "once they do get together they stop feeling alone and powerless and are ready to get moving." Note that the words are the

---

*[Alinsky died on June 12, 1972.]

same—"revolt," "disenfranchised," "frustrated," "defeated," "racists," "bigots," "stigmatized," "alone," and "powerless"—only the
target groups for minority status have been altered. Just a few years
(or was it weeks?) ago, similar themes were urged on behalf of blacks,
Chicanos, the poor. But America is still the land of opportunity, and
now everyone (the three-fourths of the population to which Alinsky
referred) can enjoy being a recognized oppressed-minority. The trouble
is that if everyone is one then no one is, so some have to be left out.

Decertification (Or in This Case, Disestablishment) of Oppressed Minorities: The Jews

There can be too much of a good thing. There must be some limit to
the proportion of oppressed minorities—for if there were no limits,
inflation would run rampant and the value of that commodity would be
entirely debased. So, knowing where to look, it is not surprising to
discover that there are informal procedures for "de-minoritizing" or
"de-oppressing" groups whose inclusion had heretofore been taken
for granted. The classic case of our time concerns another group to
which I belong: namely, Jews. The current tension between Jews and
blacks refers largely to an important event that, because it did not take
place at a specific time and was not announced, has escaped attention.
I refer to the indubitable fact—first—that sometime in the mid-1960s
blacks replaced Jews as the nation's number-one oppressed minority
and—second—that, toward the end of that decade, white radicals
succeeded in having Jews removed from the parlance of left critics of
society as a "minority," despite the fact that they constituted no more
than 3 percent of the population and were still undoubtedly subject to
minor forms of discrimination in banking, business, social life, politics,
and elsewhere. It took Christians 1,000 years to go from oppressed
minority to inquisitorial majority; those clever Jews seem to have done
it practically overnight. Let us investigate this strange case further.

During the 1920s and 1930s, Jews—not entirely without reason—
were recognized as one of the nation's oppressed minorities. Quotas
aimed to keep them out of college, discrimination out of work, and
voter prejudice out of public life. The 1950s, by contrast, was the
golden era of American Jewry, which still enjoyed its leading minority
status even though it had become, by and large, affluent instead of
deprived. Think of it: the luxurious deprived enjoying economic wealth

and a kind of social status. How did you do it all, the incredulous would ask, under these grave and continuing handicaps? What glory!

But on some as yet undetermined date in the mid-1960s (probably in the Hebrew calendar on Tishah-b'Ab, the sorriest day in Jewish history, when the First and Second Temples in Jerusalem were destroyed and tragedies too numerous to mention occurred) blacks replaced Jews as the nation's most publicized despised minority. Yet there was this consolation: Jews were still a minority, weren't they, even if they could not be number one? But no, it was not to be. This time round it was not blacks, who were too busy for ancient history, but radical whites—including Jews—who administered the coup-de-grace without so much as a by-your-leave. Without the fanfare of a public announcement or the solemn cadence of a decent burial, Jews no longer were spoken of as a minority, deprived, despised, downtrodden, or whatever. Just like that.

Really, it was a case of mistaken identity: Jews were all of a sudden taken for imperialists. Actually, it was more like guilt by association. Jews, you see, were identified with Israel, which was defeating Arabs, who resorted to guerrilla warfare, however inefficacious, which somehow gave them membership in the Third World, so that Israel *ipso facto* became an imperialist oppressor, and domestic Jews ceased being a minority. *Acta est fabula.*

Then there was also the unfortunate Jewish complicity in the crimes against black people. No, worse, because a real oppressor is out in the open and has the courage of his convictions, while a false friend (well, alright, an ineffectual one) is insidious. Were not Jews getting their kicks at the expense of blacks in contributing paltry sums to such things as the NAACP Legal Defense Fund by which they bought leadership positions, thus insulting black manhood? The objective purpose served by Jews as a minority was clearly to reconcile the oppressed to their condition. Even then they played a counterrevolutionary part. Only the most reactionary among them wondered how, while their forefathers were being pursued by kaiser and czar, they somehow were deserving guilt in America.

Aside from the return of a familiar historical figure—the Jewish anti-Semite—the withdrawal of minority status revealed the existence of a hidden talent for cost–benefit analyses. What was lost by leaving Jews out? Some would work harder than ever to show they really belonged. Others would give more as a reflex action to buy off attack. Besides, the few irreconcilables were worth the price. A club to which everybody belonged is not exclusive enough; some groups had to be kept out. Jews were the least sizable and the most masochistic.

Just as there are middle- as well as lower-class blacks, there are also poor Jews—a fact not lost on those who make a last-ditch effort to retain minority status for their religious compatriots. Like the case of the poor fellow who drowned in a pool the average depth of which was one inch, averages are misleading when they hide wide variations around the mean. These structures apply with extra force to religious or racial groups who, unlike the poor or the lower classes, must span a wide range of types. Thus, after a story had appeared in *Time* showing off the (average) financial success of Jews, an interested person—the executive director of the Association of Jewish Anti-Poverty Workers—wrote in (May 1, 1972, p. 5) to offer other revealing statistics. "Would you believe that Jews form the third largest poverty group in New York City, right after blacks and Puerto Ricans? Would you believe that there are some 300,000 Jews in New York City and approximately 900,000 nationwide who subsist at incomes below or near the federal poverty index?" The writer, S. Elly Rosen—which sounds like a Jewish name—then makes a point that could almost be considered Talmudic did it not fit perfectly with the spirit of the times. Only in our America would a member of a highly affluent group earnestly submit that the poor Jew's lot is worse than anyone else's, for "no one is poorer than the poor who is deemed to be rich."

GOG as History

Various features of the post–World War II period are made explicable by viewing the Growth of the Oppression Gap (GOG) as a major determinant of social cohesion and conflict. Take the Eisenhower years. Why do they now, in retrospect, appear so calm, so unruffled, so full of consensus? The answer cannot be that there was less oppression then than now. The proportion of poor in Ike's first term was far greater than it is now. Surely the fact that racism was kept under wraps does not mean there was greater respect among the races, nor would anyone be inclined to say that the Eisenhower administration undertook bold or extensive measures to increase social justice. No, the Eisenhower era appears to be one of good feelings because the supply of oppressed minorities and the demand for them by elites was at, or close to, the equilibrium point during the mid-1950s. The minorities recognized as oppressed (and by this time it is clear that minority status is at least partly a state of mind or a social rather than scientific judgment) were sufficient to absorb the energies of the elites who could lead them. The oppressed could find aspiring leaders, and the elites could locate willing minorities. Supply and demand had met. GOG was at rest.

Today there is a feeling that elites in the past had been lacking in courage. Why, we may ask, did so few elites in preceding decades engage in battles to help the oppressed? Why did the demand for their services exceed the supply? Why—if I may be permitted to depart from the usual dull statistical terminology—was GOG angry?

Now, I never said that equilibrium is socially desirable, or that disequilibrium is bad, or—indeed—that I might not prefer one kind of imbalance to another. The point here is that all these conditions have consequences, and we may be able to gain some insight by paying attention to them. When the oppression gap is unbalanced in the direction of recognized oppressed minorities, that condition signifies elites are unwilling to meet the demand for their services. The obvious economic explanation is that at those times minorities cannot afford to pay enough. The palpable risks are too great for the potential rewards. And so they were, before the 1950s. Jews lacked money, blacks lacked organization, and the poor lacked identity. The oppressed couldn't give what they didn't have. Elites couldn't get what wasn't there.

When people are truly oppressed, not only are they deprived materially, but their cause is considered reprehensible. Opprobrium is attached to their defense. The cards are stacked against them so the prospect of success is low and of vilification high. Who would stick up for the downtrodden under these conditions? Only a small segment of the upper, upper crust—those who had the economic wealth and the social status to withstand constant adversity, as well as some family tradition of engaging in uplift—might try. From this strain came the Roosevelts, the Harrimans, and the Rockefellers. Their commitment to basic social change was, of course, limited by the nature of the transaction. "Please help us," cried the oppressed. "We will help you," ran the implicit bargain struck by the elites, then in short supply, "if you moderate your demands and promise to be good. You must also wait in line because the temporarily disadvantaged middle classes have fallen on hard times and you will have difficulty being heard above their din. Perhaps, in doing things for them, some of the benefits will trickle down to you." With no saviors in sight, and something being better than nothing, this tacit bargain was struck.

Things are different now. The most pressing economic difficulties of the middle and working classes have been alleviated, enabling the voices of oppressed minorities to be heard and releasing energies previously occupied by the need to make a living. As elites have grown in size, their confidence has increased along with peer-group reinforcement. Punitive actions against them for supporting unpopular minorities have been much diminished, perhaps because these minorities are no longer, in fact, so very unpopular. Simultaneously the incentives in terms of social esteem, control over others, lucrative jobs, consultantships, speaking fees, and the like have become far more attractive. For activity advertised on behalf of the least fortunate, the risks have decreased and the rewards have increased.

Developments in the past 30 years can also be traced to different stages in the widening oppression gap. In the beginning GOG opened up enough to encourage action but not sufficiently to assure safety. These were indeed stirring times. During the heyday of the civil rights movement in the early 1960s, the recognized oppressed minorities were so far down that it was all the privileged elites could do to help raise them up. The early promise of these efforts—punctuated by a major Civil Rights Act and the inauguration of poverty programs—encouraged the elites to redouble their efforts and swelled their ranks, while the condition of the deprived was slowly but surely improving. Before they knew it, however, the oppression gap yawned ever wider and the elites had oversupplied themselves. A few dropped out altogether as they were unceremoniously booted by black organizations. Diverted, but not thwarted, the privileged elites—finding their supply exceeded the demand—made the best arrangements they could to keep up the price for their services. Where they were unable to ferret out, as it were, groups whose oppressed condition had somehow escaped public notice, they agreed to speak only when spoken to. Like all good experts they would be on tap—not on top—mere hirelings, birds of passage waiting anxiously for the day the rightful owners would return to reclaim the mansion, that storehouse of past sufferings upon whose failed aspirations the new society would one day arise. To legitimize their presence, the professionals among the elites developed new doctrines, like "advocacy planning," that purported to justify taking money from the poor—for their own good, to be sure, as they had previously done for the rich.

GOG as Future

It might be misleading and it would certainly be presumptuous to credit the oppression gap with causing what we all experience as "the permissive society." It would be wrong to blame all evil on GOG. People have certainly wanted to curse, fornicate, and blaspheme long before our educated elites found themselves with too much time on their hands and too few underprivileged to lay them on. Yet, if these parallel developments are coincidental, they are certainly pretty damn convenient. For if everything is allowed and nothing is prohibited, the old-fashioned distinction between majority and minority is surely going to break down. In olden times, the majority was the depository of community values and the minorities were deviants. Since there are no longer supposed to be values because all behavior is permitted, there can be no discernible departure from them. Everyone becomes a minority—that is, a person whose norms are not shared by others.

Once upon a time a champion of the despised expected to (and often did) pay a heavy price. He might be excommunicated from church, expelled from clubs, and denied the means of earning a livelihood. Around those who survived, there naturally grew up an aura of heroism. He or she might even be the object of envy, so long as it could safely remain secret. In our time the whole idea is ludicrous. The person who finds a hitherto unknown oppressed minority wins a prize of inestimable worth—not an albatross, but a medal, now hangs around her (or is it his?) neck.

Again we have arrived at the point of being able to explain a frequently observed but still puzzling series of events: the almost compulsive urge to cry suppression in the midst of the most licentious period in the past several hundred years. Acknowledgment of unfettered liberty would call attention to the fact that society has no nos. Like the lady who yells "monster in the sky" when her bloomers fall to the ground, someone is trying to divert our attention. But when she keeps saying it, we may begin to suspect that, at bottom, she is calling attention to herself. We look down instead of up. As all eyes focus on her self-induced plight, the oppressed become monsters in the sky— distant objects whose very existence is rendered suspect. They are everywhere and nowhere. If all are oppressed, none are, no man more than any other.

A supreme irony has taken from the deprived their last possession: their status as an oppressed minority. What avowed enemies could not do, professed friends have done. The oppressed have been robbed in broad daylight, but nobody notices because the thief is so well dressed. He escapes into a sideshow; and who, if life has become a circus, is to tell him apart from the other freaks?

The disease of bureaucracy is substituting the needs of the organizations for the people they are supposed to help. Elites have accomplished the same feat by displacing the goals of the oppressed with their own wants. But don't worry; it's alright. They're used to it.

The End

Super: What [gesturing vaguely] is to be done?
Ego: Not much.
Super: We can't stand (and look at) GOG.
Ego: We do.
Super: Well, it may be your bag but it's not my GOG.
Ego: Wasn't it Vladimir who said "There's man for you, blaming on his boots the faults of his feet"?
Super: You're right. What's left?
Ego: Only laughter.
Super: Is that all?
Ego: Everything.
Super: Smile when you say that, pardner.

Introduction:

Why Worry?

A headline reads that the United States has won the Cold War. The Cold War is over and we have won. So why aren't we happy? Perhaps you have observed that there has not been a great outpouring of national sentiment crying hurrah, our troubles are over. On the contrary, there seems to be some sense of foreboding that our troubles are just beginning. I think that's right. The Cold War is over in Europe, but it's just beginning in America.

Not long ago I met a distinguished scholar who told me how impressed he was that in one country after another around the world, socialistic ways were giving way to capitalistic ways. Even old-line social democratic and socialist parties were moving in a more capitalist direction. He gave as examples very good ones: New Zealand where the Labour party is privatizing everything in sight, almost as much as in Australia; and Sweden where marginal tax rates (the supply-side solution) are being systematically reduced. Somehow I thought to ask, "Can we think of any place where they are moving in the other direction?" And we looked at each other and said, together, "Yes, here, in the United States of America." That is something that requires some explanation.

It is not easy to get people to pay attention to what is right under their noses. Their familiarity with the facts persuades them not that they know it all, but rather that what is familiar to them cannot be new. They know that the Democratic party has changed but not that much. It is, after all, the liberal party. They know that liberalism American-style has altered its meaning, but not all that much. Democrats, after all, are still the party of social welfare. Now that has also

changed from programs based on universalistic criteria, such as income
and age, to particularistic concerns, such as race and gender. True, the
Democrats used to be the party of strong defense—John F. Kennedy
campaigned on that theme in 1960—and law and order. Come to think
of it, law and order, let alone prayer in the schools, had not yet been
national issues in Kennedy's time, the early 1960s, partly because
there had not yet been a pandemic of crime or, in regard to prayer, a
Supreme Court decision to the contrary, but mostly because it was
impossible to imagine any party that hoped to govern taking a position
against prayer or for crime or criminals. That the party of Franklin D.
Roosevelt and Harry S. Truman gave patriotism, law and order, and
defense to the opposition is astounding, but true.

How could this happen? Democrats must have seen something in
common between the issues they kept, like social welfare, and the new
issues they adopted, like prisoners' rights, as well as in the old
positions they abandoned. That common factor, I contend, is egalitarianism—the belief in the moral virtue of diminishing differences among
people of varying incomes, genders, races, sexual preferences, and
(especially) power. A strong preference for equalizing measures also
gives a certain consistency to reducing defense expenditure in order to
make room for welfare and to blaming the system for producing
criminals. Of course, no one favors crime. But which situation aggra-
vates the observer the most: the harm done by the criminal, or the
unfair treatment meted out to criminals who are darker-skinned and
poorer or otherwise more victimized than their victims?

Nor are we lacking astonishing stories about internal transformations
within the Republican party. How did the party of Abraham Lincoln
lose a good 80 percent of the black vote? How did the party that once
came out for the equal rights amendment find itself not only in
opposition to that piece of policy, but also somehow pegged as being
against "women's rights" in general?

Imagine that the hierarchical propensities of Republicans, which
they inherited from their Whig party forebears, had been reinforced.
Then the role of women would be stereotypified as helpmates, not as
executives. Imagine that these hierarchically inclined Republicans
were joined by individualists of the more pronounced form: Self-help
is the only moral help; self-regulation is the only moral regulation.
Then why should poor people or black people or women receive
preferment?

But why use these peculiar cultural designations when party names
or good old liberal and conservative are best? Why, one might have to

think through different categories of thought or, worse still, think differently. In this respect, radical and reactionary alike are defenders of the conceptual status quo with which they grew up. Yet, as I will show, left/right and conservative/liberal leave out important parts of political reality, especially in the division between social and economic conservatives, a division that is neatly encompassed by the cultural categories of hierarchy and individualism.

In my experience, individualists are most willing to fess up to their culture. The term "individualist" still has a favorable connotation of doing your own thing, not being bossed by anyone. Connotations of greed and selfishness, however, have become stronger. (In the future, I suspect that the expression "corporate greed" will be written as a single word, because the inequality that individualism promotes is morally unacceptable to egalitarians.) Whereas there may actually have been greater approval of individualism in the 1950s, moreover, there were fewer principled defenders. Nowadays, individualists are much more aggressive defenders of their preferred way of life than they used to be, perhaps because they face stronger opposition.

Egalitarians, by and large, do not show their colors. Fearful of being accused of vulgar radicalism (i.e., of desiring to level incomes), they tend to portray themselves, at least in my observation, as staunch believers in diversity—protectors, one might say, of endangered human species. Given any array of differences, however, they are likely to desire to diminish them. Thus one has the spectacle of academic institutions making much ado about increasing the gender and racial diversity of their faculties while actually increasing the uniformity of opinion about the subjects their new professors teach. For almost all the people hired under this principle have similar left-liberal egalitarian political opinions.

Hierarchists are least likely to admit to their cultural leanings, for they know these are reviled. The very idea that different people fit into different places in society, that there is a natural or divinely inspired structure of statuses that composes the good society, is considered laughable. Only among Mormons, Protestant fundamentalists, and Orthodox Jews do I hear overt approval of social differentiation, and that only with the knowledge that these beliefs and practices will be ridiculed on radio and television and in private. The very same people who make a fetish of spotted owls dismiss the religious as superstitious. The weakness of hierarchy in the United States at the end of the twentieth century—when you call "the establishment" no one answers—is one of its notable conditions.

My theme is cultural change. Once upon a time, the individualist and egalitarian alliance against hierarchy made the United States different than other countries. Now hierarchy is weaker still. But egalitarianism has grown much stronger than it has been since the days just before the Civil War, while individualism still remains strong. So what? In the past, when egalitarianism grew strong in our country, it was modified by the need to work with individualists and by the existence of a hierarchical party—first, after the Revolution, the Federalists; and then, in reaction to the president they called "King" Andrew (Jackson), the Whigs. After the Civil War both major parties were establishment alliances of individualists and hierarchists. Now, in our time, egalitarians have become disaffected with individualism because of fears that, unlike in earlier times, more equal opportunity may not lead to more equal results. Nor are hierarchists powerful enough, as they are in Scandinavia, to impose strong limits on egalitarians. Thus it is possible that both individualists and egalitarians will frighten each other into becoming more extreme, with hierarchists (like George Bush) too weak to enforce compromise.

The action–reaction syndrome can be crushing. Witness the Bork affair. (See Chapter 11.) Bork was brought down by converting policy differences into immoral behavior. His opponents rummaged his distant past for intellectual instances thought to be discrediting in the present. This moralizing of policy differences has led to the appointment of as neutral or neuter a person as possible—that is to say, Judge David H. Souter. Those who make public discourse—thereby risking wrong—are castigated for being out of the mainstream and cannot be considered, while those who keep their thoughts to themselves are the only candidates. Surely, over time, this syndrome will weaken the quality of both public discussion and political representation.

My concerns about the consequences of a rising radical egalitarianism are sprinkled throughout the following chapters. To avoid unnecessary suspense, I believe that rising egalitarianism will lower our standard of living, decrease our health,[1] debase public discourse, lower the quality of public officials, weaken democracy, make people more suspicious of one another, and (if it be possible) worse. Worse is the constant denigration of American life—our polity, economy, and society—with no viable alternative to take its place.

Why has this tendency to make sows' ears out of silk purses become ever-stronger since the mid-1960s? Lots of people feel that the quality of our public life has changed. But they can't put their finger on it. In the chapters to come I have tried to sum up the difference in a single phrase: the rise of radical egalitarianism. The decline of the alliance between egalitarians and individualists that once made this country different is now putting us through the shock therapy of becoming more like the ideologically divisive democracies of Europe.

Why am I worried? It is not that egalitarians are critical of existing institutions. No democracy can (or should) exist without criticism. Intelligent people should subject what they hear to critical scrutiny. My concern is with the quality and the quantity of criticism. My qualitative concern is that egalitarians make contradictory demands that demoralize government. On the one hand, they want government to do a great deal more—regulate vast areas of society, from cleaning stores to body shops. On the other hand, since they believe leadership is suspect because it signifies an unequal relationship with followers, they constantly seek to undermine authority. The egalitarian desire for bureaucracy without authority is not good for democratic government. Neither is unremitting criticism. If to err is human, I do not believe any institution peopled by human beings can survive the crescendos of criticism that surround presidents, legislators, bureaucrats, and other public officials. Weimar Germany should serve as a cautionary tale, being both far from perfection and infinitely superior to the Nazism that came after.

I am concerned that incessant exaggeration of harm from technology will leave Americans not only poorer, but sicker. In *Searching for Safety* I made an extended argument to the effect that standard of living is part of people's health and safety.[2] If expenditures that are supposed to improve safety actually do not, the loss of the resources devoted to this counterproductive task will reduce health and safety still further.

In all of the talk about lack of competitiveness—much of it, in my opinion, misplaced—there is one American institution that enjoys a continuing high reputation: higher education. The evidence is there for all to see: Many more foreigners come to the United States than there are Americans who go abroad for education. American universities are commonly regarded as among the best in the world, and the research they produce among the finest. Yet this record too is under attack by egalitarians. They do not want to make colleges and universities more knowledgeable, but more egalitarian. This comes out in demands for affirmative action interpreted as a student body, faculty, and administration that contain the proportion of women and racial minorities as there are in that state's population.* In one fell swoop the idea that America stands for the recognition and reward of talent goes by the boards. The quality of education will surely decline. By the time there is in parts of the United States a majority of minorities, so to speak, the irony will be that their places in higher education will not be worth having.

An American tragedy is taking place as blacks and other people of color are getting even with "whitey" by doing themselves in. It is well to attack the supply side of this dilemma: Education and work services, for instance, need to be conducted by people who believe that students can learn and clients can work. But the demand side of education and work—the desire to learn and to be productive—also requires emphasis. As long as those who wish to improve motivation to learn and to work are accused of blaming the victim, however, the lack of a demand-side response will stultify all efforts. Who is benefited when those who most need education and work are taught to despise the teachers and corporations that provide it? Who is helped when people who are victimized in their own neighborhoods are urged to reject police for minor harassments so they become even more subject to major crimes?

When I was a boy growing up in Brooklyn, the public school was a symbol of American ideals. We went to the common school as our affirmation of Americanism. That was true for my children too. The loss of this symbol is of inestimable value. And it will continue to be lost so long as parents do not feel their children will be safe and so long as they believe that in public schools education will be inferior. It is easy enough to accuse such parents of racism. It is harder to recognize that the reasons these parents withdrew their children are also good reasons for reforming schools so they can serve better their existing clientele and indeed attract old ones back. All they need do is provide effective and safe education. But that requires students who are orderly because they wish to learn. When we treat the deficiencies of education as if they were solely the responsibility of incompetent teachers or uncaring authorities without attending to motivation for study, we harm the very students we claim to help.

The contempt for existing institutions on the part of egalitarians is an open secret. The mixture of anger, rejection, and hostility toward

---

*In 1990 the California Assembly and Senate passed (with all Democrats in support) laws to require proportionality in all hiring. Governor George Deukmajian, a Republican, vetoed these measures.

market capitalism and political democracy by egalitarians has to be seen and heard over and over to be believed. Listen to their voices on television and look at the picture of America they portray. Joe and Josie Dope are victimized by incompetent bureaucracies and vicious corporations who make money by dealing out death in the form of unsafe products and cancer-causing foods. It is hard to say whether Americans are better off dying young to avoid being exploited by nursing homes or getting old so as to suffer the agonies of corporate-induced cancers. Doubt it? Watch the pitiful children who are, without a shred of evidence, pictured as dead or diseased victims of a vicious system. For sheer pandering, current television portrayals of the ravages of capitalism can hardly be matched. Thus, in analyzing the politics of television's treatment of environmental pollution, Michael X. Delli Carpini and Bruce A. Williams conclude,

> At the substance level of politics, all [the shows studied] adopt a liberal perspective in defining the issues posed by environmental politics. First, they all employ a catastrophic perspective on environmental problems and the risks posed by pollution. They assume that environmental pollution of all types is worse than ever, that each form of pollution poses a grave and immediate threat to humans and to nature, and that we must do something now. This may or may not be accurate, but it is certainly not the only perspective. As we have noted, there is much disagreement about the actual severity of the problems and the risks they pose. Yet, no serious attention is paid on any of these shows to scientific uncertainty, or the relative risks posed by various forms of pollution.
>
> Second, none of the shows seriously address the trade-offs between regulation and economic activity. The notion that reducing pollution may require reduced economic growth is either not addressed, ridiculed as a ploy by unscrupulous businesspeople or the shows suggest that reducing pollution will be good for the economy. In short, when dealing with environmental regulation these shows present a comfortable liberal perspective that ignores or ridicules the questions raised by conservatives.
>
> At the institutions level of politics [the shows studied] are critical of the problem-solving capabilities of political and economic institutions. Government (in the form of politicians, the EPA, or state environmental agencies) is seen as corrupt, incompetent and completely inadequate to the task of dealing with the problems posed by environmental pollution. Thus, [the shows studied] make it quite clear that we cannot count on government to help solve this problem. Nor can we count upon business to act responsibly. . . . The business sector is represented by either evasive corporate spokespersons or shady and disreputable owners. In either case, they cannot be trusted to either obey the law or to act responsibly.[3]

How much worse can it get? Stay tuned. My task is to explain why such system-blaming shows were once so scarce but are now so common, and why so few people seem to notice the difference.

The first part of this book, "Then and Now," seeks to establish that early in the political history of the United States, egalitarians—who then viewed the central government as a source of inequality—were allied with individualists against hierarchical forces who sought to use government to increase national unity. (The first chapter explains the cultural perspective and argues its superiority to the usual division between left and right or liberal and conservative.) The "Now" chapters engage in a panoramic search for egalitarian influences in order to help explain what otherwise appear to be anomalies in the American political economy.

The second part on "The Culture Wars" describes selected aspects (those I was interested in working on) of cultural conflict: the Bork nomination, the media, the bad-mouthing of the American economy, and the internal transformation of the Democratic and Republican parties so that Republicans are almost entirely individualistic and hierarchical while Democratic party activists are largely egalitarian.

Though it should be evident that my personal preferences suffuse this problem, the third part "Contra Egalitarianism" is more explicitly argumentative. There are chapters about the Catholic bishops' views on poverty, the denigration of American accomplishments, affirmative action, and a variety of other remarkable campus phenomena like the trashing of free speech in the name of equality. I end with ". . . the Fall of Academic Standards"—not blaming those students, but us professors—partly because in this speech I had to recapitulate the main argument but mostly because it is my most personal statement. It is easier to talk about things far away than those close by. Universities are where I live. Like other Americans in trouble when they know what they are doing isn't good for them or the institution in which they work, I restate the moral we should have stuck to from the beginning: just say no to any other standard but intellectual excellence.

I have tried to explain why the rise of radical egalitarianism worries me. Its proponents may well reply that my unfortunate views worry them. I hope that readers will take note of the conflicting arguments, consult their own experience as to which are more valid, and consider future events from the standpoint of whether radical egalitarianism—be it the hope or despair of the nation—actually is becoming much more powerful.

I am told, quite reasonably, that if I did not teach at Berkeley or live in the Bay Area I might not be so sensitive to the rise of radical egalitarianism. No doubt. But as soon as the concerns I voice appear to others to be limited to a few "Berzerkleyites," they are then found everywhere. So take this book as a report from an outlying province, a frontier post of strange doings that turn out to be either figments of a diseased imagination or the future that is now upon us.

Just as many of the chapters in this volume charge egalitarians with exaggeration of society's ills in order to further their cause, so too the same accusation can be leveled at me: Because I obviously do not approve of egalitarianism, I may be accused of vastly exaggerating the evils this tendency will bring about. Fair comment. But that does not dispose of the question of whether (and to what extent) what I say is true.

Why worry because the dominant egalitarian faction within the Democratic party is demanding that the domestic government be made much larger while simultaneously denying it authority? Why worry when demands for the freest speech imaginable—it is okay to piss on the sacred beliefs of tens of millions of Americans, but it is punishable to utter words on campus to which those deemed to be deprived object—are contradicted by the same people? It is one thing to engage in political conflict over whether American society and government should be more egalitarian; it is another to moralize these political differences so that the opinions of opponents are not merely considered mistaken but denounced as depraved.

No better illustration of pervasive egalitarianism can be found than in the reactions of those opposed to the war against Iraq. Whereas it took several years for a peace movement to form during the Vietnam war, roughly from the last years of the 1960s through the early 1970s, it was obviously there, waiting only for the stimulus to be activated, at the end of the 1980s and the beginning of the 1990s. One might have imagined praise for the performance of the military in a high-tech war, thus giving the lie to those who claimed that racial minorities could not perform. Instead, we hear that this war, whatever its merits, is immoral because black- and brown-skinned soldiers are disproportionately represented. The anti-missile-missiles that protect people's lives are denounced as if they took food and jobs from minorities. And to the reply that it is a volunteer military, the egalitarian response is that minorities do not have a real choice. This is how one of the great American success stories, the racial integration of the armed forces, is made into a plot against racial minorities.

In my opinion, things will get worse before they get better. For the sake of the happiness of the American people—myself included—I would be glad to be proved wrong. But I don't think that will happen, at least not until there has been a great deal more trauma. Why worry? All that is happening is a major effort to make Americans poorer while insisting that they do more to equalize their resources. A better recipe for civil war has yet to be found.

I

THEN AND NOW

1

Who Wants What and Why?
A Cultural Theory

Support for and opposition to different ways of life (the shared values legitimating social relations here called "cultures") are the generators of diverse preferences. Thus preferences come from the most ubiquitous human activity—living with other people. After discussing why it is not helpful to conceive of interests as preferences, or to dismiss preference formation as external to organized social life, I shall explain how people are able to develop many preferences from few clues by using their social relations to interrogate their environment. I also argue that the cultural division of ideologies (or biases) is superior to the common distinction between left and right or liberal and conservative. Then I apply this cultural theory to a whole range of objects from economic growth to leadership to perceived dangers stemming from technology.[1]

Always in cultural theory shared values and social relations go together: There are no disembodied values apart from the social relations they rationalize, and there are no viable social relations in which people do not attempt to justify their behavior to other people.

Interests as Preferences

Ask political scientists where preferences come from and—if they don't just stop the conversation with "haven't a clue," or refer disparagingly to the muddle over ideology—you are likely to hear that

3

ubiquitous catchall term "interests." Preferences presumably come
from the interests people have. Indeed, a sweeping review of the
literature done by Michael Thompson and Michiel Schwarz tells us
what we already suspect: The politics of interests is the mainstay of
political science.[2] Yet, if preferences come from interests, how do
people figure out what their interests are—presumably, these do not
come with the birth certificate or Social Security card—so they will
know that these are the interests they ought to prefer? For if interests
and preferences are synonymous, we still are no wiser about how
people come to have them.

"Interest explanations are reason explanations. That is, when we
explain an action by pointing to the interest that prompted, produced,
or motivated it, we allude not to a human cause but to a *reason* or
ground for acting."[3] But why do people give the reasons they do? One
explanation is that reasons and preferences are self-evident. Individuals presumably size up the situation, distinguish opposing interests,
separate the interests of others from self-interest, and choose (or
choose not to choose) the self. Instead of this understanding by sense
perception, however—interests are self-evident, chiseled in stone on
objects that force themselves as they are upon human perception—I
would rely on the convergence of strands of work in social science
according to which meanings are socially constructed.

If the interests that we consider our own are indeed the products of
social relations, then the origins of our preferences may be found in
our deepest desires—how we wish to live with other people, and others
to live with us. "The real moment of choosing," as Mary Douglas
maintains, "is . . . choice of comrades and their way of life."[4]
Preferences are formed through the organization of social relations.

Instead of a social science that begins at the end—assume interests!—I wish to make what people want (their desires, preferences,
values, ideals) into the central subject of inquiry. By classifying people
into the cultural biases that form their preferences, cultural theory
attempts to explain and predict recurrent regularities and transitions in
their behavior. Preferences constitute the very internal essence, the
quintessence of politics: the construction and reconstruction of our
lives together.

Preferences Are Internal, Not External

Ask an economist where preferences come from and you will be told
that they are exogenous, external to the system being considered.[5] The

motive force for participation in markets—the desire to do better through living a life of bidding and bargaining by competing for resources—is ruled out as a noneconomic question! Worse still, preferences are referred to as "tastes," for which, as the saying goes, there is no accounting, thus rendering them not merely noneconomic but nonanalyzable. If preferences are fixed and outside the process of choice, then we cannot inquire into how preferences are formed. The least interesting behavior—instrumental actions—may be explained by preferences; but about the most interesting—preferences themselves—nothing at all can be said. Lindblom is right: "We have impoverished our thought by imprisoning it in an unsatisfactory model of preferences taken as given."[6]

Cultural theory, by contrast, is based on the premise that preferences are endogenous, internal to organizations, so that they emerge from social interaction in defending or opposing different ways of life. When individuals make important decisions, these choices are simultaneously choices of how to live with others. People discover their preferences by evaluating how their past choices have (and by anticipating how their present choices would) strengthen or weaken their way of life. Put plainly, people decide for or against existing authority. They construct their culture in the process of decision making. Their continuing reinforcement, modification, and rejection of existing power relationships teaches them what to prefer.

Deriving Preferences from Cultures:
Four Ways of Life

Cultural theory is based on the axiom that what matters most to people is their relationships with other people and other people's relationships with them. An act is culturally rational, therefore, if it supports one's way of life.

There are only a limited number of cultures that between them categorize most human relations. Though we can imagine an infinite number of potential cultures, only a relatively small number (here I shall work with four) are filled with human activity; the rest are deserted. The latter do not keep their constituents because they cannot combine the values they share with a congruent pattern of social relations.

The social ideal of *individualistic* cultures is self-regulation. They favor bidding and bargaining in order to reduce the need for authority.

They support equality of opportunity to compete in order to make arrangements between consenting adults with a minimum of external interference. They seek opportunity to be different—not equality of condition to be the same, for diminishing social differences would require a central redistributive authority.

Hierarchy is institutionalized authority. It justifies inequality on grounds that specialization and division of labor enable people to live together with greater harmony and effectiveness than do alternative arrangements. Hence hierarchies are rationalized by a sacrificial ethic: The parts are supposed to sacrifice for the whole.

Committed to a life of purely voluntary association, *egalitarian* cultures reject authority. They can live a life without authority only by making greater equality of condition the sole norm regulating human life. Thus egalitarians may be expected to prefer reduction of differences—between races, or income levels, or sexes, or parents and children, teachers and students, authorities and citizens.

A *fatalistic* culture arises when people believe they cannot control what happens to them. Since their group boundaries are porous but the prescriptions imposed on them are severe, they develop fatalistic feelings. What will be, will be.[7] There is no point in them having preferences on public policy because what they prefer would not, in any event, matter.

But none of these modes of organizing social life is viable on its own. A competitive culture needs something—the laws of contract—to be above negotiating; hierarchies need something—anarchic individualists, authorityless egalitarians, apathetic fatalists—to sit on top of; egalitarians need something—unfair competition, inequitable hierarchy, nonparticipant fatalists—to criticize; fatalists require an external source of control to tell them what to do. "What a wonderful place the world would be," say the adherents of each culture, "if only everyone was like us," conveniently ignoring the fact that it is only the presence in the world of people who are not like them that enables them to be the way they are. Hence cultural theory may be distinguished by a necessity theorem: Conflict among cultures is a precondition of cultural identity. It is the differences and distances from others that define one's own cultural identity.

It follows that cultural context—the strength of each of the four cultures compared to the others—is crucial in explaining behavior. For it is not just what the adherents of a culture want but what they think they can get that explains their behavior.

Alone, no one has power over anyone. Power is a social phenomenon; power, therefore, is constituted by culture. But the form and extent of manipulation vary. The fatalistic culture is manipulated; fatalists live by rules others make. Manipulation is built into hierarchies; orders come down and obedience presumably flows up. The evocative language of New Guinea anthropology (the "big men" versus the "rubbish men") expresses the growth of manipulation in individualistic market cultures as some people no longer possess the resources to regulate their own lives. Egalitarians try to manipulate the other cultures by incessant criticism; they coerce one another by attributing their internal differences to the deception and duplicity of their opponents.

To identify with, to become part of a culture, signifies exactly that: The void of formlessness, where everything and therefore nothing is possible, is replaced by social constraint. Even so, individuals keep testing the constraints—reinforcing them if they prove satisfactory in practice; modifying or rejecting them, when possible, if unsatisfactory. It is individuals as social creatures, not only being molded by but actively molding their social context, that are the focus of cultural theory.

If social life is the midwife of political preferences, how do people get from culture to preferences? Is politics too complicated for most people to figure out what they prefer?

Competitive Individualism versus Egalitarian Collectivism

The single worst misunderstanding about American politics, in my opinion, is the joining together of two separate and distinct political cultures with opposing preferences for policies and institutions—competitive individualism and egalitarian collectivism—as a single entity. Between equality of opportunity, so individuals can accentuate their differences, and equality of results, so individuals can diminish their differences, there is a vast gulf.

Individualistic cultures seek self-regulation as a substitute for authority. They prefer minimum authority—just enough to maintain rules for transaction—but they do not reject all authority. If it leaves them alone, they will leave it alone. They need authority to protect property. These competitors are individualistic in two senses: They transact for themselves rather than being bound by group decisions; and they prefer as few prescriptions as possible (other than the absence of physical coercion) binding their behavior.

Egalitarians are collectivists. While they also like to live a life of minimal prescription, they are part and parcel of collectives in which, so long as they remain members, individuals are bound by group decisions. This critical distinction in group boundedness—the freedom to transact for yourself with any consenting adults as against the requirement of agreement with group decisions—makes for a radical difference in the way in which adherents of these two political cultures form their political preferences. The two cultures—individualism versus egalitarianism—differ in regard to economic growth, technological danger, taxing and spending, defense and foreign policy, the legitimacy of institutions, on and on. Yet each, because of its dependence on personal consent, is called individualist, totally ignoring the consideration that egalitarian cultures form collectives while individualistic cultures do not.

The left–right distinction that is used to classify beliefs is beset with contradictions. Hierarchical cultures favor social conservatism, giving government the right to intervene in matters of personal morality. Hence egalitarians may support hierarchical intervention in the economy when it increases equality, but not in social life when it maintains inequality. Libertarians, who are competitive individualists, protest both social and economic intervention. Triangular we stand, says cultural theory, invoking egalitarianism as well as individualism and hierarchy; but dichotomous—left or right, liberal or conservative—we fall because these categories contain insufficient variety to account for what we know.[8]

A division of the world into left and right that is equally inapplicable to the past and the present deserves to be discarded. Are the Soviet officials who resist current efforts to democratize "conservatives"? Efforts to read back the left–right distinction into American history, for instance, succeed only in making a hash of it. In the early days of the republic, egalitarians pursued their objectives through severe restrictions on central government because they then regarded the center as inegalitarian. Nowadays, egalitarians view the central government as a potential source of equality, thereby supporting its effort to diminish power differences in society. How, then, can one make sense of the Republican alliance of economic free markets and social conservatism or the Democratic combination of statism with distrust of authority? Is it the "left" that supports the authority of central government and the "right" that opposes it, or is it the "right" that respects authority and the "left" that denigrates it, or what? The confusion over liberal versus conservative is magnified by the prevailing conception of a single American political culture united in its distrust of political authority.

Individualists Are Not Egalitarians

In his powerfully argued *American Politics: The Promise of Disharmony,* Samuel Huntington sees the United States hung up between a political culture that opposes authority and the necessity of supporting institutions if its ideals of liberty and equality are to be realized:

> This gap between political ideal and political reality is a continuing central phenomenon of American politics in a way that is not true of any other major state. The importance of the gap stems from three distinctive characteristics of American political ideals. First is the *scope* of the agreement on these ideals. In contrast to most European societies, a broad consensus exists and has existed in the United States on basic political values and beliefs. These values and beliefs, which constitute what is often referred to as "the American Creed," have historically served as a distinctive source of American national identity. Second is the *substance* of those ideals. In contrast to the values of most other societies, the values of this Creed are liberal, individualistic, democratic, egalitarian, and hence basically antigovernment and antiauthority in character. Whereas other ideologies legitimate established authority and institutions, the American Creed serves to delegitimate any hierarchical, coercive, authoritarian structures, including American ones. Third is the changing *intensity* with which Americans believe in these basic ideals, an intensity that varies from time to time and from group to group.[9]

Americans do not, I contend, agree to these antiauthoritarian ideals, or to the social practices they support. Although none but the hierarchical culture supports authority, holders of these "American Creed" values are not in fact antigovernment per se.

The individualistic culture that wishes to minimize authority is not in agreement with the egalitarian culture that wishes to reject it. I emphasize this difference in motives not merely because the reasons people give may matter, but also because these rationales are integral parts of different ways of life. Hence the behavior that follows varies considerably. The individualist is content to let government do less, for instance, without challenging its right to rule; the egalitarian wishes government to reduce inequalities while rejecting its authority as prima facie inequality, which is something else again. Dispositions toward government, moreover, may well be instrumental, as the egalitarian abolitionists (previously pacifistic) showed during the Civil War. Action to increase equality led egalitarians to support coercion by the central government.[10] While what the competing cultures want may stay the same (say, greater or lesser equality), the means (central government as a source of equality or inequality) vary with their historical experience.

Intensity of belief does differ over time. But this need not mean that everyone's (that is, all cultures) dispositions become more intense or that these feelings move in the same direction. Given their varied internal organizational structures, the cultures differ markedly in their proclivities toward political passion. Is it pure happenstance that the hierarchical Federalists and Whigs stress cool consideration (self-control being a cardinal virtue), while the egalitarian abolitionists, Student Nonviolent Coordinating Committee, and Friends of the Earth are known for their passion? Do the periods of passion that Huntington stresses—the revolutionary period, the period before the Civil War, the civil rights movement—just happen to coincide with the rise of radical egalitarianism?

Huntington asserts, however, that the gap between institutions and ideals is responsible for the recurrent convulsions in American politics: "No government can exist without some measure of hierarchy, inequality, arbitrary power, secrecy, deception, and established patterns of superordination and subordination. The American Creed, however, challenges the legitimacy of all these characteristics of government."[11] So far as it goes, this statement is true, but it does not go far enough. For if there were no support for hierarchical institutions, the qualities complained about would not exist at all. Without a hierarchical political culture in the United States—albeit weaker than elsewhere—there would be no established authority to be against. No orthodoxy, no heterodoxy.

"The essence of the [American] Creed," Huntington informs us, "is opposition to power and to concentrated authority."[12] How, then, is it possible to explain why the very same people who urge American national government to undertake ever-larger measures to reduce inequalities also oppose large defense budgets? If the creed is principled, why does it vary with the issues and the times? Why do those who favor ever-larger preparedness in defense urge ever-smaller intervention in the economy? Why, to go back into American history, did people who opposed economic development by the national government (then called "internal improvements") favor the very same thing by state governments if it was governmental authority per se to which they were opposed? Once we understand that the Jeffersonians and the Jacksonians were coalitions of egalitarians and individualists, and that in those days both cultures identified the central government with hierarchy, the answer becomes evident.

It is true enough that from the beginning hierarchical cultures have been weak in America compared to Europe. It is also true that the often dominant individualist culture and the sometimes influential egalitarian culture are not exactly enamored of authority. But that is not the whole truth.

My claim is that the different attitudes toward authority in individualistic and egalitarian cultures make a world of difference in the policies they pursue and hence in the problems they pose for government. An egalitarian culture, whose adherents believe that people are born good but are corrupted by evil institutions (being basically anti-institutional), offers a far more severe challenge for the conduct of foreign policy (America pure or polluted, nothing in between, as in the Persian Gulf War) than one whose adherents are reluctant to pay for defense but basically believe the American political system is benign. An individualist culture willing to compromise offers quite different prospects for domestic reconciliation than an egalitarian culture opposed in principle to compromise. Insofar as we are concerned with the undermining of authority in the midst of expanding government—a major anomaly of our time—it is the challenge of egalitarianism, not individualism, that should occupy our attention.

There is more involved in dispositions toward authority than mere acceptance or rejection. People may also feel that while they accept the need for authority under some circumstances and within stipulated conditions, this authority is too large and/or too strong or too small and too weak. Authority may be deemed to have too broad or too narrow a scope or to be applied with too much or too little rigor.

The utility of these distinctions lies in the ability they give us to make sense out of variations in the behavior of different cultures toward authority. Hierarchies support authority as legitimate—moral, right, and appropriate. Egalitarians reject authority as illegitimate—immoral, wrong, and improper—unless it increases equality. But there is more to be said about those who accept authority but differ as to its scope and rigor. Fatalists accept authority as inevitable and uncontrollable. They can do nothing about it. Individualists accept authority in narrow and circumscribed areas, generally thinking it too broad and rigorous.

To the detriment of our understanding, adherents of exclusive hierarchies are generally omitted from analytic consideration, being
lumped in with inclusive hierarchies. Inclusive hierarchies are large,
integrative organizations that seek to accommodate diverse desires,
while exclusive hierarchies are smaller, more cohesive, and rigid,
demanding adherence to a narrow program. While accepting—even
demanding—authority, exclusivists do not necessarily support existing
institutions. These social conservatives want larger and rigorously
enforced moral and social differences. Their complaint about American society and government is not that government is too strong but
that, in regard to individual behavior, it is too weak; to them, differences between what they deem right and wrong are not enunciated
clearly enough and not enforced vigorously by governmental authority.

Even if substantial majorities of citizens and elites actually do
approve of authority in some way, therefore, the officials in power may
not gain the benefits of this support, besieged as they are by individualists who tell them they have exceeded their warrant and social
conservatives who condemn them for moral confusion and coward-
ice—let alone egalitarians who believe that authority is necessarily
inegalitarian and hence illegitimate. The attack on authority is multifac-
eted; it comes not only from egalitarians but also includes adherents
of strong and exclusive hierarchy. This three-pronged attack on authority (simultaneously too strong and too weak, too broad and too
narrow) is important to an understanding of American political history,
and never more so than right now.

Instead of considering a single American culture, I propose that
analyzing American political life in terms of conflicts among at least
three active political cultures—hierarchical, individualist, and egalitarian—will prove more satisfactory. This approach will generate fewer
surprises and provide explanations that better fit the phenomena.

Preferences Need No Inferences

The cultural hypothesis is that individuals exert control over each
other by institutionalizing the moral judgments justifying the relationships they wish to establish. But how does this social filter enable
people who possess only inches of facts to generate miles of preferences? What is it about cultures that makes them the kind of theories
that ordinary folk (and we are all ordinary outside our area of specialization) can use to figure out their preferences? The ability of people to

know what they prefer without knowing much else lies at the crux of understanding preference formation. Culture codes can be unlocked, I maintain, because their keys are social. By figuring out their master preferences, as it were—what groups they do and do not identify with—they can readily figure out the rest. A basic reason people are able to develop so many preferences is that they actually do not have to work all that hard.

Suppose a new development occurs. Without knowing much about it, those who identify with each particular way of life can guess whether its effect is to increase or decrease social distinctions, and to impose, avoid, or reject authority—guesses made more definitive by observing what like-minded individuals do.[13] Of course, people may be, and often are, mistaken. To seek is not necessarily to find a culturally rational course of action. Capitalists may try to establish hegemony over others, but they are often mistaken about which ideas and actions will in fact support their way of life. They may, for instance, use governmental regulation to institute a pattern of cumulative inequalities that convert market arrangements into state capitalism, leading to their ultimate subordination. To be culturally rational by bolstering one's way of life is the intention, not necessarily the accomplishment.

Preferences may be rationalized from the top down, specific applications being deduced from general principles. But complexity of the causal chains invoked leaves people who lack a capacity for abstract thought unable to form preferences. Reasoning in steps is also slow. Without social validation at each step—which is difficult to achieve, moreover—the chain of reasoning may snap. Fortunately, faster methods are available. People can know what they believe or who they trust and yet not how the belief is derived. It is no more necessary for a person to verbalize about culture than it is necessary to know the rules of grammar in order to speak. Mediating their perceptions through their cultures, people can grab onto any social handle to choose their preferences. All they need are aids to calculation.

Aids to the Calculation of Preferences

"How," Paul Sniderman and his colleagues ask, "do people figure out what they think about political issues, given how little they commonly know about them?"[14] They answer that three aids to calculation are particularly important: (1) likes and dislikes; (2) liberalism versus conservatism; and (3) attributions of responsibility. All these aids to calculation are "ideological" (or, to use our cultural term, "biased") in the sense of rationalizations for preferred social relationships.

Who is responsible for what, as we will see, is culturally determined. So are feelings about other people. But how does ideology help people figure out what to prefer when new issues, such as social issues, arise? An advantage of cultural theory is that it handles both economic and social issues without strain. Pamela Conover and Stanley Feldman write,

> Traditionally, it was assumed that the meaning of ideological labels and self-identifications could be easily summarized in terms of a single dimension: the liberal/conservative continuum. In recent years, however, this viewpoint has undergone some modification. The decade of the 1970s ushered in a variety of "social" issues—abortion, marijuana use, the Equal Rights Amendment—which did not fit easily into the traditional liberal/conservative spectrum. Because of this, many researchers now posit that the meaning of ideological labels and self-identifications must be interpreted within the context of two liberal/conservative dimensions: one economic and one social.[15]

Using cultural concepts makes such ad hoc category massage unnecessary. Individualists, being nonprescriptive and anticollectivist, prefer minimal economic and social regulation. Egalitarians, combining nonprescription with collective decision, prefer strong economic but weak social regulation. And adherents of hierarchy, joining hard group boundaries to heavy prescription, desire strong social and economic regulation.

Frames of Reference

Cultures answer questions about life with people: How is order to be achieved and maintained? Is there to be leadership and, if so, by whom? How are the goods of this world to be secured and divided up? How is envy to be controlled, inequality to be justified or condemned? Which dangers are to be confronted out of the multitude that might face us and which, since we cannot turn every way at once, are to be ignored? What, in sum, is the good (or, at least, better) life?

This is the critical question: What sorts of people, organized into what kind of culture, sharing which values, legitimating which practices, would behave in certain predicted ways in order to do the two things every culture (except the fatalists) try to do—make their people stronger and the opposing cultures weaker? There follow the predictions that cultural theory gives for the four cultures. I begin with envy because it sets the stage for the crucial drama about who is to blame for misfortune.

Envy

Envy must be an especially difficult problem for egalitarians because they work so hard to control it. If all members are supposed to be equal (how else get voluntary agreement on political processes and public policies?), then this egalitarianism must show in the outer appurtenances of life: plain food, meals without main courses (as in vegetarianism), simple clothes, redistribution of income, bare furniture, unornamental "worker" housing, the life of the humble style. Suspicion is on all members—but especially leaders—to see that they do not elevate themselves above others. Envy is not correlated with the size of social differences alone, but rather with their acceptability. The crucial question is not whether there are large differences in individual or group resources in most places—surely there are—but whether these are rationalized as natural or unnatural, right or wrong, appropriate or illegitimate.

The humble life would hardly be appropriate (to say the least) in market individualism, whose rationale depends on the ability of competitors to appropriate the benefits of the risks they take. Conspicuous consumption, or making a fetish out of commodities, may be a rational effort to point to where the power is so as to gain adherents in a network for future ventures. Since some people display much more of the goods of this world than others, however, envy is bound to rear its ugly head. But where egalitarians blame the system, individualists attribute personal success to good luck and/or good performance, and failure to bad. Those who complain are given the no-special-treatment response: You have had your chance (i.e., opportunity is equal) and will have it again if you work hard. Naturally, fatalists know no envy, because, for them—to use Mrs. Gaskell's evocative term—life is like a lottery. Lacking control over their lives, they take whatever comes their way.

Control of envy in hierarchy is more interesting because it is more necessary. After all, hierarchy is institutionalized inequality. Ostentation is reserved for the collectivity—grand palaces, public works, ornate buildings in which the complexity of design mimics the near-infinite gradations of social structure. Hierarchists may wear faded finery at home, but the army and the marching bands and the tombs of founders are bedecked in all splendor. As education inculcates the desirability of differences, envy is further deflected by arguing the appropriateness of specialization and the division of labor. Experts do know best. Leaders are to be loved because they reveal the sacrifice of the parts for the whole by going out first in battle, or by subsidizing medical care and pensions, or by donating museums and libraries.

Blame

When things go wrong, however—as they must in all cultures—who is to blame? Fatalists blame fate, but hierarchists cannot blame the collective. "System blame"—blaming the relationship between the parts and the whole on which they pride themselves—would amount to self-destruction. No, hierarchies are famous for their blame-shedding techniques. Responsibility is hidden or (the same thing) diffused among numerous offices. Investigations are quashed or forbidden by official secret acts. Blame is shifted to deviants. They do not know their place. They must be subject to reeducation, or they belong in asylums. (Apparently, a person would have to be crazy to object to a collective way of life.) To egalitarians, however, who reject authority, it is precisely the system (some combination of individualism and collectivism) that is insane—coercive and inegalitarian. If egalitarians had their way, suicides would be owed redress by the implacable institutions that drove them to their undeserved deaths. Were society differently organized, murderers would not want to kill their prey. Since good people are corrupted by evil institutions, the egalitarian task is to unmask authority by revealing the connection between apparently benign institutions and the cancers they actually cause. Cultural solidarity is maintained by portraying external forces as monstrous, and by accusing deviants of secretly importing evil ways ("hidden hierarchies") to corrupt the membership. Consequently, egalitarians search for insidious contamination from secret external sources—the turncoats, the oreos, the political radishes, the witches, the polluters—who have brought duplicity into their innocent garden.

Now individualists can hardly claim to be innocent; they are supposed to know what they are doing. But not entirely. The whole point is to outguess the future; if it were knowable, there would be no need for entrepreneurs. Hence, individualists can blame bad luck or personal incompetence or any combination thereof, providing only that the system—in their case, competitive individualism—is blameless. People may be dumb, as economic individualists say, but markets are always smart.

Inequality

Every regime has to confront inequality of condition. Egalitarians abhor inequality; it can never be justified. Cultures that embody it are guilty of perpetrating the silent death of institutional oppression. For fatalists, inequality is the norm; they expect to be ruled by others. Hierarchies extend assistance because the "unequals" are part of their own people for whom they feel responsible. Their justification of inequality is the same as for the system itself: Different roles for different parts is healthy for the system as a whole. In return, all members of society are supposed to get equality before the law, so that their claims may be adjudicated on a consistent and predictable basis. Adjudicating "who has the right to do what" is essential to maintaining distances and differences in hierarchies. By contrast, individualists believe in equality of opportunity, the right to enter contests to compete for the goods of life, not the right to have the same power or wealth as others.

I have argued that egalitarians advocate equality of results, that hierarchists are concerned with legal equality, and that individualists advocate equality of opportunity; that is why, though everyone (except fatalists) speaks approvingly of equality, they all mean something different. Whether policies are designed to diminish or maintain differences among people is a telltale sign—to citizens as well as to social scientists—of what political culture is preferred.

Fairness

For those who have no control over the prescriptions or people that govern their lives, fairness is fate. Life is fair for individualists when they have opportunity to enter and to benefit from competition. Failure is fair too, providing that the markets they enter are unfettered and that they have a chance to acquire resources so as to try again.

Cumulative inequalities—to use Robert Dahl's phrase[16]—would eventually prevent competition. In a hierarchical collective, fairness follows function; being fairly treated does not mean being treated like everyone else but being treated according to predictable rules affecting one's own station in life. In egalitarian collectives, fair is equal. No one is to have more of anything—especially power—than anyone else.

Economic Growth

Thus egalitarians have little interest in (i.e., they do not prefer) economic growth. Abundance increases the temptation to differentiation, which interferes with equality. Far better for egalitarians to concentrate on equal distribution, which keeps their people together, than on unequal development, which pulls them apart.

Wealth creation belongs to the established cultures, but in different ways. The promise of hierarchies is that collective sacrifice will lead to group gain. Thus they plan to reduce consumption to create capital to invest for future benefits. Should its solidarity be threatened, the collective may adopt a limited redistributive ethic—buying off discontent, limiting exchange so as to limit losers. Not so, competitive individualists. They seek new combinations in order to create new wealth so that there will be more for all and they can keep more of it.

Scarcity

The idea of resource scarcity is useful to hierarchists who can then proceed to allocate physical quantities by direct, bureaucratic means. The idea of resource depletion is also useful for egalitarians who can blame the "system" for exploiting nature as it does people, and who can then try to get the authorities to change their inegalitarian lifestyle. The idea that resources are limited, however, is anathema to individualists because it implies that exchange makes people worse off (and therefore has to be curtailed), and because it attacks the central promise of expanding wealth that will eventually make everyone better off. Shortages do not matter to fatalists who must, in any event, make do.

Leadership

Hierarchies tie authority to positions.[17] Hence hierarchies are proleadership cultures, shoring it up at every opportunity, protecting it when under attack, shedding and diffusing blame, keeping information under close control. Individualistic cultures treat leadership like any other commodity: They pay for it. They seek to make it unnecessary by self-organization through bidding and bargaining. When conditions—such as external attack—make a modicum of leadership necessary, however, it is limited in time and authority, the hope being that the meteoric leader who flames bright and then burns out will retire when the task is completed.

In a corresponding manner, each culture fears the perversion of its main values. Hierarchy, which elevates leadership, fears the charismatic leader who overturns the law; individualists fear the leader who overstays his welcome so as to become a dictator; fatalists fear the disappearance of leadership to give guidance; and egalitarians fear the very distinction between leaders and followers, for followership implies inequality. Egalitarians oppose differentiation of all kinds because they see structure as a screen to hide inequality.

Apathy

The very same failure to vote (or lack of interelectoral activity) may be appropriate or inappropriate, legitimizing or destabilizing, depending on the cultural context. Adherents of each culture select out meanings of apathy to support their preferred power relationships.

Egalitarians rationalize rejecting established authority by arguing that there is no real participation. Power is "unmasked" by showing that fatalism is the true location of the mass of citizens. Like the wonderful Steinberg cartoon in the *New Yorker,* where Manhattan grows so large the rest of the country recedes from view, egalitarians see fatalists as most of the people—a nation metaphorically populated by 4,200 oligarchs, 2,000 egalitarians, and 200 million apathetics. All the while, egalitarians seek to recruit supporters from among fatalists who, they claim, are apathetic because decisions are made for them by the establishment. The hierarchical counterclaim that apathy is functional—because inactivity implies consent—is derided as ideological window dressing. High rates of general participation across a broad scope of issues, by contrast, would undermine hierarchical rule.

How could principles of hierarchy be maintained if roles are changed and challenged all the time? Instead, hierarchies try to inculcate civic consciousness, a positive obligation to vote. But not much more than that—for citizens should participate according to their station in life. Within the sphere of competence assigned to them, however, members of hierarchies are expected to do their duty.

Individualists do not have to take the rate and scope of activity as a measure of their manhood. If it is worthwhile for people to participate, they will; if not, they won't. Should voting decline, for instance, this might indicate that the probability of an individual influencing events is so low that a rational person would not bother. Perhaps people feel the government does too much. (Don't vote, the adage goes—that will only encourage them.) Indeed, the anarchist wing of market cultures thinks of government more as the problem than the solution. (Voting makes no difference—it says—the government always gets in.)

Why, in sum, is there a low rate of voting (if, indeed, there is)? Because, egalitarians answer, the system excludes people; because, supporters of hierarchy reply, voters are so satisfied they are willing to leave things to those who are better qualified; because, individualists respond, voting is not worth the effort it takes; because, fatalists respond, voting is ineffectual.

Risk

In discussions of technological danger, one theory is that people are reacting to the actual dangers: They are risk adverse because the risks are actually rising. Another theory is psychological: There are risk-taking and risk-adverse personalities. Still another is perceptual: People are willing to accept dangers that are voluntarily undertaken, but they reject risks that are imposed on them. The most widely held theory of risk perception I call the "knowledge theory": the often implicit notion that people perceive technologies (and other things) to be dangerous because they know them to be dangerous. In *Risk and Culture* Mary Douglas and I argue that perception of danger is a function of political culture—risk acceptance going along with approval of individualistic and hierarchical cultures, and risk aversion with egalitarian opposition to these other cultures on the grounds they are inegalitarian.[18] Put briefly, we contend that the debate over risk stemming from technology is a referendum on the acceptability of American institutions. The more trust in them, the more risk acceptance; the less trust, the more risk rejection.

Consider in this context of competing explanations a variety of survey findings. The first—a survey of the feelings of a variety of elites about the safety of nuclear power plants—shows, among other things, an immense gap (far greater than survey research usually produces) between nuclear energy experts (98.7%) and the military (86.0%) saying "safe" compared to relatively tiny proportions of leaders of public interest groups (6.4%), movie producers and directors (14.3%), and elite journalists (29.4%). The difference between people who support and oppose authority is very great.[19]

Recently, Karl Dake and I used a survey of Bay Area residents to compare perception of danger from technology as opposed to danger from economic decline, social deviance, and war. Egalitarians, we found, were by far most fearful of technology. Hierarchists were deeply fearful of social deviance, and individualists greatly feared war. Knowledge of these areas of potential danger made no difference in our or any other survey reported in the literature. Those who endorse egalitarianism would also rate the risks of social deviance to be relatively low. What right has an unconscionably inegalitarian system to make demands or to set standards?[20]

Another poll compares the general public to executives of small and large corporations and environmentalists on a variety of preferences related to politics and public policy. Whereas around two-thirds of the general public and executives favor a strong defense, only a quarter of environmentalists give it a high priority. Maintaining order in the nation gets around 80 percent or more from everyone else but just 47 percent from environmentalists. On an egalitarian issue—like having more say at work—the situation is reversed, as around two thirds of environmentalists and the general public give it a high priority but only a quarter of executives in large companies and two-fifths in small ones do the same.[21] Polarization of elites is evident.

In a study of voters in the U.S. Senate, Joseph Kalt and Mark Zupan report, "It turns out that politicians consistently package liberalism and environmentalism together—the correlation between the LCV's [League of Conservation Voters] and the ADA's [Americans for Democratic Action] rating scales is 0.94."[22]

Hierarchists favor technological risk-taking because they see this as supporting the institutions they rely on to make good their promises—to wit, technology can promote a stronger society and a safer future provided that their rules (and stratified social relations) are maintained and their duly qualified experts are followed. Individualists also deem technology to be good. They hold that following market principles (and individually negotiated social relations) will allow technological innovation to triumph, conferring creative human value on otherwise inert resources. They also believe that the enormous benefits of technological innovation will convey their premise that unfettered bidding and bargaining leaves people better off. If they believe that free market institutions are intrinsically ruinous to nature, individualists could no longer defend a life of minimum restraints. By the same token, egalitarians are opposed to taking technological risks because they see such risks as supporting the inegalitarian markets and coercive hierarchies to which the egalitarians are opposed.

Egalitarians claim that nature is "fragile" in order to justify sharing the Earth's limited resources and to discomfort individualists, whose life of bidding and bargaining would be impossible if they had to worry too much about disturbing nature. On the contrary, individualists claim that nature is "cornucopian," so that if people are released from artificial constraints (like excessive environmental regulations) there will be no limits to the abundance for all, thereby more than compensating for any damage they do. In the hierarchists' culture, nature is "perverse or tolerant"; good will come if you follow their rules and experts, bad if you don't.

People who value strong equality in the sense of diminishing distinctions among people such as wealth, race, gender, authority, and so forth believe that an inegalitarian society is likely to insult the environment just as it exploits poor people. Besides, what better way to weaken the institution they believe creates inequalities—the capitalist corporation—than to claim that it causes cancer. If people cannot abide capitalism's waste products, they will not stand for capitalism.

Viewing environmentalists as protesters against inegalitarian institutions (recall their concern about "endangered species" and corporations that cause cancer) helps us understand their political alliances. Since Berkeley constitutes a kind of political-medical museum for this purpose, we can observe a member of the city council—accused of spending too much time on foreign affairs instead of local concerns—responding, "You can't explain one without the other. If the money was not going to Central America, we would have the money to fix the sewers."[23] Unless defense has an avowedly egalitarian purpose, egalitarians view the military as taking from welfare for the poor.

A striking contemporary example connecting culture and risk, based on newspaper accounts, comes from perceptions of acquired immune deficiency syndrome, AIDS. The more hierarchical the group, I hypothesize (following cultural theory), the more it minimizes technological danger as the price of progress while maximizing fear of casual contact with people who have AIDS. For, in its view, when people violate divine commandments, the Lord brings plague. Conversely, egalitarians tend to overestimate grossly the dangers from technology (because the social and economic relationships they dislike are bad for your health) while minimizing the dangers from contact with carriers of AIDS. "Gays" are good—that is, potential allies—in the egalitarian view because they are antiestablishment and because they reduce one of the main differences among people.

Defense Policy

A significant part of the opposition to the main lines of American defense policy from the mid-1960s to the present is based on deep-seated objection to its political and economic systems. This is not to say that any of these policies were necessarily wise. Indeed, at any time and place, the United States might well have been overestimating the threat from the Soviet Union or using too much force in regional conflicts. What I wish to suggest is that the across-the-board criticism of U.S. policy as inherently aggressive and repressive, regardless of circumstance—a litany of criticism so constant it did not alert us to the need for explanation—has a structural basis in the rise of a political culture opposed to existing authority. The collapse of communism in Eastern Europe and the weakening of the Soviet Union has lessened domestic conflict over foreign policy. But we can expect the same criticism to start up over other matters, i.e., the Persian Gulf.

To the extent this criticism is structural—that is, inherent in domestic politics—the problem of fashioning foreign policies that can obtain widespread support is much more difficult than is commonly conceived. For if the objection is to American ways of life and therefore to the government "for which it stands," only a transformation in power relationships at home, together with a redistribution of economic resources, would satisfy these critics. Looking to changes in foreign policy to shore up domestic support is radically to confuse the causal connections and, therefore, the order of priorities. Unless or until they face an overwhelming external threat, how people wish to live with one another takes precedence over how they relate to foreigners.

A difference between the 1950s and the 1970s and 1980s lies in what
is missing. In earlier times, a politician could be both for welfare and
for defense. Henry Jackson and Hubert Humphrey exemplified the
dual commitment to a strong defense and to provision for those in
need. No longer. Indeed, the six major candidates for the Democratic
party presidential nomination in 1988 all specified conditions for armed
intervention—completely containable consequences, impeccable
moral character, Soviet acquiesence, and the like—that could never be
met. And the Democrats (considering their representation in state
government and Congress and the loyalties of citizens) are still the
majority party in the United States. What is more, the Republican then
Secretary of Defense Caspar Weinberger's specification of the conditions required to justify military intervention was, in a different way,
just as stringent. His insistence on open-ended commitment—whatever
it takes to prevail no matter what—is impossible in practice because it
can almost never be given.

In an article in *Commentary*, Owen Harries traces the "deeper
roots" of imagining a world without force ("best case" thinking) to
the universalistic liberal tradition that denies "the reality of conflict in
the name of a fundamental harmony of interest." Since "there are no
real intractable conflicts of interest," it follows that enmity among
nations "is illusory and unnecessary."[24]

But explaining one set of ideas by another separates them from their
social context, as if they existed apart from the people who believed
them. By asking a different kind of question—what sort of people,
sharing which values and justifying what kind of practices, would act
on these beliefs in order to shore up their way of life and tear down
their opponents?—the tenacity with which these ideas are held and the
immense challenge they pose to U.S. foreign policy will become
apparent.

Does anybody actually believe in the universal harmony of interests?
I think not. The idea is recognizably wrongheaded. In fact, the very
people who argue the best-case thesis in foreign policy also argue the
worse-case thesis in domestic policy. Harmony in domestic policy,
they claim, is the ideology of the oppressor. There are irreconcilable
conflicts between the haves and have-nots, whites and blacks—conflicts that cannot be compromised but only overcome by struggle.
Foreign policy, apparently, is different. Why?

Let us ask a more varied and more interesting question: Who sees
harmony in international affairs and hostility in domestic politics?
What else do the people who claim that the U.S. government is

perforce the aggressor in world affairs believe? They believe in equality of condition. They are part and parcel of many other movements dedicated to the diminution of distinctions among people.

When I grew up, children could never do enough for their parents; now all we hear about is child abuse, state intervention obviously being required to prevent parents from doing terrible things to their young. Harmony of interests, indeed!

How can harmony abroad be reconciled with hostility at home? Take the critics at their word: Intolerable, unconscionable, unbearable, inequalities at home—they believe—are justified by paranoia about threats from faraway places. It is not that they think the Soviet system is benevolent or that it provides a better way of life. They are not that dumb, or dumb at all. It is rather that they care about how people live with other people in the U.S.A., not in the U.S.S.R. or Iraq. It is their passion for equality of condition and their anger at inequality that leads them to a portrayal of an international heaven spoiled by people bent on maintaining a domestic hell. Acknowledging a Soviet or Iraqi threat would mean agreeing with certain premises: (1) that the social system of the United States is worth defending; (2) that other systems are worse; and (3) that a morally legitimate government has the right to divert resources from domestic (i.e., egalitarian) to military (i.e., inegalitarian) purposes.

The differences voiced in the 1980s over whether the deficit should be reduced by cutting defense or domestic programs are instructive. To the extent sacrifices are being imposed, of course, sharing them among beneficiaries makes sense. When civilian pensions are being reduced, for instance, military pensions may follow suit. But there is more to it. Not only is defense being treated as just another domestic interest ("the military-industrial complex," say, as opposed to what used to be called "the common defense"), it is also being placed in a zero-sum relationship to welfare programs (canes versus guns, I suppose). Observe the complaints that the expensive Patriot missile used to shoot down Iraqi SCUD missiles takes money from programs for poor people.

Among our several political cultures, we may ask, which would interpret events to support more defense spending, or which less? Hierarchies believe in defense of the collective. Doubts about military spending would suggest that military experts and the civilian leadership cannot be trusted to appraise the situation and are incompetent to know what to do about foreign dangers.

There is not much place for competitive individualism in war—

except, perhaps, for prima donna generals. Individualist forces fear war for its coercive military draft and its disruption of agreements among consenting adults. During wars of mass mobilization, they give up their individualism in return for being sheltered from competition. During peacetime, they are reluctant to pay higher taxes. Individualist cultures make reluctant warriors, especially when there is no booty.

Imagine that the U.S. government is deemed immoral (to the more extreme, perhaps illegitimate) because it fails to provide social justice, understood as much greater equality of condition. (A current code word is "fairness.") What follows from this assumption?

Unfairness at home becomes transmuted into exploitation abroad. The Third World serves as a surrogate proletariat, its poverty being a result of domination by multinational capital led by the United States. It follows that the United States owes redress to poorer nations just as it owes reparations to its own poorer people. Assuming further a fixed limit to the world's goods (egalitarians being also anticapitalist), more for arms means less for welfare. In brief, the industrial North exploits the Third World South; the United States rules the North; capitalists rule the United States; hence an end to inequality in the United States is necessary for social justice in the world.

The antimilitary culture is egalitarian. Opposed to authority, seeing its own society as the cause of immoral differences, fearing subjugation by established institutions, egalitarians favor at most a small army. Only by sustaining a belief that their cause is entirely just, and their opponent's entirely evil, can they accept even minimal subordination to authority. Hence they respond to such unifying slogans as "The war to end all wars" or "Unconditional surrender!" Whereas in Vietnam it took several years for an antiwar movement to arise, the difference is, in the Persian Gulf it was waiting for us.

The foreign policy of egalitarianism flows naturally from its commitment to redistribution. First, there is redistribution from rich to poor countries. Second, there is redistribution from defense to domestic welfare expenditure. Third, there is redistribution of authority from government officials to mass movements, from those now in power to those—to use their favorite phrase—left out of power.

Egalitarianism Then and Now

My aim has been to link identification with one of the four political cultures to the ability of individuals and groups to form policy preferences. From here on I shall concentrate on the part played by egalitarianism in American political life, beginning with the claim that it is the alliance of egalitarianism and individualism against hierarchy that once made America exceptional. The end of that alliance, and the subsequent bid for power by "radical egalitarians" (so named to distinguish those who want greater equality of condition from individualists who prefer equal opportunity), is my subject.

2

Resolved, That Individualism and Egalitarianism Be Made Compatible in America: Political Cultural Roots of Exceptionalism

Only in America. Everyone who studies American politics (at least everyone I know) comes away feeling that it is special in some significant way without quite being able to specify precisely what that is. Me too. All who wander through American political history share the disconcerting feeling that there is a common, unifying, but mysterious element that would make sense of what happens or, at least, of what doesn't. Many reach for the brass ring only to find themselves clutching at thin air. Many theories are called forth, as we know, but few, to our dismay, are chosen. Here, as the title of this chapter says, is another hostage to fortune.

Exceptionalism in Cultural Context

Why—we ask—is there no socialism, or at least a sizable socialist party, in America? Why have trade unions been weak here compared to other democracies? Why is the United States a "welfare laggard"? Why has it had a meliorative two-party system, instead of multiparty system with radical parties? Why, I might add, is its budgetary process unlike any other, from the primacy of its legislature to its fixation in balance?

The most common answer (stemming from Louis Hartz and others) is that the United States, having no feudalism, knew no hereditary hierarchy. Yet examples that contradict this reasoning (like Argentina and South Africa) abound. How about abundant and cheap land? Other places (Russia, Canada, Australia) manage that without looking the least like America. Besides, all that was long ago. What has sustained over time whatever American exceptionalism consists of?

Attention is paid to the separation of powers and to federalism. Both sets of institutions are said to weaken central government, thus making it difficult to engage in radical transformation or to enact consistent policies.[1] Both institutional arrangements not only fragment power but also create incentives for people placed in different centers to disagree. Or so *The Federalist* says. One difficulty here is inability to determine whether these institutions are causes or consequences of behavior deemed exceptional. Thus socialism might be harder under federal arrangements, though Australia and Germany manage quite a bit of welfare policy together with a federal structure. There might be a kind of functional explanation in which consequences of federal institutions become causes of their perpetuation. In some sense this must be so, for otherwise it would be impossible to explain why any organization persists. Yet federal structure has not notably impeded wartime arrangements or social security. Nor has separation of powers stopped vast environmental legislation.

Then there are the people. Special qualities are often attributed to them, from unusual moderation to "creedal passion."[2] Unfortunately, these characterizations, all of which find supporting evidence someplace, are left in midair, suspended without a social base. As a social scientist, I am opposed to treating values as if they were disembodied, without people to institutionalize them in their social relations. (The converse is also true: No set of social relations can endure without the people involved being able to justify them.) Everything one says about America and Americans is true somewhere. Unless we are to turn to cyclical theories, which only restate the questions—who is passionate, when and why?—flesh has to be put on the bones of human and institutional nature in these United States. Are we referring to adherents of small exclusive hierarchies, or to radical egalitarians, or to warriorlike individualists?

Could it be that Americans have been brainwashed or indoctrinated or otherwise fooled into believing some things and rejecting others so as to account for their peculiar behavior?[3] Would America be more like Europe if its people were less gullible? And if true, does this thesis imply that other nations that have taken different paths are seeing through a glass clearly? If our people see differently, then that is what must be explained.

Enter the corporation and the state. Was all well in our American garden until corporate capitalism introduced such vast inequalities that it bought government, schools, churches, the media, conscience itself, until no dissent could be heard or accepted? A troublesome feature of this serpent-in-the-garden theory is that the characteristics it was supposed to have caused—weak central government, a preference for laissez-faire, state protection of private property, on and on, including features like a powerful Congress and a predeliction for balanced budgets—were part of American exceptionalism long before the industrial revolution.

My view is that all these theories have merit but are insufficient by themselves. The weakness of hierarchical forces is a perennial feature of American political life—never more so than now. The existence of large numbers of small enterprises, which is what early American farms were, is bound to influence ideas about desirable public policy. So is abundant land. And no set of relationships among people could last unless they contained mechanisms for reproducing themselves.

What is missing, I believe, is conflict, context, and culture. Instead of seeking the Holy Grail of a single distinctive American value, we have to look for conflict among people with different and opposing values—values that are not suspended in midair but serve to justify the different ways of life we call cultures. Only then can we see what combination of politically charged values distinguish America from the rest of the democratic West. Cultures are composed of people sharing values that justify different kinds of social relationships. It is the cultural context—how strong the different cultures are in relation to each other—that matters. Weak hierarchy, by itself, is one thing; combined with strong individualism on the one hand (as in America), or strong egalitarianism (as under the Khmer Rouge in Cambodia) on the other, it is something else again.[4]

Whatever explains American exceptionalism, moreover, must also explain European uniformity—that is, why other Western democracies are more like each other than they are like the United States. One reason theories of exceptionalism are difficult to formulate is that they must simultaneously explain both the American and the European experiences in terms of their differences. The same variables that

purport to explain why America is exceptional must also show why
Europe is not.

My hypothesis is that what makes America special is the deeply
imbedded belief, accompanied by supporting social relationships, that
liberty and equality—the cultures of individualism and egalitarianism—
are (or can be) mutually reinforcing. In America if not elsewhere, equal
opportunity, as in individualism, and equal results, as in egalitarianism,
may be made compatible. Where in other Western democracies egalitarians ally with hierarchists to reduce inequality, in the United States
egalitarians have historically allied themselves with individualists.

The next section of this chapter explains why cultural theory is
relevant to the problem of explaining American exceptionalism. The
subsequent section exemplifies this hypothesis through a brief recon-
sideration of several early episodes in American history. Then we look
at exceptionalism as specific promises. The section after that reviews
the rise of egalitarianism in the past 30 years. The last section asks
whether America will continue to be exceptional and, if so, whether it
will continue to be exceptional in the same way. For if egalitarians will
no longer join with individualists and if hierarchy becomes ever
weaker, can egalitarians, with their rejection of followership as inequality, rule by themselves?

Exceptionalism in Political Culture

Political cultures are solutions people craft as they jointly form institutions to solve the problem of how human beings should live with
each other. Their answers to questions of social order—who am I?
what shall I do? with whom?—are provided by their cultures.[5]

Context counts: As the cultural parts make up the societal whole,
the ways in which they are combined—who allies with or opposes
whom, the relative strengths of the contending cultures—is of great
political importance. The combination of *hierarchy*[6] and
egalitarianism[7] I call *social democracy,* after the European nations
that add a strong egalitarian element to the sacrificial ethic of hierarchy, in which the individual parts are expected to aid the collective
whole. Where egalitarianism and *individualism* combine, so that equality of opportunity is believed to be compatible with equality of results,
as in the Jacksonian era of American political history, I call the mixture
American individualism. Extreme individualism in concert with the
fatalists' dominion of authoritarianism brings forth *state capitalism.*

Authoritarianism together with hierarchy breeds *totalitarianism*. The alliance of hierarchy and individualism can go by its colloquial name: *The establishment*. (See Figure 2.1.)

The policy preferences of people in political cultures follow from the desire to reinforce their own way of life and to destabilize that of their opponents. People's intentions—supporting, opposing, minimizing authority; increasing, decreasing, maintaining economic differences—remain constant, but their ideas about what will be efficacious vary according to the conditions of the time.

For present purposes, two hybrid regimes—social democracy and American individualism—are crucial. Change tends toward the dominant culture;[8] strong hierarchies attract weaker egalitarianism in Europe, while strong individualism attracts egalitarianism in America. This difference in cultural contexts explains why America and Europe

Figure 2.1   Model of Cultures in Context
Group Strength
Number of Prescriptions

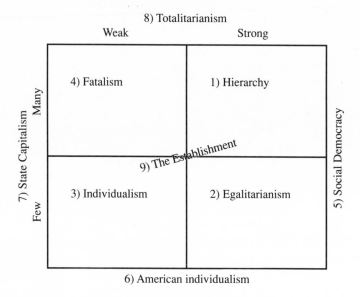

8) Totalitarianism

6) American individualism

Source: Developed by the author using a Thompson–Tuden matrix; see J. Thompson and A. Tuden, "Strategies, Structures, and Processes of Organizational Decision," in J. Thompson, ed., *Comparative Studies in Administration* (Pittsburgh, Pa.: University of Pittsburgh Press, 1959), pp. 195–216.

are different. European regimes are characterized by strong hierarchy, medium egalitarianism, and weak individualism, for instance, while the American regime is one of strong individualism, weak hierarchy, and medium-strength egalitarianism. The seemingly simple statement that egalitarianism is growing in two countries could imply quite different outcomes depending on whether there are or are not strong hierarchies to keep it in check. Thus the same explanation (if true, of course) accounts for Western European and American divergence. It takes two to differ.

What is exceptional in America is the alliance between egalitarianism and individualism. Try scanning your memory bank for European regimes that ever experienced anything similar; I come up empty. What made this combination possible in the United States? Historical study is necessary in order to trace the transmission of ideas and their institutional embodiment.

The cultural hybrid here called "American individualism" was possible because of historical circumstances that made alliance with hierarchy far less desirable than in Europe. For many (though not all) Americans, hierarchy faced a double whammy: Not only had Americans fought a revolutionary war against a distant hierarchy, but they also took their politics from the struggles within England to limit the efforts of the crown to subordinate republican government.

I have explained why many (but obviously not all) individualists opposed hierarchy (an alliance between individualism and hierarchy also being possible, as the Federalist party proves). But how were individualists able to come to terms with egalitarians who could conceivably have wished to redistribute the individualists' property? And how were egalitarians able to join individualists whose personal networks were based on achieving more than others?

What remains is to restate what has already been said in different terms. Because egalitarians were consumed by the struggle against the English hierarchy and were especially sensitive to what they perceived to be monarchical efforts to undermine self-rule, they identified the central government as a cause of inequality. Hence both egalitarians and individualists could join in severely limiting the size and scope of central government.

In a nation of small farmers, moreover, property was viewed as part of equality. How would large landowners be countered if not by spreading the holding of property? Rights in property, therefore, were commonly held to be essential to the defense of individual welfare.

Now we are on our way to an understanding of how the institutions that helped maintain American individualism—the separation of powers, federalism, and mass parties—were themselves reinforced by this compound of egalitarian and individualistic cultures. Federalism and separation of powers were partly carryovers of past practice during colonial times, partly chosen to help secure small central government, and partly maintained to join egalitarianism with individualism. Where European egalitarians have accepted the greater coerciveness of hierarchy in order to reduce inequalities, American egalitarians chose to trade some inequality for even less coerciveness. A smaller federal government was more beautiful to them. Roads and canals and economic development in general at the state level were supported by the cultural hybrid of American individualism. For it was not government per se but the purported inegalitarian character of central government to which egalitarians objected.

To have been there at the beginning, moreover, is not necessarily to have lasted until now. The separation of powers is given life by the identification of the different branches with stronger and weaker central government. Defending the institution then becomes equivalent to defending one's culture or way of life. Opposition to perceived inegalitarian measures taken by central governments also helped sustain federalism, while providing a home for opponents of central power. If central power corrupts, one would wish to oppose it even when one's own people were in office.

My emphasis on the cultural union of egalitarianism and individualism, producing a belief that equal outcomes and equal opportunity can be mutually reinforcing, is strengthened by the great American political invention: mass parties. Early on, these were not just parties as an undifferentiated mass, but specific Jeffersonian and Jacksonian parties organized to limit government severely. Andrew Jackson was the genius who created the president who acts publicly as a tribune of the people in order to diminish the size and scope of government.

Suppose, however, that the central government was eventually to become a possible source of greater equality of condition, and not the reverse. What would happen to the culture referred to here as American individualism? Before speculating about that, let us assay a preliminary test of this cultural hypothesis by briefly reviewing key episodes concerning political economy in early American history.

Selected Problems of Political Economy in the Early American Republic: Banks and Corruption

Imagine that today's left-wing liberals were opposed to the growth of government and to its regulation of business and that today's right-wing conservatives supported larger government actively intervening in the economy. That supposition would provide a much better guide to the struggles that ensued over our structure of the political economy from the founding of the republic to the Civil War than transposing current preferences into the past. Reading back current attitudes to public policy turns early political economy on its head—for the anti-federalists, the Jeffersonians, and the Jacksonians believed that central government was the source of artificial inequality that threatened republican government. Once that reversal is engraved on our consciousness—the political forces that we would now call progressive, left, or antiestablishment then identified central government with inequality—we are in a position to better understand the conflicts over Hamilton's funding of the debt, Jackson's opposition to the Bank of the United States, and Henry Clay's American system organized around internal improvements. And from these great struggles we will come to an understanding of the cultural context of exceptionalism.

The opposition to central funding of the debt, to a national bank, and to internal improvements was not opposition to business or to private markets per se. On the contrary, most families were engaged in farming, and most farmers thought of themselves as engaged in business, buying and selling land as well as produce. Market competition was in high repute, provided only that it was truly competitive—that is, uncontaminated by artificial restraints imposed by the central government. Nor was government per se the object of villification. State governments were encouraged to do the very thing denied to the central government. Why this enmity to central government?

"This measure," Jefferson wrote in *The Anas,* referring to federal assumption of state debts, "produced the most bitter and angry contest ever known in Congress before or since the Union of the States."[9] This was so, Jefferson argued, because the debt acted "as a machine for the corruption of the legislature." Now by "corruption" Jefferson and his supporters did not mean financial dishonesty; he knew Hamilton to be personally honest. Rather, drawing on their fears of the reestablishment of monarchy (read "hierarchy") in America, they meant the perversion of judgment caused by giving men with a financial stake in the debt a special interest in and an enhanced capacity for undermining the independent judgment of Congress. This political corruption, this fear of the decay of the foundations of disinterestedness required by republican government, is traced in Lance Banning's reconstruction of the struggles between the party of the king and the party of the country in England half a century earlier.

Ministers could . . . call upon additional inducements in the form of governmental offices or pensions for their parliamentary supporters. Patronage and governmental influence in elections . . . made it possible for ministries to exercise a certain measure of executive control of Parliament. . . . Court money was employed in parliamentary elections, purchasing the representatives and debasing the electors: "the little beggarly boroughs" were "pools of corruption."[10]

The source of this power, according to Bolingbroke's description of his quarrel with Walpole, was—in Banning's words—as follows:

Growing revenues and higher taxes make it possible for ministers to create a horde of officers, who fill the Parliament and exercise a rising influence in elections. The civil list provides vast funds for the corruption of Parliament, and the practice of anticipating revenues creates supplies. In fact, the means available to ministers have grown to such a great extent in recent years that the crown has now, through influence, powers just as great as it once had by prerogative. The fate of English liberty depends on a union of good men against the progress of corruption.[11]

This—just this—is what Jefferson meant when he charged that "Hamilton was not only a monarchist, but for a monarchy bottomed on corruption."[12]

Commerce and agriculture and artisanship, yes; but large-scale industry, no. James Savage sums it up:

Jefferson's great fear was that a central government burdened by deficits and debts would undermine its republican and constitutional foundations while promoting widespread social and economic inequality. This inequity would emerge through two simultaneously occurring events. First, speculators, bankers, and the moneyed aristocracy could gain the financial leverage and profits derived from financing the national debt. Second, the government itself would spend its added revenues by promoting an industrialized economy through Hamiltonian policies resembling those of mercantilist and corrupted England. Once again, England served as the model to be avoided, for just as its government was corrupted in no small way due to its enormous debt, English society and its moral values were also corrupted by a system of manufacturing and industry that created vast social and economic divisions.[13]

All this was to be undone by keeping the central government small, by paying off its debts, and by preventing the Hamiltonian machine from being driven by the engine of a national bank.

Republican thought, memorialized in writings of the anti-federal-ists,[14] considered substantial inequality of resources and a large-scale government to be incompatible with personal liberty. Their egalitarian views called for small agricultural communities in which an educated electorate—not far from one another in economic status and geo-graphic distance—would handle their affairs on a face-to-face basis.

By President Andrew Jackson's time, commerce had developed, the industrial revolution had begun, and banking was considerably more important than it heretofore had been. Jacksonians faced certain choices: If they controlled markets, thereby preventing inequality from growing, they risked losing personal liberty and gaining unwanted governmental growth; if they tried to remove impediments to markets, thus allowing more people to compete, the end result might be enduring inequality with its pernicious consequences for democratic life. In the end, they denied there was any conflict between economic competition and political equality.

The widespread belief among those contemporaries who theorized about Jacksonian democracy—a belief apparently shared by their supporters in the citizenry as well—was that equality of opportunity, meticulously followed, would lead to an approximation of equality of result. The operation of economic markets, unimpeded by the federal government, would eventually approximate real equality of condition—as closely as innate differences in human ability will permit. At the very least, central government would not add artificial to natural inequality, thereby preserving representative government. It is this belief—not in equality undefined, or in just one kind of equality, but in the *mutual reinforcement of opportunity and result*—that made Amer-ica truly exceptional.

Individuals would be allowed, and indeed encouraged, to keep all gain that resulted from the unfettered use of their own talents. But everything artificial and unnatural, everything government imposed on man in his free state—such as charters, franchises, banks, and other monopolies—became anathema. If every man could not be his own government, he could (and many Jacksonians advocated he should) become his own banker. As William M. Gouge argued in discussing money and banking, "a man has . . . a natural right to . . . profits," but the distribution of wealth depends on a nation's institutions. Once the granting by government of "peculiar commercial privileges" lays the "foundation of the artificial inequality of fortune," therefore, "all the subsequent operations of society tend to increase the difference in the condition of different classes in the community."[15] "Every corporate grant," as Theodore Sedgwick, Jr., put it, "is directly in the teeth of the doctrine of equal rights, for it gives to one set of men the exercize of privileges which the main body can never enjoy."[16] The remedy was clear: Abolish the "monster" bank.

If you believe that central government–chartered banks produce "artificial inequality,"[17] you would also agree with Jackson's attorney general, Roger Taney, that the Bank of the United States should not be rechartered because of "its corrupting influence . . . its patronage greater than that of the Government—its power to embarrass the operations of the Government—and to influence elections."[18] You would also understand why Jackson pledged that if he became president he would pay off the national debt "to prevent a monied aristocracy from growing up around our administration that must bend it to its views, and ultimately destroy the liberty of our country."[19] No wonder Jackson celebrated, in his own words, his "glorious triumph" when he "put to death, that mamouth of corruption and power, the Bank of the United States."[20]

Once inequality was laid at the door of central government, competitive markets could be reconciled with egalitarian outcomes, equality of opportunity with equality of result, by claiming that an attack on hierarchy (i.e., central government) could increase equality of opportunity, which would then, once artificial fetters were removed, naturally lead to tolerable equality of result. If, in hearing about American "equality," the citizen cannot tell whether the word refers to opportunity or result, and if, in regard to American "individualism," the citizen remains unaware of whether the culture referred to is individualist or egalitarian, that is the idea. The disagreement over meaning is the price of agreement on the term.

The Promise of Exceptionalism: Equal Opportunity and Equal Condition Are Compatible

Is the proof that America is exceptional—one may well ask—exemption from history? Has the abundance of the land, its dazzling array of resources, the conditions of its settlement, or the blessings of providence, made America invulnerable? Daniel Bell summarizes this notion of exceptionalism as

the idea that, having been "born free," America would, in the trials of history, get off "scot free." Having a common political faith from the start, it would escape the ideological vicissitudes and divisive passions of the European polity, and, being entirely a middle-class society, without aristocracy or *bohème,* it would not become "decadent," as had every other society in history. As a liberal society providing individual opportunity, safeguarding liberties, and expanding the standard of living, it would escape the disaffection of the intelligentsia, the resentment of the poor, the frustrations of the young—which, historically, had been the signs of disintegration, if not the beginning of revolution, in other societies. In this view, too, the United States, in becoming a world power, a paramount power, a hegemonic power, would, because it was democratic, be different in the exercise of that power than previous world empires.[21]

Disagreeing with this conception, I do not believe that, as Bell continues, "today, the belief in American exceptionalism has vanished with the end of empire, the weakening of power, the loss of faith in the nation's future."[22] The promise after all is not external, but internal—a promise about how Americans might live with one another, not a promise of power over strangers. What, I ask by way of summary, is the faith reflected in American exceptionalism?

America is about possibilities, not certainties. You can (but you don't have to) get rich. America is about promises. Here class divisions do exist, but they don't have to matter. Because, in America, competition can be compatible with equality, there is the promise of classlessness. Exceptionalism is the doctrine that justifies the promise.

The promise is in two parts. The first part—the promise of entry—is that competition will be possible. Entry is not equality. On the contrary, it is the promise that despite inequalities of all kinds—in formal education, literacy, ethnicity, status, wealth, and so on—advancement will still be possible. The related promise is that failure, when it occurs, need not be permanent. Robert Dahl's notion of "cumulative inequalities" tells us what America promises won't happen: that whatever inequalities exist will not grow so far in a single direction as to preclude the possibility of self-government.[23] Thus the second part of the promise is that, if artificial—that is, governmentally sponsored—is not added to natural inequality, we-the-people can still run our own lives.

The critical importance of balance in American political life is that it is meant to check cumulative inequalities by dividing power. Hence the importance of federalism and the separation of powers. The redundancy that results[24]—multiple institutions for doing practically anything, uncertainty over who is supposed to do what—shares power in the service of keeping the promise. Redundancy adds to reliability.

When the doctrine of exceptionalism holds that equal opportunity may be made compatible with sufficiently equal results as to make self-government possible, it both justifies inequality and seeks to prevent its institutionalization. When the argument goes beyond the prevention of cumulative inequalities to claim that inequality per se is incompatible with self-government, so that substantive equality must be achieved before equal opportunity (and hence the political system itself) may be deemed legitimate, exceptionalism American-style is over. For then egalitarianism becomes incompatible with individualism. Indeed, individualism has first to surrender its desire for differences before it can be accepted as legitimate. Social democracy—the European alliance of egalitarianism with hierarchy—becomes the remaining alternative. Or does it?

Among Lincoln's greatest achievements was the development of a Republican party in which individualism was the dominant force with hierarchy subordinate, thus reversing the cultural context of the Whig party. Never before had there been a party within which individualism was supreme. How, then, after the Civil War, did the heirs of Jefferson and Jackson slowly alter their heritage so as to give a greater role to government? How was "corruption" taken from central government and placed on corporate capitalism as the source of inequality? How did "states' rights" give way to national power as the preferred mechanism for equalization? How did Populists, the heirs of Jackson, shake off his time-honored view of the inherent corruption of government and change it into one in which central government became a force for equality? And how did the Progressives, heirs of the Whigs, get away from the party's self-denying ordinance on executive power (a reaction to their fear of "King Andrew" as a charismatic leader who would overturn the system)? If we knew the answers to these questions, we would know more about how America remained exceptional through depressions and wars.

And now, with the contemporary revival of egalitarianism in the form of feminism, gay rights, civil rights, animal rights, environmentalism, and the rest, we must ask whether American exceptionalism has or will soon come to an end. Will egalitarians return to their historic alliance with individualism, seeking to make opportunity serve autonomy, or will they go the European way toward hierarchy? Will egalitarians, in other words, embrace state power, accepting some coerciveness in order to gain greater equality? Or will egalitarians attempt the wholly unprecedented by ruling alone?

The Misleading Decade and the Past 30 Years

Thirty years ago, in the 1950s, there were no homeless people; there were only bums, drunks, psychos, and transients. The difference is that way back then people without homes were characterized in ways that made it clear that they—and not society—were responsible for the ills that befell them. In egalitarian parlance, in those days the victims were blamed. "Homeless" sounds like everybody else was given their fair portion but some, through no fault of their own, got left out. If people are home-less, presumably the remedy is for those who have neglected them to make them home-full—that is, to provide public housing.

Perhaps, as in the case of the homeless, it is well to begin comparing the 1950s to the 1980s with other categories of people who certainly existed then—sometimes in shocking conditions—but whose political presence was minor if not miniscule. In the 1950s (as distinguished from today) most people hardly noticed or talked about women's rights, gay rights, children's rights, or "grey power." What the groups acting under these rubrics have in common is a belief in "rights" conceived as greater equality of condition. All (yes, even animal rights) are committed to reducing differences among people. Of course, everyone you ask denies wanting everyone to be the same; on the contrary, they all feel that their way will lead to a renaissance of true individuality based on personal not social or economic differences. Nevertheless, given the usual array of differences, they will think these are too large and ought to be reduced.

I left out civil rights so as to accentuate its importance. It was known and discussed in the 1950s. But how different that discussion was. The civil rights issue was conceived to be equal opportunity, not equal condition: Wouldn't it be wonderful if racial bias, which gave preference to whites, were overcome so black people could vote and learn and work without discrimination? It would have been unthinkable for any group of distinguished people—let alone two former presidents, as Ford and Carter did recently—to hold up equality of condition as the norm for judging achievement. Ford and Carter are able to say that conditions are getting worse for black people because as a whole they have not caught up with whites, though most are doing considerably better. In earlier times, such visible social commentators would have— as the song says—accentuated the positive.

The 1950s journalist was cynical but supportive. American institutions were good; the more the pity, then, that public officials did not always live up to them. Reporters—recall the frenzy at the Iran–Contra press conference—were not yet Paparazzi. Imagine in the 1980s a President Kennedy, contrite over the Bay of Pigs, not only telling the American people that the whole thing was so bad he wasn't going to talk about it again—but getting away with it. Or think back to President Eisenhower confronting Soviet Party Secretary Khrushchev over the U-2 incident and not getting savaged by the media for duplicity. The tolerance for error, the point is, has grossly diminished. I hereby allude to the fact that John F. Kennedy's extramarital affairs were kept out of public view, while Jimmy Carter's mental temptations became headline news and Gary Hart's political career was ruined. Both survey evidence and analysis of media content reveal that the major media have an egalitarian bent.[25]

The reader possibly has been given sufficient background—a rise in system blame, a decline in system support—to appreciate a quality of the 1950s that occasions much difference of opinion. Talk to a Hungarian refugee or anyone whose main political memories date from that time, and you will find a near-idyllic America. Stability, amicability, consensus were the bywords. After the demise of McCarthyism, no major movement appeared to threaten the tranquility of American life. Not so, a few radicals cried, pointing to poverty, racism, militarism, and other sources of discontent they assumed to be seething beneath the surface. Asked to put up or shut up, their voices could find no popular echo.

I think both sides were right: There was tranquility, *then;* there were also people wanting to be liberated and issues waiting to be born, *later.* So what else is new? Change is part of life. True, but not so true if one takes the 1950s as the standard against which to measure other times. Looked at through the lenses of the decades before and after, the 1950s were a lot less turbulent. It may be that unexpected prosperity after the World War II created a wave of optimism that, for a time, dampened conflict. The awakening to worldwide responsibilities, reluctantly but adventurously pursued, may have focused conflict outward. Whatever the reasons, support for the status quo was stronger and for change was weaker than it had been or would be.

Think of America's churches. In the 1950s, Protestant fundamentalists were not active in politics. It took Supreme Court decisions permitting abortion and forbidding prayer in public schools to do that. The World Council of Churches was an international do-good organization, supporting the United Nations, foreign aid, and—along the way—American foreign policy. From the mid-1960s through the mid-

1980s, while retaining its internationalism, the WCC has directed it toward opposing the foreign policy of the United States. The WCC's posture is egalitarian—that is, supporting the Third World against the First. As for the Catholic church in the 1950s, its bishops were largely hierarchical, a posture ameliorated by traditional social doctrine, which called on the better-off to help the worse-off, and the identification of many of its ethnic parishioners with the Democratic party. Nowadays the Catholic bishops' conference has become egalitarian.[26] What a long way from the more-reactionary-than-thou Cardinal Spellman of my youth. Unless memory plays me more than its usual tricks, I recall him breaking a strike of not-too-well-paid gravediggers in Catholic cemeteries by using labor recruited from the young men of the seminaries. No chance of something like that happening in our time.

Worrying whether the United States would become addicted to excessive force in the international system, toppling regimes in the Dominican Republic and Iran, as in the 1950s, is quite different from wondering if its people would support a two-week war (one week longer than Grenada, the longest "war" conducted by the Reagan administration). So far, in Panama, the Bush administration has not exceeded that record (though it has in the Persian Gulf). It is apparent that support for armed intervention has declined greatly. It is also apparent that there is far more disposition to challenge government than there was 30 years ago. Against this view it could be said that there was considerable conflict over foreign policy in the 1950s. True but, again, misleading. True, the war in Korea became unpopular; true, also, that questions like "Who lost China to the communists?" and (if I am permitted a year's advance) slogans about the "missile gap" were prevalent; the point, however, is that those were conflicts over means— how best to defend against communism—not about the justness of the cause. The moral tone today is much different than it was 30 years ago. The question was whether McCarthyism would win—that is, whether basic liberties would be preserved from forces wrapping themselves up in the flag—not whether the flag would escape burning.[27]

The most distorting impression left by the 1950s—one that colors American politics in the wrong hues even today—concerns the nation's two major political parties. Party policies and presidential candidates are still viewed, so it seems to me, as if they were the same or similar to those we saw in the 1950s—conservative, pragmatic, centrist—and made more so by competing for the same moderate nonideological electorate. Of the mass electorate, this description may have more validity; but of party activists, nothing could be more mistaken.

The activists who dominate the major parties and the public officials who represent them have undergone a radical transformation in the past 30 years. The Democratic party of Hubert Humphrey and Henry Jackson is no more. Which of today's leaders carries on their belief in a strong welfare policy coupled with a strong defense? What is more, the meaning of "liberal" has dramatically expanded. Where it designated a belief in modestly more welfare protection—perhaps a Fair Employment Practices Commission to ward off the worst discrimination and that was all—to be a liberal now signifies that one subscribes to most all of the following positions: more welfare; less defense; less prayer in public schools; more women's rights, including the right to abortion; more environmental expenditure; fewer property rights; and discrimination in favor of designated groups. In short, the Democratic party is now under the control of activists who believe generally in greater equality of condition.

The Republican party of President Eisenhower is no more. As Republicans have moved south and conservative Southern Democrats have converted to the Republican party, each party has become more like its main tendency. Among Republicans, this means Northern and Western liberals are a vanishing breed. Republican activists now come in two kinds: free market conservatives and hierarchical-patriarchal conservatives, popularly known as economic conservatives and social conservatives.

The days when *le homme bourgeois* could sleep well before the election—knowing that whichever party won wouldn't matter that much—are over. It remains only for contemporary opinion to catch up with the past 30 years.

Will America Continue to Be Exceptional?

Hierarchy is growing weaker. Every large-scale integrative institution, from parties to unions to churches, is weaker than it was. Individualism remains strong but is being challenged by egalitarianism.[28] Empathy for (and sympathy with) capitalism—whether it be on the part of Catholic bishops or Democratic party activists[29] or public interest lobbyists[30] or major journalists[31] or academics who, like Charles E. Lindblom, refer to "The Market as [a] Prison"[32]—has declined. There is still a sneaking admiration for capitalism but not, among egalitarians, positive moral support.

Democratic party activists—the most radical segment of the party—are egalitarians.[33] They see government as a vastly expanded compensatory mechanism whose purpose it is to make up for past inequalities. Their cultural forebears, at the dawn of the American republic, saw central government as engaging in reverse redistribution. When these old exceptionalists blamed "the system," they had in mind central government acting to increase inequality, which is what made their alliance with individualists possible. When today's left-liberal Democrats blame the system for inequality, they want government to do things it is not now doing or to do more of what it is doing, mostly through higher taxes, which leads individualists to oppose them. By the system that is blameworthy, the new egalitarians no longer mean central government but market individualism.

Who, if anyone, will today's egalitarians ally themselves with? They oppose capitalism as based on unfair competition that increases inequality. The egalitarian desire to use central government to redistribute resources suggests that modern-day egalitarians might be willing to ally themselves with hierarchical forces. But that would make it difficult for gays, feminists, and other elements of the egalitarian constituency to coalesce. Egalitarians appear hostile to social no less than economic conservatives. Moreover, American hierarchists seem too weak to be worth allying with. Can egalitarians rule by themselves?

The only effort to organize a unicultural regime in the United States, so far as I know, was President John Tyler's ("His Accidency") in 1840. It failed. The only effort at cultural fusion, combining the three cultures, was President James Monroe's during the so-called Era of Good Feelings. It lasted a few years before party conflict took over. The only other regimes with significant egalitarian content—Jefferson's and Jackson's—had large (and some historians would say dominant) individualist influence.[34]

America, it appears, will remain without strong hierarchy. Whether it will retain its old exceptionalism in which equal opportunity is made compatible with equal results, or whether it will turn to a new exceptionalism in which equal opportunity is rejected in favor of far more equal outcomes—a regime based on equality—is now being decided.

In sum, I agree with those who see in the strength of individualism and the weakness of hierarchy clues to historic American exceptionalism. I agree also with those who see in American institutions, its land, its frontiers, its people, and its institutions (federalism and separation of powers) further clues to what makes America special. I have argued not that these insights are mistaken, but that they need to be combined through the analysis of conflicting cultures so that there are not ideas without people or social relations without justifications but all together in cultural context.

The frontier hypothesis is famous for its attractiveness, its contradictions, and its vagueness. Perhaps what makes America special is the huge tracts of vacant land. Why Canada, Australia, Brazil, the Soviet Union, and Argentina do not manifest the same negative attitudes toward authority then becomes puzzling. If the availability of frontiers siphons off discontent, as is often claimed, why has the United States remained relatively content compared to most European countries both before and after its geographic frontiers diminished? And why were the areas left behind often more volatile (e.g., the Civil War) if the most volatile people were allegedly drawn off? If, as cultural theory claims, however, exceptionalism is imbedded in cultural context—so the American people carry it with them wherever they go—the reproduction of exceptional behavior becomes more understandable. And so would the end of American exceptionalism when the cultural alliance that called it forth is no longer in existence.

Why has there been no socialism, no successful socialist party, no intense class conflict in America? The short answer is that Americans institutionalized beliefs that worked against such developments. The strength of individualism and the weakness of hierarchy—to start where agreement is greatest—mean that nationalization of industry is widely regarded as wrong. Not only large corporations and small businesses, who help make individualism powerful, but also egalitarians of all stripes reject that solution. Instead they once hoped to make individualism-cum-capitalism contribute to equality by depriving it of special privilege. Before the Civil War, that meant keeping central government small and weak. After the Civil War, that increasingly has come to mean using the central government to regulate big business. Though the tactics differ according to the conditions of the time, the purpose remains the same: making liberty and equality compatible.

One can (and some do) look on this belief as naive, foolish, or—worse—a justification of exploitation. One can also (as I do) look on it as worthy, heroic, even romantic—a part of the world's endangered political species, of which, when gone, there may be no more.

3

The Internal Transformation of the Major Political Parties: Democratic Activists Are Increasingly Egalitarian, Republicans Individualist and Hierarchical

The received wisdom is that there has been no transformation of American political parties since the New Deal era of the 1930s. By "transformation" is meant the change of party loyalties from one major party to the other by a significant proportion of the electorate. It is agreed that such a transformation is taking place in the South as formerly conservative Democrats become Republican and as liberals, black and white, become even more Democratic. There has also been a movement of Republicans into the South.

Too little attention has been paid, in my opinion, to the alteration in character of the most active members of each party. In cultural terms, Democratic activists, who used to be culturally heterogeneous, are becoming monolithically egalitarian, while Republican activists are more individualist as well as hierarchical than before. Consequently, the Republican party of Nelson Rockefeller and Dwight Eisenhower is no more, while the same can be said of the Democratic party of Harry Truman and Hubert Humphrey. In their place are party activists far more extreme (pure or consistent, if you like) than in the recent past.

Adapted from Nelson W. Polsby and Aaron Wildavsky, *Presidential Elections,* 7th ed. (New York: Free Press, 1988).

I am often asked for evidence of increased egalitarianism in American political life after I have just made a demonstration of it. When I see it everywhere and others claim it is nowhere, demonstration becomes difficult. On probing, I discover that those who perceive our polity as woefully inegalitarian tend to believe that anything short of radical restructuring shows nothing has happened. Because equality of condition is not a recognized way of life or ideological tendency, as are market individualism and hierarchical collectivism, many tend to miss it when it does show up. Thinking of equality as redistribution of economic resources, moreover, tends to blind people to its larger meaning as "diminution of distinctions"—from race and gender to power and professorships.

It is true that in recent years the distribution of income has become slightly more unequal, though governmental programs make income somewhat more equal. Unless one is an economic determinist, however, that does not negate the fact that other areas of life show pronounced egalitarian influence. Thus increased income inequality is offset by redistributive spending programs.

My aim in this chapter is to demonstrate the vast changes in the ideologies of party activists since 1968. This provides evidence in depth of growing egalitarianism among people active in politics.

Party Ideology and Political Polarization since 1972

The major study of the 1976 and 1980 convention delegates—Warren E. Miller and M. Kent Jennings's *Parties in Transition*—found "large absolute differences in terms of what are widely recognized as conservative and liberal positions."[1] (See Figure 3.1.) Dramatic differences between the parties, which "provide striking evidence of party polarization at the elite levels," were also displayed in the evaluations of 13 groups on a thermometer of feeling.[2] (See Figure 3.2.) Miller and Jennings report,

> The basic data demonstrate more than simple differential affinity; they also demonstrate differential antipathy. Using 50° on the feeling thermometer as the midpoint of positive–negative affect, it turns out that Republicans granted only one presumptively liberal group a mark of 50° or higher, and that group is the broad population grouping of Blacks. All of the patently liberal groups were rated below 50° on the average, often far below that midway point. For their part, the Democrats accorded no

Figure 3.1   Interparty Differences on Issue Positions among Convention
Delegates, 1972–1980
(Entries represent the Republican mean scores minus the Democratic mean
scores. The larger the difference, the more conservative Republicans are
compared with Democrats.)

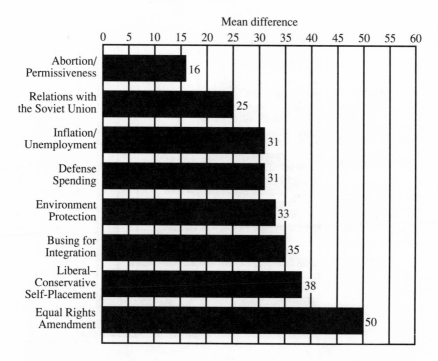

Source: Warren E. Miller and M. Kent Jennings, with Barbara G. Farah, *Parties in Transition: A Longitudinal Study of Party Elites and Party Supporters* (New York: Russell Sage Foundation, 1986), p. 164.

conservative group a mark above 50°, whereas all liberal groups except
that of Gay Rights were scored above 50°.

This element of differential rejection and antipathy, when coupled with
the element of differential approval, not only produces the extreme
differences between the parties in terms of group evaluations, but it also
implies a marked polarization of attitudes toward groups going well
beyond varying degrees of favorableness. In this sense the opinion
cultures of the two elites are truly antagonistic.[3]

What explains this party polarization? The more continuously active
the delegates over the years, Miller and Jennings show, the greater the

Figure 3.2   Interparty Differences on Group Evaluations among Convention Delegates, 1972–1980
(Entries represent the Republican mean scores minus the Democratic mean scores.)

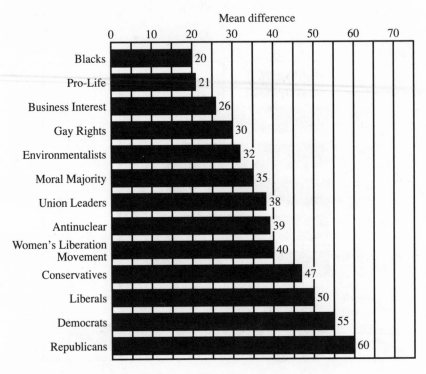

Source: Warren E. Miller and M. Kent Jennings, with Barbara Farah, *Parties in Transition: A Longitudinal Study of Party Elites and Party Supporters* (New York: Russell Sage Foundation, 1986), p. 167.

polarization among Republicans and Democrats.[4] In fact, partisan conflict was considerably less among the 1972 delegates who later dropped out of presidential nominating politics than among those who stayed in. Both turnover and individual change resulted in greater party polarization by 1980.[5]

Prior to 1972, Democratic delegates were closer in issue preferences to Democratic voters than were Republican delegates to those who voted for Republicans. That older relationship—first measured and identified by Herbert McClosky in 1956—reasserted itself in 1976.[6]

What accounts for the greater distance between Republican activists and voters in 1980 compared to 1972? The least conservative activists and hence those closest to the rank and file tended to drop out. The activists who replaced them were more conservative. And those who remained active from 1972 onward themselves became progressively more conservative.[7] Apparently there were profound internal changes among the population of delegates.

A glance at the pie and bar charts prepared by the University of Michigan Center for Political Studies from 1984 data on delegate issue preferences and preferred spending allocations reveals that the party activists remained polarized (Figures 3.3 and 3.4). The only issues on which there was consensus between the rival activists were spending less on foreign aid, more support for science, and fighting crime. Every other issue—domestic policy, defense policy, foreign policy, the environment, prayer, abortion, even social security (which for years was uncontested between the parties)—reveals large differences.[8]

The university analysts concluded, moreover, that there was "a deep schism among Republican delegates, much deeper than those which separated the policy preferences of supporters of the major Democratic candidates." On only one issue—busing (which is declining in saliency)—were Democratic delegates more disunited than Republicans. Everywhere else—even on defense spending, Star Wars, prayer in schools, and abortion, on which the Reagan administration had taken a definite stand—Republicans were far more divided than Democrats.[9] This division occurs, I believe, because Democratic activists are overwhelmingly egalitarian while their Republican counterparts are divided among individualists and hierarchists.

Among Democratic delegates, women were consistently the most liberal on most issues, especially in their positive appraisal of spending on health and welfare services and their negative view of defense. Though their differences with already liberal Democratic male delegates are not large, Jennings concludes, "they definitely bespeak an element of liberal ideology that serves to alter the ideological cast of the Democratic conventions and, at a further remove, the composition of the party cadres and leaders." Though Republican women are moderately more liberal than the party's male delegates, Democratic women "are infinitely closer to Democratic men than to Republican women."[10]

Thus party still matters more than gender in organizing the political preferences of party activists. As Jennings says, "the vast dissimilarities in ideological orientation according to party tend to swamp what modest differences are provided by gender."[11] But the influx of women

Figure 3.3 Policy Preferences among National Convention Delegates, 1984

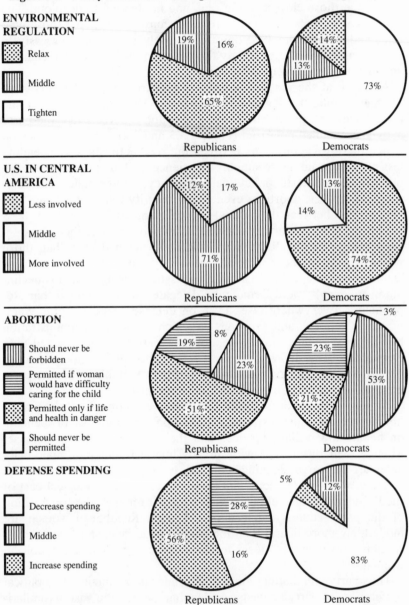

Source: Center for Political Studies, Institute for Social Research, "Convention Delegate Study: Report to Respondents," University of Michigan, Ann Arbor, 1985, p. 4.

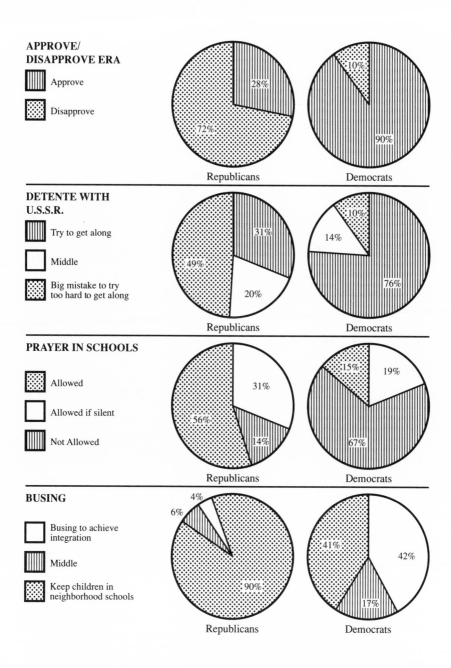

APPROVE/
DISAPPROVE ERA

▦ Approve

▨ Disapprove

Republicans

Democrats

DETENTE WITH
U.S.S.R.

▦ Try to get along

☐ Middle

▨ Big mistake to try
too hard to get along

Republicans

Democrats

PRAYER IN SCHOOLS

▨ Allowed

☐ Allowed if silent

▦ Not Allowed

Republicans

Democrats

BUSING

☐ Busing to achieve
integration

▦ Middle

▨ Keep children in
neighborhood schools

Republicans

Democrats

Figure 3.4 Preferred Budgetary Allocations among National
Convention Delegates, 1984

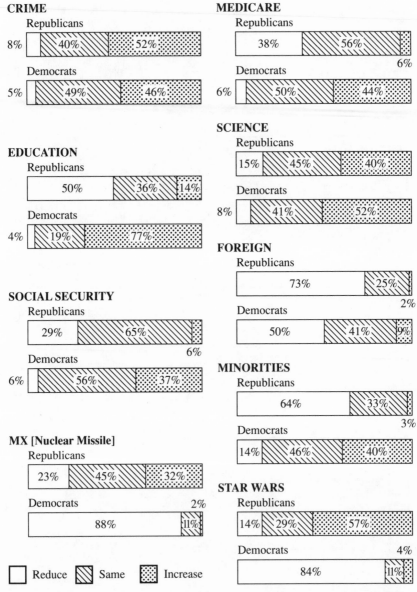

Source: Center for Political Studies, Institute for Social Research, "Convention Delegate Study: Report to Respondents," University of Michigan, Ann Arbor, 1985, p. 5.

has added to the Democratic party's liberal stance. Republican women are relatively conservative for women but are nevertheless liberal for Republicans, and so the net effect of their growing participation has somewhat diminished the ideological cohesion among Republican delegates. (See Figure 3.5.)

A study by Barbara G. Farah on the composition of delegates from 1944 to 1984 reveals that the big demographic change over that time lies in a four-and-a-half-fold increase in women.[12] From 1972 to 1976, a good half of female Democratic delegates were employed in the public sector, either in government itself or in public education. This was also true of a little over a third of Democratic male delegates. Among Republicans, somewhat more than a third of female and just under a fifth of male delegates were some sort of government employee. More than a quarter of all delegates were union members, most of them teachers or from other public-sector unions. For women in particular, then, Jennings concludes, "Public employment is a key route to the avenues of party power."[13]

As the traditional party of government, it is to be expected that Democratic delegates would come more heavily from the public sector. This may also explain why they seek higher spending on domestic

Figure 3.5 Delegates' Decline in Party Support, 1972–1984

PERCENT SUPPORTING POLITICAL PARTY "VERY STRONGLY"

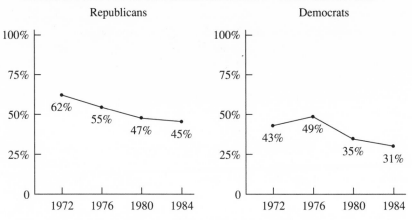

Source: Center for Political Studies, Institute for Social Research, "Convention Delegate Study: Report to Respondents," University of Michigan, Ann Arbor, 1985, p. 2.

programs. But there is nothing inherent in public-sector employment that would necessarily lead to a preference for lower spending on defense, or against military intervention in Central America, or for liberal positions on social issues. For that we must look to an ideological explanation. Jo Freeman conjectures,

> The 1984 conventions solidified the direction in which both parties had been moving for the previous ten years. The Democrats adopted the feminist perspective on all public issues directly affecting women and made it clear that women, under feminist leadership, were an important part of the Democratic coalition. The Republican Party adopted antifeminist positions on almost every issue. Its public script was written by Phyllis Schlafly. But it didn't repudiate women; instead it affirmed their importance by showcasing them extensively and devoting more real resources to help women, as individuals, get elected, than the Democratic Party has done.[14]

What happens when party and ideology conflict? A "requirement of participating in the mainstream of the party," Freeman says, "is that one not become an electoral liability. NOW [National Organization for Women] demonstrated its awareness of this rule by endorsing Democratic men running against Republican feminist women, arguing that anyone who supports Reagan's economic program, and that doesn't support pro-choice [on the abortion issue], is not really a feminist."[15]

Evidence from representative governments throughout the world demonstrates that voters have more moderate views than elected officials, who in turn are more moderate than party activists.[16] In 1984 there was poll evidence sustaining this view, showing Democratic voters to be slightly and delegates vastly more liberal than the average of the general population, except on national health care. (See Table 3.1.) Moreover, Democratic delegates grew more liberal from 1980 to 1984.[17]

While the general public prefers smaller government and lower taxes far more than do Democratic activists, the public also likes welfare and health spending a lot more than Republican activists do. Where the rank and file are 32 points apart on the scoring system used by Warren Miller (whose findings these are), party activists are 108 points apart—more than three times further away.[18] (See Table 3.2.) We conclude that, when party activists talk about the great issues that separate them, they are not talking about the public, which is much more moderate, but about themselves.

Table 3.1 Democratic Delegates to the Left of Rank and File and the Public at Large, 1984

	Public	Democrats	Delegates
Ratify ERA	60	64	91
Blacks are long way from the same chance as whites	55	63	85
CIA should help friendly governments and undermine hostile governments	40	36	14
Reinstitute the draft	49	51	26
U.S. should take all steps including force to stop communism	63	59	22
Government should raise taxes to deal with deficit	23	22	53
U.S. can meet security obligations with smaller military budget	49	59	85
Government should stop building nuclear power plants for safety reasons	56	64	65
Government should institute national health-care program	71	81	70

Source: From Peter Begans, "The ABC News/Washington *Post* Poll," surveys 0122–0125, 1984, p. 4.

Democratic activists agree on a wide range of issues that differ from those faced by their party predecessors. Franklin Roosevelt, Harry Truman, John Kennedy, Lyndon Johnson, and their party supporters regarded themselves as insiders whose talk it was to moderate the injustices of capitalism through mild redistributive measures, while building up national defense to support international commitments. Nonpresidential exemplars of this view were Senators Hubert Humphrey and Henry Jackson, who combined a pro-welfare stance with a strongly internationalist posture. Because the Democratic party had a significant Southern base and was otherwise diverse, until the 1948 convention it was silent or very cautious on civil rights measures and would not touch social issues. This posture of an active central government intervening in pursuit of economic growth, economic redistribution, and internationalism was typical of the American brand of liberalism until the late 1960s.

Nowadays Democratic activists agree substantially on more social welfare but less defense spending, more environmental regulation but less foreign involvement, more affirmative action but fewer subsidies to industry, more restriction on prayer in schools but fewer impedi-

Table 3.2   Ideology and Policy Preferences, 1984, for Partisan Activists and Rank-and-file Party Followers

	Democratic Party		Republican Party	
	Activists	Rank and File	Rank and File	Activists
Ideological self-designation	64	12	−40	−84
Abortion	57	20	10	−28
Moral Majority	94	15	− 1	− 2
Aid to women	65	21	−11	−45
Women's movement	73	49	−26	−53
Blacks	76	54	45	− 1
Busing	4	−61	−80	−83
Defense	84	16	−27	−42
Détente	69	9	−26	−16
Central America	65	33	9	−66
Average	+65	+17	−15	−43

Note: Minus means more conservative, and plus more liberal.

Source: Warren E. Miller, Blazer Lecture on "Ideology and Polarity in American Politics," University of Kentucky, Lexington, March 9, 1987.

ments to abortion. Democrats are, in short, increasingly committed to equality in the outcomes of social and political life. In its rules, in its party platform, and in its congressional programs, the Democratic party seeks not only to reduce gaps in income, but also to diminish differences in power between men and women, black and white, gay and straight, young and old. Thus a commitment to greater equality leads to lower defense spending, because defense takes from welfare; greater governmental intervention to secure jobs and investment opportunities for minorities, women, and others who have not had their fair share; but less intervention against people, such as gay men and women, who have been treated unequally.

In the 1930s, Republican party values were highly individualistic, favoring both less domestic and less foreign involvement by the government. The struggle within the Republican party to nominate Dwight Eisenhower was an explicit attempt to change these values—a fight between the Main Street and the Wall Street factions of the party. During the Eisenhower presidency the Republican party came to a grudging acceptance of social security and related measures and a more active stance in the international arena. Making the Republican party safe for internationalism was Eisenhower's central goal in office. Thus Republican disputes with Democrats from the 1960s onward were largely confined to domestic (bigger versus smaller government) issues. The Republican party today is a coalition of economic libertarians and social conservatives. A successor to the Whig party, which believed in social hierarchy, the Republican party has always had a traditional belief in the importance of social order. Integral to this view was a belief that there are inherent differences among people that justified their taking on different roles in society. Recently the Republicans have received an influx of fundamentalist Christians who have a hierarchical conception of desirable social differences, with a corresponding belief that there are large moral differences between right and wrong.

With Democratic activists increasingly professing belief in reducing economic and social differences among people, and Republican activists desiring to maintain or increase such differences, the parties have found new grounds for opposition. This distancing has taken place not only on questions of economic redistribution, popularized by the New Deal, but even more so on social issues and on defense policy. Democratic activists have moved toward such policies as affirmative action and the Equal Rights Amendment (ERA). Republican activists have rallied to the defense of existing institutions: the family, the market, and even the government as a provider of law and order at home and abroad. Opposing Democrats, however, is not quite the same as achieving agreement among Republicans.

On social issues, the Republican party's free enterprisers have not been happy with their party's opposition to abortion or its advocacy of prayer in schools. Economic conservatives frequently believe that defense spending is too high. The party's growing number of female activists, while generally opposed to ERA and abortion, have been less opposed than Republican men.

As for the party's social conservatives, their emphasis on family, order, and obedience to a strict moral code has led them to dislike government intervention in economic affairs that individuals should handle for themselves or within their community. Believing in hierarchical principles, however, they are somewhat more disposed than free marketers to approve of social welfare, especially medical programs.

Thus, although Republican activists remain far more socially homogeneous than are their Democratic peers, ideological differences among active Republicans have increased. The great contemporary divide between the parties is whether equal opportunity (Republican) or more equal outcomes (Democratic) should be the guiding norm for American public policy.

Now we can guess why in the midst of a considerable change in policy preferences, wholesale party realignment fails to appear: The major parties have realigned themselves internally. This is most evident in the South as newcomers and young voters have become increasingly Republican.[19] There is also considerable movement in and out of each party, thus facilitating their greater homogeneity. Whether and to what degree the electorate supports the new directions of the parties remains to be seen. But the older view that the major parties were essentially alike, which was never true, is even less true today.

4

Is Egalitarianism Really on the Rise?

with Brendon Swedlow

In making claims about the rise of radical egalitarianism in the United States, we are sometimes met with the counterclaim that in fact the United States is becoming less and less egalitarian. We cite the evidence: Compared to the 1950s or any other earlier decade, people who wish to diminish distinctions among other people and those who empathize and sympathize and support them are much more influential. In the 1950s, for instance, gay and lesbian individuals and groups were occasionally seen but rarely heard from; certainly they had virtually no political influence. Indeed, to be identified as gay or lesbian was equivalent to disqualifying oneself for public office and opening oneself up to discrimination and worse. Now things are radically different.

And among heterosexuals, feminism—which calls for breaking down distinctions as to who is supposed to do what in the home and on the job—has gained significant support among American women and men. Ethnicity, particularly among those with foreign-sounding names, which used to be something to hide or at least not to parade about, is, as we say, "in"—a fact to which Wildavsky can testify. Rules and regulations proscribing what business cannot do and prescribing what it must do have grown greatly since the 1950s. While business in general has influence, it is nothing like what it was in the past. Everywhere one looks—or so it seems to us—one finds people trying to diminish differences; whether it is those between black and white adults (civil rights) and parents and children (children's rights) or people and animals (animal rights) or trees and rivers and people (environmentalism) or old and young (grey power), the trend to reducing differences is unmistakable. How else, for instance, can one explain the extremity and the rapidity with which retirement ages—so long ensconced in our institutions—have been swept away, with hardly a word of protest. Nowadays those who wish to maintain distinctions (e.g., virginity, deference, patriotism) have to explain why the behavior indicated ought to be enacted, whereas in the past those who wished to erode distinctions had the onus of proof.

There are those who claim there is now less equality than there had been before. As evidence they point to what they consider the reactionary Reagan years and the inability to elect people they consider mildly liberal as Republicans sweep the presidency. Most of all they refer to recent trends in which the distribution of income has become somewhat less equal than it was in the 1950s or 1960s. Now this distribution has been stable and considerably unequal for 200 years. It changes only glacially. And it is true that it has become somewhat more unequal in the past 20 years. At the same time, however, governmental transfer payments have reduced this inequality. And if it is per person and not per family income that is counted, income inequality declines even further. Overall, taking into account the tendency of the private sector to result in somewhat more unequal outcomes and of the public sector to result in moderately more equal outcomes, the overall result is either that nothing much has changed in income distribution or that the public sector offsets the private sector's tendency toward somewhat greater inequality.[1]

Most important of all, perhaps, to those who perceive increasing inequality in American society, or at least no decrease in inequality, is that what has been classically called the "life chances" of various kinds of people are still substantially different. They point to very poor people in general or to minorities or to the handicapped or to those they consider permanently disadvantaged. In response, those who see more opportunity in American life point to rapid rates of both upward and downward mobility. Thirty years ago, say, it was unusual to hear ethnic names as heads of corporations, and now it is quite common. Lots of people whose families had a good deal of money and considerable educational advantage do not do so well, whereas others with the opposite characteristics are now thriving.[2] Much depends, as the reader can tell, on which part of American life one chooses to focus on. Is it the poverty and poor educational performance of certain minorities in central cities or is it the rapid rise of Indians from India or the Vietnamese or Koreans who come to the United States? If the system persistently discriminated against people of color, one would not find these disparate results. If the system created genuine equality of opportunity, as its proponents claim—the other side says—we would not find certain groups statistically doing worse in quality of life over considerable periods of time.

One difference between those who see equality as growing and those who see it as declining lies in what they consider most important. If the economic sphere is considered dominant, obviously there is going to be a lot less equality than if one considers the cultural sphere, family, art, literature, and the rest. The portrait of business in the movies and television, for instance, is one of almost unrelieved condemnation. Yes—the other side might possibly agree—but business executives have so much more income and other resources than ordinary Americans they must be more powerful.[3] Selective perception on both sides is powerful.

A lot of the difference depends on the kinds of examples people choose to emphasize. Some people see those with wealth as undeserving, uncaring, and far too powerful. We ourselves tend to notice how often they disparage their wealth or use it for egalitarian purposes. Like what? Like the long list of foundations, all based on private wealth, whose main purpose in life is to secure egalitarian outcomes. Like the most recent example we have run across. In the June 10, 1990, edition of the San Francisco *Examiner* we read of the "power wedding"—as the press dubs it—between the scions of two prominent political families: Kerry Kennedy, a daughter of the late Robert F. Kennedy, and Anthony Cuomo, son of Governor Mario Como of New York. Their occupations are instructive. In addition to being a political advisor to his father, Anthony Cuomo is head of a New York foundation to help the homeless, and Kerry Kennedy is head of a human rights foundation named after her father. They are out of the money-making business and into the do-gooding business. What kind of good? Most interesting are their vows. Can any reader recall people getting married who swore—as the newspaper put it—"mutual commitment to the oppressed"? Like who? Like "the people who have disappeared in El Salvador, the children in shelters in New York." Both instances chosen represent implied rebukes to the political system in the United States. Why is our country allied with those in El Salvador who are responsible for the disappearance of innocent others? And why does our system permit people to be homeless? Of course, it would be possible to say that children in shelters in New York are unfortunate but not necessarily "oppressed"—a word that suggests they are there not because of happenstance or because of the misfortune or failure of their parents, but because some nasty people or system put them there and keeps them there.

With the effort of egalitarians to show that virtually every group or grouping in the United States—aside from white males—is oppressed, it is not surprising that rival equalities sometimes conflict. Equal one way is often unequal another. In 1989, for example, a Fair Housing Act was passed containing provisions that make it unlawful to discriminate against families with children. Unless more than 80 percent of the people in a housing complex are over the age of 55 and it also provides special facilities for the elderly, it must admit children. These provisions do not accord with the desires of elderly people who are active and independent but do not wish to live near children. If the elderly have the right to live among their own and families with children have the right to find housing where they can, somebody's right will have to give way.[4]

Global Exchange is an education, research, and nonprofit action center in San Francisco that takes people on rough-and-ready tours of Appalachia—designated as the "Third World of the United States"— in order to encourage them to engage in community activities to break stereotypical differences between the First and Third Worlds. From this we would conclude that Global Exchange is an egalitarian organization that seeks to reduce differences between rich and poor countries by encouraging activism along egalitarian lines. Could one venture to say this much, the reader might wonder, with so little to go on? The tour coordinator, Laurie Adams, answers the question by telling us why she believes there are similarities between Appalachia and Third World countries:

> The resources, such as coal, are extracted for the benefit of rich outsiders while local workers live in poverty and face dangerous working conditions. A lot of the control is in the hands of distant politicians and corporate boards, not in the hands of local people. Environmental destruction is wrought by things such as the coal mining industry. And health care, education and transportation systems aren't fairly distributed.[5]

One hears crude materialist explanations so often nowadays, accompanied by some version of the old English song "It's the rich what gets the pleasure; it's the poor what gets the blame,'' that one hardly notices when it occurs.

The Signs of the Times

The signs all point, we insist, toward a rise in egalitarian culture. Among other indicators, this culture is recognizable by its adherents' preference for equality among humans along every dimension, by their shared belief that nature is fragile and humanity naturally good, by their aversion to the technology they believe supports inequality, and by their tendency to blame "the system" when things go wrong. People who hold these beliefs and values tend to cluster or "culture" together because these beliefs and values are mutually reinforcing. They go together just like the people who hold them.

The criteria we cite for a rise in this egalitarian culture are of several kinds, some of which have been discussed at various points and to varying degrees in this book. First, perhaps, are the increasing *numbers* of people who hold one or more egalitarian beliefs or preferences among political activists.[6] Whether the general public holds such views is not yet known. Second, related to this is the *intensity* with which such beliefs and values are held by egalitarians. In addition to survey questions that ask respondents to specify the intensity of their preferences, increases in the numbers of radical egalitarian groups doing increasingly radical things in defense of their way of life would be evidence of an increase in the intensity with which egalitarian beliefs and values are held.

Third, another indicator of the rise in egalitarian culture is their *organizational and institutional presence.* Are there not only more people who hold egalitarian beliefs and values more intensely than before, but have these people organized themselves into new groups and/or have they taken over existing (groups and) institutions? Most significantly, have egalitarians been able to alter existing institutions by more than just their physical presence in them? Have they been able to change rules or laws? Have they left "institutional marks" that have survived or are likely to survive their physical absence? The number and types of increasingly egalitarian groups and institutions, as well as the extent to which egalitarians have penetrated them, would provide evidence of a rise in egalitarian culture.

This book is filled with examples of egalitarians' new organizational and institutional presence, as well as some evidence of their alteration of existing institutions. The rise of single-issue groups is noted (especially in Chapter 5). In addition, egalitarians have made significant incursions into established organizations like the ACLU (see Chapter 9) and institutions like the national news media (Chapter 6), the Catholic church (Chapter 13), the Democratic party (Chapter 3), Congress (Chapter 8), and the Supreme Court (Chapter 11), which Republican presidents are now trying to alter.

The ACLU has gone from defending civil liberties to defending equality of condition. Drastic changes in the Democratic party have been noted of late, as reported by both scholars and journalists. The national news media has shifted its attention to the desirability of reducing disparities in power and wealth, to the unmasking of hidden hierarchies, and to the criticism of the system and its authorities in business, sports, and religion. The World Council of Churches used to support U.S. foreign policy. Now it opposes it.

Meanwhile, in Congress and the Supreme Court, the egalitarians' incursions have taken the form of rules and laws that will probably survive their physical departure, should such a time come. In Congress there has been a general leveling of the internal organizational hierarchy, with less emphasis on seniority, more and better committee assignments, and more staff. The courts have also moved from an emphasis on protecting property to an emphasis on protecting civil rights, including those of prisoners and the accused. In the law of personal injury (tort law) there has been a similar egalitarian shift to system blame; fault is less of a requirement in payment for injury.

Egalitarians have also left their institutional mark in the form of "sunshine laws," open meetings requirements, and freedom of information acts, all of which serve to reveal what egalitarians call "hidden hierarchies." The greater (than Europe) U.S. regulation of health, safety, and professional behavior also reflects an egalitarian desire to punish inequality. Attacks on U.S. defense policy are largely framed in egalitarian terms, the latest being critiques of intervention against the conquest of Kuwait by Iraq on the grounds of vulgar materialist motives (i.e., oil).

Fourth (to resume our general listing), a further indicator of a rise in egalitarian culture would be *a shift in the terms of the public policy debate*. Is the (local, state, national) public agenda more dominated by egalitarian concerns than it was in the past? Have the terms themselves changed? Old terms like "bums," "drunks," "psychos," and "transients"—have they been replaced by new ones like "the homeless"? Has the word "liberal" been given a new more egalitarian meaning?

Fifth, and related to the foregoing, a rise in egalitarian culture would be indicated by any *"cultural surprises" that might persuade people to adopt an egalitarian view of the world*. For some of those who believed that man can improve on his natural surroundings through technological innovation, the discovery of backyard toxic wastes and the possibility of mass destruction through nuclear weapons must have come as something of a shock. Likewise, when people who were neither bums, drunks, or psychos began showing up on the streets, some who believed that you have to be one of the above or you would have a roof over your head may have had their faith in the system shaken. Such breaches between a culture's promises and practices may surprise its adherents and may cause them to look for another way of life—like egalitarianism. Of course, the extent to which egalitarians "assist" others in coming to the conclusion that their way of life is inadequate should not be underestimated. Events have no inherent meanings, only more or less plausible interpretations. Adherents of a way of life are surprised when the interpretations of those with a different world view are more able to account for events than they are.

In late January 1991, CBS showed Mike Wallace interviewing young Iranian men who had been prisoners of war in Iraq. These men had been tortured. Asked what they thought of their captors' behavior, the Iranians replied that the United States was to blame. If it is not obvious who has tortured you what could be so obvious as to be inherent in the events?

Sixth, a final indicator of the rise in egalitarian culture is therefore the *decline of the other cultures* along all of the above discussed dimensions. Declining political institutions in America share three characteristics: (1) hierarchical organization; (2) concern with multiple issues; and (3) integration of diverse views.

In sum, evidence for the rise of an egalitarian culture may be found via these six indicators: (1) the numbers of people professing egalitarian beliefs and values, and the number of these beliefs and values held concurrently by individuals; (2) the intensity with which they are held; (3) the creation of new egalitarian groups, the organizational and institutional incursions of those holding egalitarian beliefs and values, and the institutional residue of rules and laws that these egalitarians leave behind when (and if) they leave these institutions; (4) egalitarian shifts in the terms of policy debate; (5) the presence of cultural surprises that could serve to convert individualists and hierarchists into egalitarians; and finally, (6) the decline of the other cultures along all of these dimensions.

In this chapter, we will take two approaches to the evidence. For one thing, we look at the development of several egalitarian interests since the 1960s. Among these are the animal rights and environmental movements, land use regulation in New Jersey, religious revisionism, and feminist interpretations of abortion and pornography. These realms of action are deliberately varied in order to demonstrate the ubiquity of egalitarianism. If one expects to find egalitarianism among feminists, it may come as a surprise to find it also in the animal rights movement. The other approach to the evidence covers more ground fast. The written newsreel in the "Looking Around" section aims to scan contemporary American life, and show the amazing variety of egalitarian activity within it. Even better than taking our word for it, however, look around yourself. It is close at hand. Simply take another look at today's newspaper, with our six indicators in mind. We think you will agree that there has indeed been a rise in egalitarianism.

The Development of Egalitarian Interests

The Animal Rights Movement

Some of the better evidence for a rise in egalitarianism is found in the animal rights movement. First, animal rights activists are exemplary in having all the indicia of the "egalitarian," as that term is being used here. Second, animal rights activists are perhaps the latest example of the creation of an egalitarian group, having their beginnings in the early 1980s. Consequently they are probably the freshest sign of the rise of an egalitarian culture. Third, animal rights activists are members of a number of other egalitarian groups, thus providing a starting point for charting the rise in egalitarianism through a number of seemingly unrelated social movements. The Mobilization for Animals coalition, for example, was composed of holistic health groups, radical feminists, nuclear freeze advocates, environmentalists, Buddhists, and antifluoridation adherents.[7]

Like all egalitarians, animal rights advocates value equality more than freedom or (hierarchical) order. Unlike other egalitarians, however, the equality these advocates are most directly concerned with is between animals and humans. That animals and humans share equal moral status has been called the "central assertion" of the animal liberation movement.[8] Of course, to speak of humans as if there were no distinctions among them is simultaneously to assert that they are all equal as well. Not surprisingly, then, the movement draws heavily on analogies to battles over human equality. "Speciesism" is analogized to racism;[9] and placards at demonstrations ask, "Why have women abandoned animals to the crimes of patriarchy?"[10] Animal research is viewed as the "moral equivalent" of the Holocaust or slavery, and as a consequence a number of activists "openly espouse terrorism" to stop it.[11]

The drive for equalizing humans and animals is directly imbedded in beliefs about nature and human nature that are shared by egalitarians. If man treats his natural surroundings delicately, he will be rewarded with a good, pure, and healthy existence. Consequently, the ultimate goal of animal liberationists is the "restoration of harmony between humans and nature" through the achievement of animal rights.[12] Animal liberationists have claimed that, when the human body gets in harmony with nature, then interventive techniques like surgery— developed through animal research—will become unnecessary.[13] Animal liberationists have also claimed that "all human suffering and disease" would be prevented in the future through a vegetarian diet and healthful environment, since in their view "all disease was caused by the pollution of the natural body with unnatural foods, vaccines, and chemicals."[14] This is equivalent to the view that human beings are born good but corrupted by evil institutions. In short, structures that divide people are the source of evil. Distinctions are seen as the beginnings of inequality, an hierarchical ordering of the world. Consequently egalitarians guard against such differentiation and seek to erode it wherever possible.

Animal rights advocates, like other egalitarians, prefer social relationships to be equal as well. This preference creates a need for organizations that are nonhierarchical. Egalitarian groups consequently try to avoid assigning their membership fixed roles. The very act of assigning roles would be coercive. If this form of organization is to survive it requires that egalitarians keep their focus on the group, rather than on each other. Members' attention to the group is generally maintained by allowing the only distinctions to be between themselves and what lies beyond or outside their group boundaries. In fact, egalitarians have a tendency (or so it appears to us) to exaggerate the differences between themselves and outsiders even as they concern themselves with leveling other distinctions. Thus, animal rights advocates see themselves as holding the unimpeachable moral upper hand.

Unlike humans, who may have played some part in bringing on their own misfortunes, animals are "totally victimized," coloring advocacy on their behalf with an uncomplicated "moral purity."[15] Meanwhile, researchers are seen as "at best" unconscious dupes of a corrupt system, "if not cynical, cruel, or insensitive."[16] Liberationists believe researchers are motivated by money and career concerns, and will not even consider the notion that many do their work with the conviction that it is humane.

Animal researchers are just the human manifestations of science and medicine, which disciplines are themselves merely the "institutional representatives of an exploitative system" that "suppresses ethical and spiritual values for materialistic goals."[17] Animals are seen as representative of a natural world "increasingly beseiged by technology."[18] "Animal experimentation," says Susan Sperling, "is the key metaphor for the abuses by technological society of living organisms and the ecology,"[19] a "key symbol" for "the perceived manipulation and corruption of nature by human technology."[20] This "apocalyptic vision of the destructive potential of technology"[21] has two effects. For one, it gives animal rights advocacy the inescapable millenarian tone[22] characteristic of egalitarian movements, pointing to the end of inequality and ushering in an era of social justice. It also serves egalitarian organizational needs by keeping members' attention focused on group goals rather than on individual concerns.

Animal righters see themselves as combatting one of the most unnatural technologies ever created: modern medicine. They claim that the creators of this technology, for the most part, are exceptionally left-brained—that is, cold and linearly rational—white males.[23] And the movement's emergence also appears to be linked more generally to just those kinds of "cultural surprises" that were predicted, in our list of indicators, to persuade people that egalitarians have a clearer view than the other cultures of the way the world really is. Animal rights activists often speak in terms of this recently changed general awareness; one of them put it this way: "The specter of a nuclear holocaust, the reality of toxic dumps, of deformed babies, dead rivers, extinct species, have pierced the shroud of numbness and paved the way for questioning authority and wanting to see for oneself. The horrors of the labs and factories are no longer hidden."[24]

"Awareness" is an ambiguous term, however. This same activist also acknowledged the attention-directing effects of the various egalitarian movements.

The antiwar movement, the civil rights movement, the women's movement, the environmental movement, the antinuclear movement, the peace
movement, Watergate, Vietnam, Love Canal, Agent Orange, Cointelpro,
the lesbian and gay movements, liberation struggles in South Africa,
Central America—all contribute to increased awareness, sensitivity, involvement, and connection.[25]

Watergate, Vietnam, and Love Canal are real events, but their meanings are made by human beings. The fact that they are surrounded
here by references to consciousness-raising movements is indicative of
the extent to which every event is also its evaluation.

The rise of egalitarian culture is further indicated by an egalitarian
alteration of the terms in which humans and animals are discussed,
and a related egalitarian shift in the boundary that divides culture from
nature. "A literature has developed over the last two decades," says
Sperling, "that anthropomorphizes primates, animalizes humans, and
fits monkeys and apes into the role formerly occupied by 'primitive
humans.' "[26] The effect of this literature is to blur the boundary
between culture and nature, while at the same time pushing what is
left of that boundary further back into nature. As a consequence of
this egalitarian redefinition of "natural boundaries," public discussions
of animal rights "take place across an abyss."[27] Sperling reports, "The
university administrator talks about cleaner cages, while the activist
challenges the fundamental assumption of [a] border between humans
and animals as false and emblematic of a hubris that is destroying the
world."[27]

The animal rights movement has made considerable inroads into the
media. As another activist put it, "I've noticed newspapers have more
stories about animals, and there's more stuff on TV than there ever
used to be. I ask other people, 'Is it just that I'm noticing it, or is it
really there?' I'm beginning to say it's really there. So it has something
to do with the fact that the media has caught on."[28]

But the most significant institutional changes have been in the
transformation of state laws. Many states have repealed laws permitting animal researchers to use pound animals,[29] and as of 1986 fully 80
bills restricting animal research were pending in state legislatures.[30] In
California, animal rights activists were almost successful in getting the
state legislature to deny funding to UC-Berkeley for a new multimil-
lion-dollar animal care facility.[31] Undoubtedly this is why the attention
of the Berkeley Faculty Club was recently directed to the "stuffed
animal heads on the wall of the Great Hall" by the Academic Senate

Committee on University Welfare. "Whatever may have been the
mores in earlier times," the committee remarked, "we need to recognize a pervasive new sensitivity to animals."[32]

It should be remembered that this "pervasive new sensitivity to
animals" is just the most recent elaboration of a rising egalitarian
culture's sensitivity to the plight of humans, conceived as entirely or
largely due to inequality of power. Humans, like animals—egalitarians
believe—are oppressed by hierarchical institutions and their invasive
technologies. One of the activists quoted in Sperling's book said, "We
are very concerned about human rights; we are focusing on animal
rights. These movements are all related because there's the same basic
underlying attitude of supremacy that permits and perpetuates the
racist, sexist, speciesist attitudes and concomitant crimes against
creatures."[33]

Imbedded in animal rights activists' concern for equality between
species, in other words, is a concern for equality within a species—the
human species.

Environmentalism

Attempts to protect the environment are prevalent but perhaps somewhat less obvious evidence of a rise in egalitarian culture than attempts
to diminish power differences between people, or between people and
animals. We have argued that these pursuits are mutually reinforcing.
Egalitarians believe that the environment is threatened by man-made
things, just as man is. Humanity's institutions, in the egalitarian view,
are no less the source of inequalities among humans than they are the
source of destruction for the environment. To defend the environment
is therefore is erode inequalities.[34]

Because these pursuits are mutually reinforcing, this statement can
also be read, believed, and acted on in the opposite direction. Egalitarians believe that eroding inequalities serves to protect the environment,
or that the environment cannot be protected until inequalities are
eliminated. "The unequal control of land is largely responsible for
poverty and environmental destruction in El Salvador," asserts *Greenpeace* magazine.[35] "What can a poor farmer do?" asks an unnamed
leader of Peru's National Association of Farmworkers. "He starts
working what little land he does have too intensively, year after year,
without letting it recuperate. Soon the land becomes barren and
doesn't produce. This isn't the fault of the farmer, but of the people

who own most of the land and refuse to make it available to those who need it."[36]

Another way in which egalitarian concerns for equality and for the environment are linked is through claims that certain categories of people are disproportionately affected by pollution. For example, Gerry Stover, executive director of the Environmental Consortium for Minority Outreach, claims that "in this country 4 out of 5 toxic-waste dumps are in or near minority communities. These people have as much stake in what happens in mainstream America, maybe more."[37] Egalitarian objections to individualist plans for market-based control of pollution through the buying and selling of government-created pollution permits take a similar form. "The market," notes *Time* in an article entitled "Giving Greed a Chance," "might distribute the permits in such a way that some cities would get more pollution, while others get less."[38] There is perhaps no more direct way than this to associate egalitarian concerns for equality with the desire to protect the environment.

There is hardly stronger evidence for the rise of egalitarianism than a culture's control of the terms in which an issue is discussed. Mainstream media have become so thoroughly imbued with the egalitarian version of the relationship between humanity and the environment that the dissenting voices of those with other cultural commitments are only rarely and then barely heard. For example, in all of its recent attention to environmental issues, including the hosting of a symposium and a number of cover stories, *Time* magazine has devoted solely a single page to those who see Planet Earth differently than egalitarians. On that page, Berkeley biochemist Bruce Ames is allowed his opinion that "eating vegetables and lowering fat intake will do more to reduce cancer than eliminating pollutants" before he is dismissed by an egalitarian authority, while three such countervailing opinions follow on Woods Hole statistician Andrew Solow's speculation that "it's possible that the U.S. will be economically impoverished because it unilaterally imposed draconian measures in anticipation of a greenhouse warming that never arrived."[39] This minimalist and dismissive coverage of alternative views of the dangers of pollution in general and global warming in particular is all that *Time* affords its readers.

Business also appears to be buying into environmentalism, even if only to make money. The Body Shop, a 14-year old British company with branches in 37 countries, is an example of an environmentally conscious enterprise. The shop sells 300 creams and lotions; most are made from plants, and are definitely not tested on animals. These

creams and lotions come in simple plastic bottles, which can be
returned for a discount on the next purchase. Wood interiors devoid of
endangered tropical hardwoods complement shop windows filled with
displays protesting the slaughter of whales and the dumping of waste
in the North Sea. Moreover, recycled paper is used throughout these
Body Shop businesses, from toilet paper to stationary.[40] The demand
for environmentally sound products exemplified by the Body Shop's
success has carried over to a demand for "green labels" on other
products. A Green Seal now marks toilet paper, light bulbs, laundry
cleaners, and facial tissues that pass an environmental panel's muster.
Similarly, a Green Cross will mark recyclable products in four national
supermarket chains.[41] The demand for products deemed "environmentally sound" has even entered the capital markets. "The Dreyfus Third
Century Fund," touts one advertisement, "is a common stock fund
with socially oriented goals." Then, in a rather compact listing of
interrelated egalitarian concerns, Dreyfus outlines what it means by
"socially oriented" goals. "The Fund," the ad continues, "considers
a company's record in the areas of protection and improvement of the
environment, occupational health and safety, consumer protection and
equal employment."[42] Observe that Dreyfus quite rightly equates equal
employment with the physical environment. These new markets for
environmentally conscious products and services are certainly among
the more striking indications of a rise in egalitarianism.

The general public also appears to be embracing the egalitarian
version of man's proper relationship to nature. A recent poll reportedly
reveals that 8 out of 10 Americans favor more strenuous environmental
efforts "regardless of cost."[43] The first 26,000 copies of *50 Simple
Things You Can Do to Save the Earth* sold out within days. The 75,000
copies of its second and third printings were also quickly gobbled up,
additional printings being limited only by the supply of recycled paper
available in bulk quantities.[44]

Children seem to be on board this environmental movement, as well.
Like their parents, they have their own publications to guide them in
doing environmentally correct things, and they are doing them even
where their parents aren't environmentally inclined. *The Lorax,* a Dr.
Seuss book, has been required reading for Laytonville, California,
second-graders for two years. The book, among other things, tells
children to "Grow a forest. Protect it from axes that hack." The town,
among other things, is heavily dependent on logging. Parents of these
second-graders have called for censorship, but the school district has
so far resisted.[45] Slightly older kids are taking environmental matters

into their own hands. Some high-schoolers in New Jersey and North Carolina have persuaded their school boards either to stop using nonbiodegradable Styrofoam servingware, or else to recycle it.[46] Kids Against Pollution—an international organization with 800 chapters started by some New Jersey fifth-graders three years ago—has forced McDonald's to do the same thing at hundreds of its outlets.[47] Is this bad? Not necessarily. It may be good if the harms at which this action is aimed are genuine, if the alternatives adopted are better, and if the children involved do not learn how to be coercive no matter the cause. A staple of radical egalitarian criticism is that the educational system brainwashes children into believing that their political economy is good. Neither of us recalls anything so powerful or so conformist in our school days as environmentalism is today.

Another indication of the strength of environmentalism is the rapid rise in the number of groups with environmental concerns. To give two examples: in 1984 the National Toxics Campaign—a Boston-based organization that provides technical assistance to local environmental groups—was in contact with 250 of these groups. Now they are in contact with more than 1,200. The Citizens Clearinghouse for Hazardous Wastes—a similar organization in Arlington, Virginia—reports just about as dramatic an increase in local groups. In 1985 it was helping 1,700 such groups. Now it assists around 7,000. "Today the power is being regenerated through the grass roots," says Arizona's former governor Bruce Babbitt. "Just as the civil rights movement began at the neighborhood lunch counter, this new environmental movement is beginning at the neighborhood pond."[48]

A challenge to classifying people or groups as egalitarian is the apparent gradation among them; after all, people or groups can be more or less egalitarian. And so they can. The point is that those who are strongly rather than weakly egalitarian are becoming more powerful. A good way to look at the differences between weaker and stronger egalitarianism lies in perusing a chart of anti–nuclear power groups divided into local intervenors, who are concerned about what is happening in their neighborhood and do not make a habit of this sort of activity, and the direct-action alliances like the Abalone Alliance on the West Coast, the Clamshell Alliance on the East Coast, and the Catfish Alliance in the South. (See Tables 4.1 and 4.2.)

Observe that the goals of the local intervenors are much more limited: They want to stop their local reactor, whereas the direct-action groups want not only to stop all nuclear power but to encourage radical social change. The tactics also differ in their severity from the

Table 4.1   Differences between Members of Local-intervenor and Direct-
action Antinuclear Groups

	Age	Occupations	Reasons for Opposing Nuclear Power	Prior Political Experience
Local inter venors	Middle-aged (86% over 30)	Housewives, re-tired, profes-sionals, farm-ers, teachers (most are prop-erty owners)	Concerns about safety; noise; effects on com-munity, prop-erty values, etc.	Many active in civic organiza-tions, church groups, commu-nity improve-ment, etc.
Direct-action alliances	Young (20–30; some leaders are 30–40)	Students, teach-ers, writers, clerical and ser-vice workers, farmers	Concerns about safety, view of nuclear energy as undemo-cratic, unneces-sary, sympto-matic of money-hungry deper-sonalized soci-ety	Many active in previous protest movements, es-pecially antiwar movement

Source: Katherine Riggs, "Anti-Nuclear Groups: The Goals, Tactics, and Composi-tion of the American Nuclear Movement," typescript, 1980, pp. 78–79.

talk and publicity practiced by the local-intervenor groups to the demonstrations, occupations, and blockades of the direct-action groups. The reasons these two different intervenors give for their actions explain a great deal. The local intervenors give reasons involv-ing danger and immediate inconvenience; the direct-action alliances give political rationales as well—namely that nuclear energy is un-democratic, is based on money-hungry activities, and leads to a depersonalized society. When one then looks at the internal decision-making structure of the two types of groups, the direct-action groups have strict rules involving the prevention of any particular person becoming too prominent, as well as a process for building consensus.[49] The more egalitarian the group, the more directly forceful its activities.

Anthony Ladd, Thomas Hood, and Kent Van Liere see that the antitechnology and simple-living themes of these activist groups emerge "not only out of ecological orientations but also as explicit critiques of the consumerism and commodity production that underlie

Table 4.2 Differences between Styles of Antinuclear Groups

	Goals	Tactics	Internal Structure
Local intervenors	Stop local reactor	Interventions in NRC hearings; publicity of issue; make nuclear power an issue in local political campaigns; talk to legislators	Loose "cells" based on personal contact; leaders self-appointed; little formal structure
Direct-action groups	Stop all nuclear power; reform distribution of energy; major social change	Publicity, leafletting, teach-ins, political pressure, demonstrations, occupations and blockades of reactor sites.	Strictly egalitarian, no leaders recognized; careful subdivision of alliances and large groups into affinity groups; all decisions by consensus

Source: Katherine Riggs, "Anti-Nuclear Groups: The Goals, Tactics, and Composition of the American Nuclear Movement," typescript, 1980, pp. 78–79.

capitalist systems." Their interviews of 420 nuclear activists persuade them that they "are essentially anti-capitalist, anti-military, anti–big technology in nature." The relationship between a desire for greater equality of condition and opposition to capitalism is relatively straightforward: Since capitalism is based on competition, and competition tends to lead to grossly unequal outcomes, capitalism is opposed as inegalitarian. "Moreover, the movement strongly identifies with other citizen-oriented, anti-bureaucratic movements and views itself as comprising the cutting edge for larger social change." Not surprisingly, the researchers also found that the style of decision making in these activist groups is antihierarchical, seeking consensus as opposed to majority rule.[50]

The increasingly shared egalitarian vision of the proper relationship between man and nature has been translated into concrete changes. The successful battle to protect the northern spotted owl is as good an example as any. Under pressure from environmentalists, the federal government recently listed the owl as a "threatened" species, the first step toward making the bird an endangered species under the Endangered Species Act—itself a recent (1973) piece of egalitarian legislation.[51] The effects of this threatened-species listing, however, extend far beyond protecting the spotted owl, of which there are believed to be 3,000 pairs. For in order to protect the owl, its habitat must be protected, which—the environmentalists argue—means that logging may have to be drastically cut back in three Northwestern states. A panel of biologists has advocated a reduction in logging by 50 percent in 17 national forests in Washington, Oregon, and Northern California. The government estimates that this will result in a loss of 28,000 timber jobs over the next ten years. Bringing logging to a standstill was the intent of environmentalists from the start. The endangered-species status of the red cockaded woodpecker likewise has been used to stop clearcutting in Texas and throughout the bird's range in the Southeast.[52]

What could be a more visible destruction of nature than cutting down trees? Unless, of course, it's the Barstow to Las Vegas motorcycle race. "You've seen the photographs," begins an article in the Sierra Club's Legal Defense Fund newsletter *In Brief;* "1,200 motorcycles, 200 abreast, charging into the desert."[53] The article goes on to describe how the Endangered Species Act was used by fund lawyers to stop the races in 1990. Once the Fish and Wildlife Service added the California desert tortoise to the endangered-species list, the Sierra Club had the legal handle on which to hang the off-road motorcyclists.

This same strategy has been used repeatedly by environmentalists to halt what they consider to be man's technological intrusions into the environment. In this case it was the "nobby tires" of "howling machines," which "rip up fragile desert plants and crush burrows for desert tortoises and other rare and shy creatures" and leave tracks that were "all but permanent." For the motorcyclists, who are for the most part probably individualists, the desert is—in contrast—one vast proving ground for man and machine; and the challenge is to see which marriage between man and self-made alteration of off-the-rack technology will most readily be able to survive 160 miles of inhospitable nature, including surprise collapses of those (damn) tortoise burrows.

Development's threatening of endangered species has also been the basis for halting construction of an observatory in Arizona, an irrigation project in New Mexico, and logging roads in Montana. In the first case, the endangered species was the Mount Graham red squirrel; in the second, it was two kinds of fish in the San Juan River; while in the third it was grizzly and gray wolves in the Flathead National Forest. Environmentalists' opponents are quite aware that egalitarians not only are interested in protecting isolated endangered species, but see their protection as a proxy for halting the advance of what other people consider to be civilization. These egalitarian dislikes are what cause others to fear the environmentalist desires to reintroduce gray wolves into Yellowstone National Park. As Carl Haywood, legislative assistant to Idaho Republican Senator James McClure put it, voters fear that, once there, the wolves will be used as a surrogate for environmentalists' real agenda of "getting ranchers, miners, loggers and motorized recreationists off public lands."[54]

The Endangered Species Act is not the only new piece of environmental legislation. Recent legislation includes the Migratory Bird Treaty Act, the Outer Continental Shelf Lands Act, the Ports and Waterways Act, the Rivers and Harbors Act, the Dangerous Cargo Act, the Refuse Act, the Superfund Act, the Clean Water Act, the Clean Air Act, and/or amendments to these acts. For example, 1990 amendments to the Clean Air Act effectively made California's strict clean-air standards the law of the land.[55] And these are just some of the egalitarian changes in the law at the federal level. "Congress and the states," says Ridgway Hall, a Washington lawyer, "have created thousands of new laws governing the environment."[56]

Until recently Americans' relationship to nature has been mediated by a compound hierarchy of not only engineers—with their various projects to make nature conform to man's requirements—but Army engineers at that. With their T squares and triangles, rivers were tamed so that what had been floodplains could be developed into cities like Los Angeles, an egalitarian nightmare. Now little groups of egalitarians are donating their weekends to break down man's channels, so that rivers can find their own way, as all of nature will do—in their view— if left alone. Since egalitarians don't see nature as hostile, they are apparently unconcerned about flooding, and what other people would call "natural disasters." The only disasters in the egalitarian view are concrete-pouring institutions like the Army Corp of Engineers.

Land Use Regulation in New Jersey

Beliefs about people's proper relationship to the environment, we have argued, are intimately associated with beliefs about people's proper relationship to each other. Here we show that regulation of the use of land, at least in New Jersey, has been taken in a direction that supports the egalitarian preference for equality among people. In the past two decades, the Southern Burlington County chapter of the National Association for the Advancement of Colored People (NAACP) has

twice sued the Philadelphia suburb of Mount Laurel to force it to
provide housing for low-income people. Both cases were appealed to
the New Jersey Supreme Court, and in both instances the NAACP was
victorious.

In the first decision, in 1975, the state supreme court ruled that
developing communities like Mount Laurel had to set aside some land
for low-income housing. Wrote Justice Hall for the majority,

> We conclude that every such municipality must, by its land use regula-
> tions, presumptively make possible an appropriate variety and choice in
> housing. More specifically, presumptively it cannot foreclose the oppor-
> tunity of the classes of people mentioned for low and moderate income
> housing and in its regulations must affirmatively afford that opportunity,
> at least to the extent of the municipality's fair share of the present and
> prospective regional need therefore.[57]

The court's emphasis on "variety and choice in housing" would, on
its face, appear to be supportive of individualist values rather than
egalitarian ones. Indeed, nothing less than this apparent individualist
emphasis would seem to be required by the New Jersey Constitution.
The first section of the first article in that constitution reads, "All
persons are by nature free and independent and have certain natural
and inalienable rights, among which are enjoying and defending life
and liberty, of acquiring, possessing and protecting property, and of
pursuing and obtaining safety and happiness."[58]

Yet the court's decision is not supportive of individualist values so
much as egalitarian ones. Their constitution says that New Jerseyites
have a right to acquire, possess, and protect property. It does not say
that they have a right to property—rental or otherwise—in a particular
place in the state, such as Mount Laurel. The effect of the court's
holding is, however, to create such a right and—to the degree that it
does so—to take away the right of others to acquire, possess, and
protect the property that the court says must be set aside for particular
classes of people in every developing community. Consequently, the
effect of the ruling is to restrict variety and choice in housing at the
state level, where the constitution would appear to require it. The
ruling requires each developing community to house everybody, making municipalities more alike. This diminishing of differences between
communities gives the court's conclusion its egalitarian bent.

In the second Mount Laurel case, decided in 1983, the state supreme
court reaffirmed its holding in the first case and took on the responsi-

bility of determining exactly what Mount Laurel's "fair share" of the regional need for moderate- and low-income housing was. Thus, this decision did not represent so much a further shift toward egalitarian values as the determination of the court to see that those values were realized in practice. After Mount Laurel lost the 1975 appeal, it attempted to comply with the supreme court's ruling by setting aside 20 acres for low-income housing. The 1983 court found the results inadequately egalitarian. "Papered over with studies, rationalized by hired experts, the [zoning] ordinance at its core is true to nothing but Mount Laurel's determination to exclude the poor," wrote Chief Justice Wilentz for the majority.[59] The chief justice then directed the relevant lower court to appoint a special master to determine Mount Laurel's fair share. This special judge had the power, among other things, to require municipalities to require builders to reserve a specific proportion of their new housing (usually 20%) for low-income people, to participate in housing subsidy programs for these low-income people, and to build their own low-income units first.[60] Townships could even be required to "over-zone, i.e., zone to allow for *more* than fair share," to ensure that communities would in fact become more equal.[61]

The court's emphasis on diminishing differences between New Jersey communities, is what marks both these opinions as egalitarian departures from precedent and from the state constitution. The court was willing to admit as much when it wrote that "the doctrine does not arise from some theoretical analysis of our Constitution, but rather from underlying concepts of fundamental fairness."[62] It neglected only to say that nowadays "fair" means equal. Yet elsewhere in the same opinion the court characterized its ruling as following upon a "constitutional obligation." "The basis for the constitutional obligation is simple," wrote Chief Justice Wilentz; "the State controls the use of land, *all* of the land. In exercising that control it cannot favor rich over poor."[63] (But how does a market in housing favor the rich other than by enabling them to use their property, a right presumably guaranteed by the constitution?) When the court says that it cannot favor "rich over poor," there can be no doubt it is the egalitarian concept of "fundamental fairness" that it has in mind: equality.

Egalitarian Believers

Chapter 13, which will discuss the Catholic bishops' pastoral letter on poverty, does not actually come close to revealing the extent of and the passion with which a variety of religious groups have come to see equality as their main concern. Examples range from sermons in Reform synagogues on high holy days not about religion or personal morality but about environmental concern as the model for reducing disparities in society (personal observation), to meetings of the Protestant World Council of Churches in which connections are made among such societal matters as racism in the United States, damage done to Third World poor countries by richer ones, and reliance on nuclear weapons. (Somehow our minds run to an article entitled "Against Selling Bodily Parts," in which the author refers to "the plundering of poor people's [in the Third World] parts for profit.")[64]

In an interview with Roman Catholic Bishop Patrick Cooney of Detroit, who quite understandably wants the U.S. government to concentrate on "building a more just world," Cooney employs a line of argument that is a staple of egalitarianism—namely, that "the West uses 80 to 90 percent of the wealth of the world." The implication is that we are consuming far more than our fair share of the world's resources, whatever that would be. Whether if people in richer countries consumed a great deal less that would similarly increase consumption in poorer countries is extremely dubious. But the line serves very well as an egalitarian tool for imposing guilt trips.[65]

Bishop Maurice Dingman of Des Moines, when asked what he thought of the then-existing large increases in Soviet weaponry, replied in an egalitarian manner, to wit: "Both we and the Soviets have hierarchical systems that are outdated. We have to move into networking." Presumably that is what Bush and Gorbachev are trying to do. At that time, however, it was not so clear who had won the Cold War. The Stalin–Brezhnev U.S.S.R. and the U.S.A. are morally equivalent in egalitarian eyes because both societies and systems are inegalitarian. In his support for maintaining farm subsidies, Bishop Dingman asks rhetorically, "Why do we have 20,000 acre corporate farms in Kansas? What has happened to the family farm?" He answers his own questions in an egalitarian manner: "So the rich get richer, and the poor get poorer, and the rich start working with the military."[66]

The bishops are also strongly antiabortion—a position usually connected to those of a hierarchical rather than an egalitarian disposition. True. But listen to how they formulate their opposition: "Basic human rights," the bishops wrote in a revised pastoral plan, "are violated in many ways, by abortion and euthanasia, by injustice and the denial of equality to individuals of various groups of persons, by some forms of human experimentation, by neglect of the underprivileged and disadvantaged who deserve society's concern and support." Thus the bishops are doing their best to maintain their all-time stand against abortion while shoring it up with their current views on the desirability of greater equality of condition.[67]

Given the prominence of one type in the media, it is easy to believe that all Protestant fundamentalists and evangelicals are conservative-patriarchal. Not so. Any issue of the *Sojourners Magazine,* in which virtually everything imaginable is equalized, should convince anyone of the egalitarian element in evangelical Protestantism. Sojourners do indeed oppose abortion and have a strict view of personal morality. But there the coincidence with conservative fundamentalists ends. "The radicals translate the Bible's calls for justice and peace into demands for disarmament, ending the death penalty, and changing society to help the people they believe God favors—the poor."[68] The founder of the Sojourners, Jim Wallis, puts it like this: "Now I understand why the most important things I ever learned were learned from the bottom. Jesus is there, in the very particular, dressed in the disguise of the poor."[69] An undated letter from *Sojourners Magazine,* "Dear Friend," tells us that "the cries of the poor go unheeded by a world system which relegates growing multitudes to abandonment, misery, and death. The earth itself is ravaged by the machines of profit and progress, while the vital resources upon which we depend for life are fast running out." Here we have today's typical connection between damage to the environment and inequality. "The church," the letter continues, "is becoming a new source of resistance to policies which crush the poor and move us ever closer to nuclear war."

No reader of the *Sojourners Magazine* could ever doubt its connecting—indeed its absolute equating—of social justice and equality. It is not so surprising, then, to learn that "Sojourners work closely with Roman Catholics, including Pax Cristi, many of the more peace-minded bishops and Catholic workers." In explaining this, Catholic Archbishop Rembert Weakland of Milwaukee observes of his church that "we've become much more biblical in vocation and orientation since Vatican II."[70] Historically, the Catholic church has played down the Bible in favor of mediation through its institutions.

Why should the churches be divided if they all agree on the decisive importance of equality? As John Fife, called the founder of the sanctuary movement to protect refugees from Central American wars—which is generally on the side of insurgent movements—states, "God does take sides in the world today. People are beginning to realize that the divisions are no longer between Protestant, Catholic, and Jew, but between the rich and the poor." How's that for putting equality on the line? Fife's preference is for "communities of faith," rather than "hierarchies of control." And he is consistent in the manner of radical egalitarians. Asked whether he thinks it desirable to establish a national sanctuary organization, Fife replies, "Our assumption is that this kind of structure will kill (sanctuary). I've seen the civil rights movement and feminist movement grow into a national organization and get killed as a result. That's why you do it in grassroots communities of faith."[71] Here we have in real life—as it is said—a direct connection between egalitarianism and the absence of structural differentiation.

Feminists and Gender Equality

Like egalitarians everywhere, feminists are concerned with equality, though in their case the power differences they desire to diminish are between men and women. Over time, in fact, this focus on gender equality has been elaborated to include a concern for the differences between men and women of different classes, races, and cultures in a variety of contexts. Thus, turn-of-the-century feminists were predominantly upper-class white women concerned with equality in the public sphere, particularly in the voting booth. Then came the 1960s feminists—more middle than upper class, but still very white—who rallied around the slogan that "the personal is political," extending the concern for gender equality into the private spheres of work and family life. Under criticism by nonwhite and poor women, this feminism further evolved in an egalitarian direction, embracing a concern for race, culture, and class-specific differences between men and women. Moreover, today's feminism is not just concerned with gender inequalities, but also with racial and other inequalities, including those between humans and animals. Thus, many feminists find themselves attracted to the animal rights movement because of certain parallels they see between the way women and animals are treated by men in society, and because they see women as being more in harmony with nature than men are. As one feminist animal-rights activist said, "I identified with the air, suffocating in industrial waste. Like the air, the earth and the water, like the animals, woman is seen as an object to be controlled and manipulated for the ends of man."[72]

The convention of using honorifics in newspapers and magazines has been cut by 75 percent from 30 years ago, when all publications used the titles "Mr.," "Mrs.," and "Miss." Today, not even "Ms." is an acceptable honorific. One editor recognized this as a drive to "streamline and equate everybody, a sort of egalitarian push."[73] This "egalitarian push," moreover, does not end with popular newspapers and magazines, but extends to publications that claim to have been handed down from on high. To eliminate gender-based discriminations, the "Word of God" is presently being revised by a committee of 30 translators.

The chief translator of this new version of the Bible, Rev. Bruce Metzger, says that the most important changes circumvent the "inherent bias of the English language toward the masculine gender." Thus, where Psalm 8:4 in the 1952 version queries "What is man that thou art mindful of him, and the son of man that thou dost care for him?," the 1990 Bible asks, "What are human beings that you are mindful of them, mortals that you care for them?" And where in 1952, I Timothy 2:5 held that "There is one mediator between God and men, the man Christ Jesus," the same verse in 1990 has been neutered to claim, "There is also one mediator between God and humankind, Christ Jesus, himself human." This ungendered and therefore more fully "human" version of the Bible follows, furthermore, on a decade in which the National Council of Churches has thrice rewritten its passages in response to what *Time* called "insistent feminist demands." In these revisions, God is referred to as "Father and Mother" and never as the "King." Nor is Jesus ever called the "Son of God" or the "Son of Man." Instead, the gender bias of the Bible is actively countered by the insertion of women's names that do not appear in the original.[74]

Feminist egalitarians have been pushing on other conventions and institutions as well, and with equal success. In 1985, the California Supreme Court ruled that the Santa Cruz branch of the Boys' Club would have to admit girls.[75] Even better proof of feminist incursion, however, is the fact that 80 percent of California's 133 Boys' Clubs have already gone coeducational on their own since 1973, and 25 percent of their 140,000 members are now girls. Men's clubs have undergone a parallel transformation, though not so willingly. Recent lawsuits against the Jaycees (1984), the Rotary Club (1987), and the New York State Club Association (1988) have all met with similar success in the U.S. Supreme Court.[76] In all three cases the Court upheld local antidiscrimination statutes against the clubs' claims that rights of free association were being violated, forcing these clubs to admit women as full members.

Universities around the country have undergone similar gender-conscious egalitarian transformations in recent years. The faculty at Bucknell University in Pennsylvania, for example, just voted to abolish fraternities and sororities because, in addition to promoting "racism, elitism, and anti-intellectualism," the faculty blamed the clubs for heightening sexism. Other universities are forcing fraternities to go coed. The trustees of Vermont's Middlebury College, for example, recently declared single-sex social organizations to be "antithetical to the mission of the college." Two of Middlebury's fraternities have opened their doors to women in compliance with a deadline imposed by the trustees, while three others are pleading for more time so that they can persuade their national organizations to revoke prohibitions against women that in some cases have stood for hundreds of years. Commenting on these changes, Michael Gordon, vice-chancellor of Indiana University of Bloomington, notes, "We are heading toward a whole new understanding of what a fraternity is. First they were seen as literary gatherings, then drinking clubs. What they will be in the future is living–learning centers." And according to John DeMatte, vice-president of Sig Ep, a Middlebury fraternity that recently pledged 16 women, what is being taught in these "living–learning centers" are egalitarian values, at least regarding women. "We're getting a gender-awareness lesson every day," he says.[77]

Another gendered university "institution" that has come under egalitarian scrutiny of late is the cheerleading squad. The University of Minnesota recently banned its 16-woman dance line from athletic events, claiming that their performances "sexually stereotyped" them; while the University of Illinois is considering a ban on the "pompon performances" of its 28 cheerleaders. At Illinois, a Campus Task Force on Sexual Assault, Abuse, and Violence made its recommendations after concluding that cheerleading was one of the "activities that project women as sexual objects," and that such objectional projections were a factor contributing to sexual assaults on campus women. The University of Minnesota apparently arrived at its already imposed ban in a similar manner, since one of the cheerleaders complained, "We feel we're intelligent enough to know when we're considered objects."[78]

In Massachusetts, at Wellesley (Women's) College, the students seem to make the same claim. The egalitarian interest in diminishing differences—particularly, in this case, gender differences—was evident in their selection of a commencement speaker.[79] Alice Walker, (feminist) author of *The Color Purple,* was the students' first choice.

Barbara Bush was their second; and she acknowledged this egalitarian valuation when she said, "Instead, you got me, known for the color of my hair." The First Lady then urged the graduates to "respect difference" in the life choices that women make, generally arguing that it was alright and even laudable for women to be homemakers—a feminist (and egalitarian) heresy. This is exactly what the students had dreaded hearing from this woman who left college at 19 to marry George Bush.

Two further examples of feminist attempts to diminish the differences between men and women should serve to make the point that these changes are best understood in cultural terms, and that the changes do in fact indicate that there has been a rise in egalitarianism, at least with respect to preferences regarding relations between the sexes. Feminist understandings of womanhood, which set the parameters for the debate over abortion in the late 1960s and came under challenge in the 1980s, appear to be reasserting themselves in the 1990s—albeit in a form that appeals to both egalitarians and individualists. Feminist understandings of gender-based discrimination also seem to be forcing their way into the controversy over the nature of pornography. The tilt in the debate over the practice of abortion and the place of pornography in American society, then, is further evidence that egalitarian notions of gender relations are on the rise.

Feminists and Abortion

In February 1985, the National Press Club hosted a debate on abortion in the Old Executive Office Building next to the White House. The debaters were Judy Goldsmith, president of the National Organization for Women, and the Reverend Jerry Falwell, president of the Moral Majority. The reverend reportedly carried the debate; the interesting thing, however, is not that he "won," but how he gained and maintained the upper hand. "We are reframing the debate," he said. "This is no longer a religious issue but a civil rights issue." What did he mean by this? Quite simply that "the unborn are the last disenfranchised minority with no civil rights." In case there was still any doubt about what kind of an argument he was making, he finished by saying, "We only want equal rights for the unborn—their constitutional guarantees."[80]

This emphasis on equal rights is of course an appeal to adherents of the egalitarian culture. It is the same appeal that pro-choice women made in the 1960s to gain abortion as a woman's right.* They felt women could never be equal to men until women had as much control over their bodies as men had over theirs. One of the earliest recruits to the Society for Humane Abortions, the group of women that organized to repeal California's restrictive abortion laws 20 years ago, made the argument this way:

> When we talk about women's rights, we can get all the rights in the world—the right to vote, the right to go to school—and none of them means a doggone thing if we don't own the flesh we stand in, if we can't control what happens to us, if the whole course of our lives can be changed by somebody else that can get us pregnant by accident, or by deceit, or by force.[81]

Kristin Luker, a sociologist whose *Abortion and the Politics of Motherhood* is the best study available on the politics surrounding abortion, called this argument for equality the "most significant" one made by pro-choice women. "They argued that this right to abortion was essential to their right to equality—their right to be treated as individuals rather than as potential mothers."[82]

Thus, in the debate over the legal status of abortion, both sides have found appeals to egalitarian values to be the most effective ones that they can make. This in itself is powerful evidence for the rise of egalitarian culture in the United States. But what of the active participants in the debate over abortion? Are there egalitarians on both sides of this battle? The answer is yes, but it has to be carefully qualified—for the ultimate effect of being an egalitarian on either side of this issue is to strengthen a rival way of life. Feminists who are "pro-choice"—which is to say, most of them—ostensibly seek equality with men. But the effect of achieving the kind of control over their bodies that the right to abortion gives them is to allow them to define their own roles, to enter the marketplace, and compete with men. The kind of things pro-choice women are after—their beliefs, values, and preferred social relations—makes them more individualists than egalitarians. For pro-choice women, equality of condition is just a stepping-stone to equality of opportunity. Their very slogan—"pro-choice"—is an individualist slogan.

---

*Judy Goldsmith's rejoinder to Jerry Falwell in their 1985 abortion debate did not rely on the gender-equality arguments made in the 1960s. Rather, she conceded considerable ground to Falwell and the pro-life forces by arguing for an approach to abortion that "balanced" the rights of the fetus with the rights of the mother.

Feminists who are "pro-life"—and there are some—ostensibly seek equality for the unborn. A group called Feminist for Life, says Luker, "argues that abortion is opposed to everything feminism stands for, especially the championing of the rights of the weak and socially dispossessed, including the embryo."[83] But the effect of arguing for equality along this dimension is to make women beholden to their bodies. Rather than being able to define her own roles, a woman, once pregnant, has her role defined for her. If abortion is not an option, or only an illegal and therefore dangerous and difficult-to-exercise option, the pregnant woman becomes a mother. Contemplating this prospect— or so pro-lifers believe—will cause women to confine sex to marriage, because it is only through that institution that they get the support they need to allow them to be mothers. Thus, the effect of arguing for equality for the unborn is to strengthen the building blocks of hierarchical culture: patriarchical families. Roles of women and men are defined when making babies follows sex. In becoming mothers, women usually also become wives and, generally, the family "nurturers." And women won't become mothers until they find men ready to become husbands, fathers, and, generally, the family "providers." Thus, arguing for a woman's right to abortion has the effect of weakening men's and women's traditional roles in society, while arguing for the fetus's right to life has the effect of strengthening those roles. Pro-life forces thus transformed the abortion debate from one about the relative rights of men and women, where women were seen as being oppressed, to a debate about the relative rights of women and babies, where babies were seen as being the more oppressed people. The appeal, however, in both cases was egalitarian.

Feminism and Pornography

In 1984, the Minneapolis City Council passed an ordinance intended to outlaw pornography. The sweeping scope of this antiporn amendment was not, however, so novel as its freshly concocted rationale. In the past, left-liberal progressives perceived attempts to regulate pornography as threatening civil rights. The Minneapolis ordinance altered this usual understanding by making pornography itself a threat to civil rights. This alteration, however, is not quite what it seems, since the rights in each case are different. But this change is yet another example of the rise in egalitarian culture. In this instance, feminists successfully redefined the pornography issue as a case of gender discrimination, and hence pornography as a threat to women's civil rights.

Pornography for egalitarians represents an assault on the equal protection of the laws, thus placing the Fourteenth Amendment in conflict with First Amendment guarantees of free speech. What follows is our edited version of the Minneapolis City Council's "special findings on pornography."

> The council finds that pornography is central in creating and maintaining the civil inequality of the sexes. Pornography is a systematic practice of exploitation and subordination based on sex which differentially harms women. The bigotry and contempt it promotes, with the acts of aggression it fosters, harms women's opportunities for equality of rights in employment, education, property rights, public accommodations, and public services; . . . and undermines women's equal exercise of rights to speech and action guaranteed to all citizens under the Constitutions and laws of the United States and the State of Minnesota.[84]

The declared purpose of the accompanying amendments to the Minneapolis civil rights ordinance was to "prevent and prohibit all discriminatory practices of sexual subordination or inequality through pornography."[85] Pornography was then defined as the "sexually explicit subordination of women, graphically depicted, whether in pictures or words," including one or more of nine other elements. Among these elements, the most inclusive completed the definition of pornography by looking for women "presented dehumanized as sexual objects, things, or commodities," "women's body parts . . . exhibited, such that women are reduced to those parts," or women "presented as whores by nature."[86]

With pornography defined in this way, the ordinance then criminalized trafficking and "coercion" in pornography. Keeping with the egalitarian bent of the ordinance, public libraries were allowed to maintain collections of pornography, but not display them; while the formation of private porno clubs was made into a "conspiracy to violate the rights of women."[87] "Any woman," the section criminalizing trafficking concluded, "has a cause of action hereunder as a woman acting against the subordination of women."[88] The section criminalizing coercion, for its part, gave "any person . . . who is coerced, intimidated, or fraudulently induced . . . into performing for pornography" a cause of action against everyone from the maker to the distributor.[89] As defined by this section, a porn star may be found to have been coerced even though "that person signed a contract, or made statements affirming a willingness to cooperate in the production of pornography, . . . or appeared to cooperate actively in the photographic sessions or the sexual events that produced the pornography," among other things.[90] At the hearings leading to the passage of this ordinance, the star of *Deep Throat,* Linda Lovelace, testified that "every time someone watches that film, they are watching me being raped."[91]

At these hearings, too, were the feminist scholars Catharine MacKinnon and Andrea Dworkin; it was they who persuaded the city council to adopt the proposed antipornography amendments, relying on their new gender-based discrimination rationale. In a memorandum to the city council (which had hired them as consultants), MacKinnon and Dworkin repeatedly emphasized the relationship between pornography and inequality. "That pornography is the systematic relegation of an entire group of people to second class status is a new idea," they wrote. "When real women claim not to want inequality or force," they continued, "they are not credible compared with the continually sexually available 'real women' in pornography." MacKinnon and Dworkin hooked the First Amendment into their Fourteenth Amendment argument, by saying that pornography denies women equal freedom of expression. "Equal access to the means of speech, which pornography discriminately denies to women sexually and socially," they argued, "is a First Amendment goal that is furthered by this law."[92] This concern for freedom was shown by Dworkin's own writings, however, to be an elaboration of their basic equality theme. "I find," Dworkin wrote, "the civil liberties stance to be bourgeois hypocrisy a lot of the time. We're talking about the oppression of a class of people."[93] MacKinnon also left no doubt about her central reason for opposing pornography by distinguishing "erotica" as "sexually explicit sex premised on equality."[94] While "it is tempting to proceed one step at a time, disallowing the explicit violence while allowing the dehumanization, objectification and submission," they counseled the council, "this would leave the *inequality* intact."[95]

Both egalitarians and hierarchists view pornography as a "defamation of womanhood."[96] The phrase is taken from a Women against Pornography flyer, but could just as well be heard coming from the Moral Majority camp. The very reason that adherents of the two cultures can both assent to this characterization of pornography is that they define womanhood differently. For hierarchists, "womanhood" means motherhood. Pornography, by denigrating sex for procreation, denigrates the role of mothers in society. Pornography suggests that women could be going through the motions (of making babies) but not following through with the serious responsibility of raising a family. For egalitarians, "womanhood" is a struggle against manhood. Man is not a husband and father of one's children in their view, but—as Dworkin sees it—"a parasite on females."[97] What feminists object to about pornography, in others words, is no different from what they object to about male–female relations generally: the inequality. Family relations between men and women are no better than pornographic ones in their view.

Looking Around

Without claiming that what we see is all there is or the only thing there is to be seen, we present a newsreel of events that were very rare indeed in the decades of the 1950s or earlier and are now quite commonplace. Evidence for a rise in egalitarian culture in the United States is no farther away than the nearest national newspaper or newsmagazine. Look and see.

Miss Saigon is a recent remake of *Madama Butterfly*. Like that musical, *Miss Saigon* is an interracial love story—in this case, about a Vietnamese prostitute and an American soldier. The continuing attractiveness of the theme says something about the American (if not worldwide) desire to close the racial divide that separates nations and the people within them. The controversy surrounding the casting of *Miss Saigon*'s Eurasian pimp, however, says even more about the egalitarian times in which we find ourselves. Jonathan Pryce, a Welshman, played the role in London; but before the show could come to New York—where it already had ticket sales of $25 million—Actor's Equity, the theatrical union here, voted to bar Pryce from playing the part. The union, under pressure from Asian American actors, decided that the role should be filled by an Asian. After days of heated media discussion, and producer Cameron MacKintosh's cancellation of the show, Actor's Equity decided to reverse this decision.

Though egalitarians lost this battle, the closeness of the fight and, even more so, the fact that the war could be waged at all indicates a climate that supports the diminishing of power differences between people. After all, Equity initially did go to the mat for its minority actors, saying that the union "could not appear to condone the casting of a Caucasian in the role of a Eurasian."[98] Equity also cited a clause in the production contract that called for the parties to pursue "a policy of nondiscrimination." The ensuing culture war neatly reveals not only the different values that the combatants were trying to maximize, but also the way in which egalitarians have come to believe that those values are interdependent. The producer of the show responded to Equity's casting requirements, by saying, "We passionately disapprove of stereotype casting, which is why we continue to champion freedom of artistic choice. Racial barriers can only undermine the very foundations of our profession. Indeed, Equity has rejected our application solely on the grounds that Mr. Pryce is Caucasian."[99]

This statement reveals an individualist view of the world, where individual freedoms are considered the paramount value. The claim is that artists should be uninhibited in their expression. A producer should be unimpeded in selecting a cast, guided by whatever it is that makes a particular actor or actress right for the role. If a producer chooses to use race as a criterion in making the selection—individualists believe—he should be free to do so. "What is appropriate," said Pryce, "is that the best person for the job should play the role." But the producer should not have any selection rules imposed on him. That would be coercive—a limitation on artistic license. It is for this reason that individualists reject typecasting, or any discriminations that don't originate with the individual but are imposed, as they were by Equity on the producer MacKintosh and the actor Pryce.

Egalitarians do not like coercion either, but that is because they see coercion as creating inequalities. Since they equate coercion and inequality, they view using coercion to erode inequalities as an undoing rather than a heightening of coercion. Egalitarians feel that because equality has been corrupted by institutions like slavery, present freedoms only serve to perpetuate inequalities. "At this point, nontraditional casting isn't a two-way street," says Ken Naraski, a San Francisco actor.[100] "We cannot even begin to fight for *nontraditional* casting if audiences are not given permission to accept us enacting characters of our *own* colors," B. D. Wong wrote to Equity in the push that led to the barring of Pryce.[101]

"Nontraditional casting" had been a theater-industry policy intended to please both egalitarians and individualists. It gave producers the artistic freedom to cast actors in roles regardless of race or gender, while it allowed minority actors to play more roles than they would have been able to play if producers just parceled out acting parts by the racial types called for in scripts. As evidenced by this casting controversy, however, what egalitarians really want is for minority actors to be able to get as much work as white actors. As long as nontraditional casting served this goal, it was acceptable to egalitarians; but when producers continued casting whites—like Pryce—in roles scripted for minorities, the policy compromise fell apart. In other words, egalitarians believe that we cannot have freedom before equality is realized. "Until minority artists have the same opportunities as their white counterparts," write Tisa Chang and Dominick Balletta of the Pan Asian Repertory Theater, "culturally specific roles . . . must be portrayed by members of those races."[102] In other words, egalitarians argue, the best person for the job cannot be Pryce—regardless of his talent, regardless of the producer's inclinations—until the day when race no longer limits people's equality and so their freedoms. This equality of result by race is, in the egalitarian view, a prerequisite for equality of opportunity regardless of race. Believing that freedom depends on equality is how egalitarians justify giving equality precedence.

Egalitarianism shows up in the lyrics of popular music, as well. To be sure, for every song that is strongly egalitarian, there is another that is antiegalitarian. (Two current hits are "I Wanna Be Rich" and "I Want the Power.") Many rap groups and heavy metal groups are criticized for being antigay and antiwoman. The vast majority of songs, in fact, are neither egalitarian nor antiegalitarian. They are about love, and so forth. All we mean to say here is that egalitarianism is certainly present. For instance:

> While they're standing in the welfare lines
> Crying at the doorsteps of those armies of salvation
> Wasting time in the unemployment lines
> Sitting around waiting for a promotion
>
> Poor people gonna rise up
> And get their share
> Poor people gonna rise up
> And take what's theirs.
> > Tracy Chapman, "Talkin' Bout a Revolution,"
> > 1988

> And there's a shadow on the faces
> Of the men who send the guns
> To the wars that are fought in places
> Where their business interest runs.
> > Jackson Browne, "Lives in the Balance,"
> > 1986

What've we got to say
Power to the People, no delay
To make everybody see
In order to fight the powers to be.
                    Public Enemy, "Fight the Power,"
                                        1990

And kings will rule and the poor will toil
And tear their hands as they tear the soil
But a day will come in the dawning age
When an honest man sees an honest wage.
                    U2, "Van Diemen's Land,"
                                        1988

If we bring up examples of egalitarianism from, say, the peace movement, the retort is that people have plenty of reasons for the position they take (we agree with that) and that this has nothing to do with equality (we disagree with that). Let's look around now at a 1985 meeting of peace activists, who met to consider the future of their movement. Notice the egalitarian rationale these activists give for wishing to cut deeply into defense spending: "The argument here is that the Pentagon's massive outlays sap funds from social, economic, and educational programs that benefit a wide spectrum of Americans."

Whom do the peace activists want to recruit to their cause? Those who believe the argument that defense spending takes away from social welfare will do for starters. According to Darrell Rogers of Citizen's against Nuclear War, "black people and Hispanics can be made to see that the peace issue is their issue—something 'that addresses their needs.' The same tactic can work with unemployed and precariously employed blue-collar workers." A great deal of the participants' time is taken up in discussing how to create a "peace and justice culture." Well, yes, but what is egalitarian about that? This culture creating is "impelled by a general feeling here that questions of war and peace have to be made inseparable from the issues of social and economic equality."[103] That is how peace comes to equal equality.

In American egalitarianism, equality means being treated as a person of equal merit. In ordinary American talk, equality has always meant being treated according to what you do, not according to who you are.

The radical egalitarians of today believe that past freedoms caused inequality, and moreover that to be truly free—to have the opportunities to develop our individual capacities to the degree that the individualist culture promises us we can—we must become more equal first. In effect, what is different about America today is that radical egalitarians have completely reversed what made it exceptional in the first place.

II

The Culture Wars

5

The Three Cultures: Explaining Anomalies in the American Welfare State

In the late 1940s, at Brooklyn College, I became aware of a political anomaly: Some of my fellow student activists were neither capitalists nor socialists nor reformists. Certainly they were on the left (involved with civil rights, folk music, plain foods, and opposition to the college administration) but exactly where they belonged I could not tell.

During the 1950s, Lionel Trilling called this group the "adversary culture." He said it was a critical culture, and he was critical of it, but I could get no sense of its internal dynamics from his description. The adversary culture clearly was opposed to traditional values in art, literature, and other realms, but what form of social and political life this criticism was designed to keep together remained obscure.

In the 1960s, Irving Kristol redubbed this group the "new class." He was referring to upper-middle-income intellectuals, suffering, perhaps, from status anxiety and relative deprivation, who cleverly got government to provide them with jobs and amenities paid for with general tax monies. Unfortunately, no one was able to explain why members of the new class behaved so differently from others—like their critics—who shared their social and economic status.[1]

This new class, in my view, is neither new nor a class. What it represents is a cultural impulse—egalitarianism—an impulse as old as

This chapter first appeared as an article in *Public Interest,* no. 69 (Fall 1982). It has been somewhat revised for the present volume.

101

society itself. It has been in America from the beginning and has been elsewhere from the earliest times. The mistake, in my opinion, has been to look for a class instead of a culture.

Recent cultural conflict takes place through the decline of established orders and the rise of a critical culture—critical because egalitarian. This rise is more pronounced in some areas of life than others, but present in all. It is a rise merely in degree, but nevertheless a rise sufficient to change the fabric of our lives in startling ways. We all notice it, even if we do not quite know what to call it.

In the United States today, every major integrative institution that tries to accommodate diverse interests—political parties, trade unions, mainstream churches, the presidency—is under severe attack and is undergoing decline. By contrast, disintegrative movements—single-issue special interest groups, charismatic religions, candidate-centered political movements, a critical press—are flourishing. The disintegration of institutions has been accompanied on the personal level by the diminution of distinctions that once separated moral from immoral behavior, authority from disorder. Even a short list of eroded distinctions is impressive: male and female fashion; young and old; virginity, and generally who can go into and out of the body and under which conditions (rape more restrictive, intercourse more open); the roles of parents and children, teachers and students. As old boundaries are breached, new ones begin to take their place: Smokers are separated from nonsmokers, polluted areas from unspoiled nature, pure wilderness from impure money-making, affirmative discrimination from the negative kind.

Egalitarianism, I suggest, is at the root of this revolution in our times. Boundaries that supported past patterns of authority and morality are declining in favor of different distinctions. In whose interest is it to change old patterns of practices? And how will these new patterns affect American culture and politics?

The Three Cultures

The central questions and challenges societies face are universal: How is social order to be achieved and maintained? Is there to be leadership, and by whom? How is envy to be controlled, inequality to be justified or condemned? Which dangers are to be confronted and which ones ignored? The questions are universal; the answers are different from culture to culture.

The answer of one culture, *hierarchical collectivism,* is to impose order centrally through a division of labor. Inequality is deemed necessary to safeguard the collective, each element being taught to sacrifice for the whole. Envy is controlled by teaching people their places, by reserving ostentation for collective bodies (such as the state or church), and by examples of sacrificial behavior by the elite.

The culture of *competitive individualism* imposes order by maintaining agreement on the basis of freedom of contract. Leaders are chosen like every other commodity, by bidding and bargaining. There is no permanent leadership, only different leaders for different purposes. Envy is mitigated by showing that everyone can have a chance, or by blaming failure on personal incapacity or bad luck. For individualists, risk is opportunity as long as winners can personally appropriate the rewards.

Taken together, the alliance of these two cultures—hierarchy and individualism—constitutes the modern social establishment. From hierarchy comes order (including the rules for competition), and from individualism comes economic growth. To be sure, there are tensions between them: Hierarchies care more about the strict division of labor—"who ought to do what" defines their culture—so they are far more prone to substitute regulation for consent.

Egalitarianism is opposed to both establishment cultures. Where competitive individualism believes in equality of opportunity, egalitarian collectivism believes in equality of result. Those who wish to reduce authority so as to promote individual differences and those who reject authority so as to reduce individual differences are far apart. While individualism encourages all transactions that maintain competition, egalitarianism rejects all bargains that increase disparities among people.*

---

*Are there any conservative egalitarians? No. But there are small hierarchies that may look like egalitarians by virtue of their opposition to what they see as the normlessness of the larger society. The essential difference is that egalitarians embrace the voluntary way, recognizing no imposition of authority, whereas the principles animating hierarchies are just the opposite. From this fundamental difference in social organization flow the political differences with which we are familiar. The demands of the radical right are for acceptance, not rejection, of authority. These conservatives—even reactionaries—want obedience to a larger, not a smaller, number of prescriptions. They want to regulate individual, not business, behavior. They want to enlarge, not diminish, differences among moral rules, and hence among the people who are supposed to inculcate and enforce them. A woman's right to control her own body reduces the differences between her and men, whereas obedience to God's law not to take life—interpreted by His hierarchy—increases this difference. That is why egalitarians are counted on the left, while the small hierarchies to which they bear a surface resemblance are on the right.

The animating principle of the egalitarian world view in the United States today is this: organization without authority. Whether they be religious or secular, egalitarians choose to live a life of purely voluntary association. From rejection of all authority—people who have authority tell other people what to do—come their other political choices. Egalitarians choose equality of condition because that is the only way people will agree to live together without authority. They choose criticism because painting the society "out there" in lurid colors keeps them unified. For them, leadership either should not exist (hence the endless discussions inside egalitarian groups seeking consensus, for voluntary consent implies no coercion, meaning no majority rule) or it should be perfect (hence the appearance of the charismatic leader). Envy may be mitigated by surface signs of equality: plain food, simple clothes, sharing wealth. Since perfect equality is rare, however, envy is also handled by expulsions and schisms as would-be leaders are driven out for usurping authority. Wealth creation is not the egalitarians' concern, partly because they find it difficult to tax their members, and partly because they can take the creation of new wealth for granted while still criticizing individualism for failure to redistribute the wealth that already exists.

The rise of egalitarianism is responsible, I contend, for many anomalies that puzzle us in our public life. When we ask why the growth of the welfare state is severely criticized by those who demand it, why permissiveness in personal life goes hand in hand with regulation of public activity, why, in the end, there is condemnation of established authority without anything to take its place, the egalitarian hypothesis offers a consistent and persuasive explanation. It is therefore worth asking where it came from, what sustains it, and whether anything should or can be done about it.

Of Integrative and Disintegrative Institutions

The political consequences of egalitarian culture are nowhere more apparent than in the changing fortunes of our integrative and disintegrative institutions. Why have American political parties, for instance, declined in terms of membership, of allegiance among the citizenry, and of support by politicians? Why are they no longer able to keep divisive issues, like abortion and busing, out of national life? Why have parties become less popular even while they reform their procedures to make themselves more democratic?

The textbook definition of a political party is an organization that nominates candidates for office. If this vital function is transferred to primaries, where voters cannot know the candidates, and where no deliberation about their qualifications can take place among knowledgeable politicians, then parties can no longer integrate various political viewpoints. Coalitions that will help candidates govern cannot be formed before the election. For one thing, candidates no longer need parties—they need not even be politicians—because party leaders cannot help them get nominated. Nominee selection has been so disintegrated into numerous primaries and rules for delegate selection that the only people now excluded from the process are in fact the majority of the population, whose votes are needed for election, and the majority of officeholders, whose support is necessary to govern.

Nothing shows the strength of egalitarianism so much as the excess of issue-making over issue containment. The desirability of issue expression is one of the egalitarian trademarks. Political parties, egalitarians argue, should be far apart; they should give voters a clear choice by differing sharply on as many issues as possible; they should stick to their principles without compromise; above all, they should not put the forming of coalitions to win elections ahead of maintaining the purity of their positions. Bargaining is dirty; only unyielding adherence to principle is clean.

There is a connection between public apathy and regulations requiring proportional representation of gender and racial groups. By choosing delegates among self-selected activists, according to nonparty criteria, the nominee selection process produces politicians who are far more extreme than their party's voters.

The story is the same in Congress: The more it reforms itself to encourage expressiveness by individual members, so they can show their moral sincerity, the worse its collective performance becomes. As each congressman becomes more influential—through downgrading of seniority, better committee assignments, more staff, and other such equalizing devices—Congress as a collectivity becomes less cohesive. Congressmen do spend more time catering to their constituents today, and this affection is mutual. Voters love their congressmen; it is only Congress they dislike. Just as presidents do best campaigning against "the government," so congressmen run against Congress.

If Congress is regarded as an organization devoted to the reelection of its members through service to selected constituents, it undoubtedly has been successful. Incumbents are reelected with far greater frequency today, and specific services (the congressional caseload) have grown exponentially. But if Congress is viewed as a governing body, aggregating and reconciling preferences, it is doing worse. The increasing frequency with which congressmen are refusing to seek reelection, and the denigration of the institution by its members, are two important indicators. In the budgetary process, the size and frequency of deficits, the growing gap between authorization and appropriations, the delay in passing the budget, the prevalence of continuing resolutions (a classical sign of dissensus), the wholesale escape from the appropriations process itself ("back-door financing" through direct drafts on the Treasury, loan guarantees, off-budget expenditures, and so on), all indicate a lack of connection between the whole and the parts.

Not long ago, the American people displayed their distrust of power by approving a constitutional amendment limiting a president to two terms in office; since that time, they have found only two presidents able to serve two full terms. The long-term decline in presidential popularity, the decrease in the time in office of Cabinet members and top officials, and the willingness of the media to criticize presidents are all indicators of an institution in trouble.

Matching the failure in integrative institutions is the apparent success of disintegrative institutions. Single-issue special interest groups (the designation rolls off the tongue now as if it were a single word) are known by what they do *not* do—take positions on a wide range of issues and attempt to reconcile preferences and establish priorities among them.

The Political Anomalies: Ends without Means

Why, for example, as government grows bigger, is it subject to a corresponding crescendo of criticism? We understand the critique of individualists who were always opposed to a large public sector, but how do we explain the hostility of those on the liberal-left who were and still are its strongest supporters? The egalitarian hypothesis explains that both positions—a preference for programs to redistribute income, and opposition to the authority the government represents— make sense to people in a political culture that favors equality of result but not the exercise of hierarchical authority. And if government is simultaneously told that its welfare programs are woefully insufficient *and* that they lead to abject dependence and coercion, that is all to the good, as far as egalitarians are concerned. Caught between coercion and inequality, established authority is conflicted.

There is a torrent of criticism of these established institutions; we all see that. But why is it so unrelievedly negative? Despite the disarray of democratic institutions induced by the Vietnam War and the Watergate scandal, there has been no rival program or party or leader to profit from the situation. Why not?

Except for brief periods, egalitarians cannot govern. Governing accepts responsibility; responsibility implies limits; limits require choice; choice necessitates compromise; compromise means sacrificing the best for the good. "Sectarians," as Max Weber called egalitarians, "Cannot enter into an alliance with the political power." They want government to reduce inequality, but they must also condemn its exertion of authority.

Are presidents responsible for redressing every evil? Or should presidents only step in when other institutions fail to do their duty? Ambivalence about the answers to these questions among presidents and their publics reveals an institution uncertain of its role. The expansion of presidential responsibility, together with uncertainty about whether it is appropriate to exert authority on so vast a scale, is unlikely to occur in a culture of individualism. A purely individualistic regime would have a limited government. A hierarchical regime might take on large objectives but then, willing the end, it would also will the means. Only supporters of an egalitarian culture would so expand the aims of leadership while refusing to sanction the state apparatus necessary to achieve them.

The combination of opposition to economic growth and the demand that it be redistributed is peculiarly egalitarian. Egalitarians oppose growth because it increases inequality, thus strengthening the established, immoral order.

While egalitarian culture, expressed in the term "the permissive society," sets aside many rules formerly acknowledged to guide personal conduct, its opposition to authority forces it to set out even stricter rules governing the behavior of public officials. Officials must divest themselves of assets connected with the interests they are supposed to regulate, thus converting what was formerly the advantage of expertise into the disability of "contamination" by selfish interests. "Getting things out in the open," sunshine laws, open meetings, and freedom of information acts all serve to reveal hidden privilege. And we observe, along with Lady Macbeth, that the more government cleanses itself, the dirtier it gets; the ineradicable stain, as egalitarians have known all along, lies in the authority that constitutes hierarchy, and in the inequality of result embodied in individualism.

Bureaucracy without Authority

In order to see how egalitarianism affects government policy today, it is useful to distinguish the European and American welfare states along three lines: social insurance, subsidies, and regulation. Europe does much more than the United States to provide social welfare programs because hierarchical collectivism is much stronger there and competitive individualism much weaker.

The important difference between the American and European welfare states is in regulation. Why is there so much more regulation in the United States, especially in regard to health, safety, and professional behavior, than in Europe, where the tradition of governmental intervention is so much stronger? Ordinarily, individualism rejects regulation and hierarchy favors it. But hierarchies also favor specialization because it confers expertise; a major rationale for the acceptance of inequality is that people in the proper position and with the appropriate credentials really do know best. Hence hierarchies are not disposed to place fetters on professionals; hierarchies would make it difficult, for example, to file or to win medical malpractice suits. The same goes for risk. Both management and union hierarchies are concerned about safety, but raising alarms over this or that food or chemical would be regarded as undermining the assurance of control that hierarchies seek to give. Hierarchies cannot accept the main arguments for regulating risks—that dangers are hidden, involuntary, and irreversible—because that would constitute condemnation of the culture that did such awful things to its adherents.*

The dramatic turn that America has taken from the welfare to the regulatory state is attributable to the egalitarian desire to punish departures from equality. Damage to nature, in the eyes of egalitarians, is a mirror of damaged social relations. So they impose regulations on their enemies and affirm the connection between business ethics and bad health.[2]

Regulation wreaks havoc with localism. If evil is evil and good is good, then the more evil is prevented, and good is spread, the better. But if egalitarians view state and local governments as resisting virtue, how do they reconcile the nationalizing effect of regulation with their

---

*Individualists, like Adam Smith in his *Wealth of Nations,* argue the opposite: The benefits, not the dangers, of markets are hidden from view. The benefits, especially economic growth, are involuntary—people need not know they are producing them— irreversible, and will tend to make everyone better off in time.

abhorrence of large, bureaucratic organization? Easy—they blame big business. The large corporation stands for the alliance of internal hierarchy and external markets—the establishment to which egalitarians are opposed. They justify regulation for public health and safety by the inegalitarian concentration of power in corporations, and they cite the increases in corporate size necessary to cope with the regulations as justification for their fear that society is threatened by bigness.

An egalitarian political culture demands both increasing bureaucracy and decreasing authority. This explains why, as science and scientists are increasingly involved in debate over public policy, they are decreasingly respected. On the one hand, those who wish to show that the cultures they criticize (hierarchy and markets) cause contamination must invoke scientists and scientific knowledge on their side. It wouldn't do, in our time, to quote medicine men. On the other hand, their egalitarian social order has a congenital distrust of expertise because it suggests inequality. Expertise is a justification for hierarchy, not for egalitarianism. Bureaucracy coexists with lack of authority under egalitarianism when people sharing similar values and preferring similar practices want the same things—enforcement of regulation throughout the country and decline of the inequality that allows certain people to decide for others on grounds of expert knowledge.

Fairness without Responsibility

To expand the contradictions we are considering, why is it that the same people who support populist democracy (one person, one vote) also support judicial activism, which appears to negate this principle? Judicial activism is encouraged on behalf of causes—such as abolition of the death penalty, the rights of accused, damage from defective products—that blame the system rather than the person. "Blaming the victim," as egalitarians see it (or "personal responsibility," as the establishment prefers), justifies existing social relations. Blaming the system, requiring it to clean up its messes, holding it responsible for untoward events is peculiarly useful to egalitarians who see themselves as judges of a corrupt society. Judges would be deemed undemocratic only if they supported the establishment by holding to personal instead of systemic guilt.

This attitude toward the courts makes it apparent that concepts of fairness and responsibility differ according to the way of life each culture is supposed to support. For individualists, fairness is equal opportunity in competition. It is not success but failure (in theories, elections, or business) that is crucial, because markets for ideas or goods evolve for the better by selecting out of the worst. That is why political democracy is mostly about getting people and parties out of office, and has very little to say about what they should do when they get there (other than to leave gracefully when they lose).

Fairness in a hierarchy is about following the forms specifying the relation between the parts and the whole. Being treated fairly means being allowed to fulfill the responsibilities of one's station and supporting superiors who do the same. Fairness follows function in observing the division of labor and the boundaries between each specialty. The soldier must obey the superior officer, but the general may not invade the subordinate's home.

To egalitarians, fairness follows outcome; fair is equal. Equality makes it possible to do without responsibility or authority. If people are not responsible for their personal success or failure, then inequality is unjust and unfair. Since the absence of authority is difficult to measure directly, it is tested indirectly by the absence of distinctions that might confer advantage. Redistribution of income is bolstered by other egalitarian choices—informal dress (formality goes with hierarchy), bare "worker housing," meals without a main course—that protest against the artificial distinctions introduced by hierarchical organization. Egalitarians are distinguished, so to speak, by their lack of distinction. What could be more fair?

History without Winners

"The seller's market for guilt" that historian C. Vann Woodward finds pervasive in American public life is, as he says, different from anything we have known before.[3] "It is something congenital, inherent, intrinsic, collective, something possibly inexpiable, and probably ineradicable." For "the curious thing" about this criticism is that it includes ancestors as well as contemporaries, extends to "the founding fathers and founding mothers, who have come to be regarded as the guilty parties—or at least the original sinners." With authority identified as coercion, and inequality as injustice, it is no wonder that "American history becomes primarily a history of oppression" with no redeeming features, neither a civil war against slavery nor a foreign war against despotism.

Attention in historical writing, Woodward informs us, has shifted from oppression to the oppressed. Why, we may ask, has America gone from being "the land of liberty" to "the home of the oppressed"? American women have gone from being the freest women in the world to being the victims of male chauvinism. The elderly have exchanged their reputation for wisdom for a designation of "disadvantaged." Youth receives preferred treatment at Democratic party conventions. Entire regions seek official designation as "underprivileged," as if it were a badge of honor. American blacks, Chicanos, Native Americans, and other ethnic minorities are now considered "Third World" peoples as if they lived in a regime controlled by foreigners. That government subsidizes these categories, paying people to fit into them, is a triumph of egalitarian doctrine.

No one is considered a winner in American history, nor are there any self-declared winners today. On all sides there is gloom; each side claims it is losing. Everyone concerned, I think, is correctly perceiving the situation from their own perspective. The establishment, made up of collectivist and individualist cultures, is under attack. And, compared to where it was, has been losing. Corporations live within a web of regulations far more restrictive than in the past. The presidency, which is the closest thing the government of the United States has to a central, hierarchical institution, has had its authority much diminished. (The scope of the presidency—its involvement in major matters of foreign and domestic policy—has been much enlarged, but its formal prerogatives have contracted.)

The situation is quite straightforward on the egalitarian side: *Egalitarians exist not to be satisfied.*

Egalitarianism Is a Contradictory Culture

The anomalies in American politics that I have attributed to a rise in egalitarianism may be summarized by saying that its adherents impose contradictory demands on government and society. They insist that equality increase, while demanding that government stay small. They insist on bureaucratic regulation, to show that government is ridding itself of moral impurities, while challenging governmental authority. The very government that egalitarians call into action to enlighten the public is the same one that is always acting underhandedly to deceive the people.

The phenomenon of ungovernability, which has been said to afflict Western democracies in the era of the welfare state, undoubtedly has many causes. It may be, as both conservatives and Marxists contend, that buying votes leads to ever greater demands (the electoral spending cycle) until there is a "fiscal crisis of capitalism." Quite possibly, government has taken on tasks it cannot perform or that its people will not support. Were this the whole matter, the sense of crisis would not be in the air. Rather, one would hear of modest retrenchment, of a pause in the growth of the welfare state until the costs of oil or of pensions could better be accommodated. There is nothing surprising about outrunning one's resources, or spectacular about the difficulties of allocating a modest decline in standards of living. Why not just produce more and distribute more? No sweat. But when those who demand redistribution also oppose economic growth, and when those who expand government also condemn it for being too big, we may be pardoned for thinking that government is being programmed for failure.

Collectivism and individualism are balanced cultures; the strong group boundaries and strong prescription of behavioral norms in hierarchies reinforce one another, as do the weak boundaries and lack of prescriptions in individualistic markets. The established cultures can govern alone; egalitarian culture cannot. Egalitarians make inconsistent demands because the rejection of authority and redistribution of resources cannot be reconciled.

In the past, the term "sect" was often preceded by the modifier "powerless." Egalitarian sects either rejected the main society and moved to the wilderness, or so enraged the establishment that it destroyed them. Today, egalitarians are part of the system that imposes regulations on their opponents. They are powerless no longer. What has transformed these insignificant sects into generators of major social change?

Government, that's what happened (with an assist from modern technology). The use of computerized mailing lists permits egalitarian entrepreneurs to tap contributions from large numbers of people who do not participate directly in their group activities. This opportunity for vicarious participation has not only produced ready cash but has also simplified the task of leadership. Instead of satisfying an active membership, which might make contradictory demands, only the top leadership need be considered. *Sectarianism without sects is the clue to the comparative advantage of egalitarianism in modern politics.* Taken together as a statement of political economy, the costs of entry (a few dollars per mail-order member) and of activity (lobbying and legal work) in influencing government have been vastly reduced. The benefit of interaction with government has increased while the cost has declined.

Egalitarians want to separate themselves from evil (inegalitarian, coercive) social orders. Yet in a modern technological society most people cannot flee. And faced with a market economy populated in part by large corporations, egalitarians alone cannot compel their opponents to transform their common existence. What can egalitarians so situated do?

What they can do, and what they have been successful in doing, is get government to coerce other interests without themselves being responsible for the consequences. Environmental regulation is a case in point. This makes our egalitarians very powerful. They must find the irony delicious: Instead of being subject to other people's rules, they impose, through government, a large number of rules on their opponents. So egalitarians get stronger as their opponents are made weaker.

6

The Media's American Egalitarians

Bias. adverb. In a slanting manner.
Bias. noun. Systematic error . . . encouraging one outcome or answer
over others.
Webster's New Collegiate Dictionary, 1977

You are listening to public radio or viewing network television news or reading a major newspaper or news magazine. You are certain they are biased—that is, slanted, systematically favoring one view over another. Yet media people deny that they favor one political party or political ideology over another. They are not party hacks—they tell us with visible irritation—nor are they—in all exasperation—ideologues. They are, instead, professionals devoted to exercising as much objectivity as fallible beings under constant pressure can muster. Perhaps they do prefer the dramatic to the prosaic, for they must beat the clock by selecting from a potentially huge menu a much smaller number of items that can fit into a vanishingly small news hole. To guard against bias, they have institutionalized precautions. They split off hard news from soft opinion, writers from editors, news pegs (events of the day) from staged events. They cannot give mere opinion, for their stories must have a source (usually some governmental official) for anything they say. And if reporters are biased, a slew of editors are there to counter it. Their focus on conflict is real—they say—but it is also

---

The first part of this chapter appeared in *Public Interest*, no. 88 (Summer 1987), pp. 94–104. Added to this here is "Where Bias and Influence Meet," *Public Interest*, no. 91 (Spring 1988), pp. 94–98. Slight changes have been made to both.

exciting for the lay public that has to be wooed to the news—necessary to meet the competition—and yes, it does suggest there is more than one side to the story. Whatever their inadequacies—this typical defense continues—the personal political biases of media men and women do not intrude into their stories in any systematic manner.

Doubt it? Consult academic studies. These show that, except in 1984, when anti-Reagan bias was prevalent, television and national network reporters did not favor one party over another, nor were their stories markedly more liberal or conservative. How, then, to explain why both liberals and conservatives claim media bias, to the consternation of those on the receiving end of these criticisms?

A clue is provided by a leading student of the media, Michael Robinson, when he sums up the prevailing view of scholars by concluding that "the national press is biased against everybody, but in near equal proportions."[1] Another clue was provided by a friend who told me that "media people are not ideologues; it is just that they hate authority and believe that money is the root of all evil." Now that combination of values may not be everybody's idea of an ideology—it does cut across familiar left–right distinctions—but it is nonetheless a distinct world view with strong implications for the behavior of those who adhere to its tenets. Since all perception is selective—without leaving some things out it would be impossible to focus attention on anything—an ideology that denigrates authority as a form of inequality does form a distinctive (albeit insufficiently known) bias.

I shall argue that the national media has a characteristic bias that could be called American egalitarianism. This bias is not recognized by those who hold it, partly because it seems natural to them (as our biases appear natural to us) and partly because it does not fit neatly into the liberal–conservative or Democratic–Republican dichotomies to which all of us are accustomed. The fact that members of the national media are criticized across the usual political spectrum solidifies their view that they are distributing their blows impartially. Because scholars have not tested for American egalitarianism, they do not find it. A well-known research phenomenon—you only find what you look for—may explain why some of us find biases while many studies deny it.

The liberal–conservative or left–right distinction is adequate for capturing issues of economic redistribution. But it fails miserably to capture differences on social issues. Thus, social conservatives generally prefer market solutions but favor governmental intervention in private life to support community norms. Economic conservatives, by contrast, dislike governmental intervention in both economic and private life. We used to think of liberals, American style, as favoring a greater economic role for government but opposing state intervention in personal life. How, then, do we explain their support for governmental intervention in the family to prevent child abuse or their interest in regulating pornographic material that places women in a demeaning position? If conservatives favor less government, moreover, why do they want higher defense spending? And if liberals are big spenders, why do they want to spend less on defense?

Use of a triangular scheme of world views will correct these anomalies. First, individualists are people who prefer self-regulation to authority. They attribute success to individual initiative, and failure to personal incapacity or governmental intervention. Individualists want minimal government in all spheres except where law and order (local or international) is concerned, so they will remain free to transact with others as they see fit. Stories that stress individual achievement or the desirability of deregulation or the virtues of markets would be biased in their direction.

Second, adherents of hierarchy believe that social order requires the regulation of private life. They believe in and seek to enforce large moral and social differences. Individuals, in their view, are born bad but may be reformed through good institutions that inculcate desirable behavior. Success stems from following the rules, and failure from disobeying the authorities. Therefore supporters of hierarchy believe that authority ought to adhere in formal position. Power should go with place. Giving their emphasis to the value of the collective, members of hierarchies expect the parts to sacrifice for the whole. Hierarchies practice state intervention in all spheres, moderating their demands only when in alliance with individualists who won't stand for it. Stories that praise traditional moral norms or excoriate deviance or defend the nation and its institutions would reflect a hierarchical bias.

And third—just as individualists believe in equality of opportunity so as to expand the available resources within which some people can do better than others, and hierarchists believe in equality under the law so that people of different status can be judged according to their positions—egalitarians believe in greater equality of condition so as to reduce disparities in power. Accordingly, they want to diminish differences between rich and poor, black and white, women and men, children and parents, Third and First Worlds, and so on. Because authority is a prima facie case of inequality, they reject it. Failures are blamed on the system (the combination of coercive hierarchy and

inegalitarian markets they call "the establishment"), and successes
are attributed to following egalitarian principles. They view defense as
an egalitarian issue because it takes resources away from social welfare, because rich governments should not gang up on poor ones, and
because the established authorities deliberately overestimate the for-
eign/Soviet threat—for instance—in order to perpetuate an unjust (i.e.,
inegalitarian) system. Stories on the desirability of reducing disparities
in power or wealth or that criticize existing authority or unmask hidden
hierarchies in public life reveal an egalitarian bias.

Egalitarians do justify coercion if it is directed against "crimes of
inequality": rape, racism, child abuse. Inequality may also be justified
on an exceptional basis on the grounds that it helps "the unequals" in
their struggle against an oppressive establishment. This is the justification the national media give for their special privileges and protec-
tions.

I call members of the national media "American egalitarians" to
distinguish them from their foreign counterparts. Because individualism has been so strong in American life, egalitarians who are also
Americans stop short of income leveling. Their egalitarianism is thor-
oughgoing but incomplete: no nationalization, no confiscation, no total
equality of incomes.

Egalitarianism makes the finding of little partisan bias in the news
explicable. When election contests or policy divisions elicit media
feelings about institutions or authorities, the treatment is uniformly
negative irrespective of party. But when feelings about authority and
institutions reinforce feelings about equality—that is, when American
egalitarians line up all their ideological ducks—we can expect an
especially strong negative reaction. It was not the major media's liking
Walter Mondale in 1984, after all, but their disliking Ronald Reagan's
policies so much that increased their bias.

None of four recent books about the media I am reviewing here has
anything to say about how the public perceives the news. They all do
tell us a good deal about how certain members of the media treated
specific stories, about the personal political views of these media
members, and about how public officials deal with them. It is up to us
to bring something to the discussion so as to make sense out of this
disparate material. Let us see whether the books considered, viewed
from a triangular perspective, can shed light on allegations of media
bias.

System Blame in the News

If the unexamined life is not worth living, the examined life does not exactly inspire confidence. To the adage that if one wishes to enjoy either sausages or politics one should not see how either is made, we can now add the news. I thought I knew what I needed to know about Westmoreland versus CBS and Sharon versus *Time*; Renata Adler's *Reckless Disregard*[2] has convinced me otherwise. Her luminous intelligence and her controlled passion make us aware that these court cases point to similar morals. For this is one of the few times—in my reading, the only time—that reporters and commentators have been subject to the same pitiless examination (deposition and testimony going minutely over the same ground) as is now routinely meted out to public officials.

How can I convey the sheer shoddiness of the reporting? Were it possible to make the evasiveness of the White House Watergate crew look candid, *Time*'s reporters would be able to do it. And were it conceivable that the slant in the explanations of the Daniloff and Iran affairs—what, swap hostages for spies or arms, not us!—could be made to appear truthful, the crew of the CBS documentary on Westmoreland would do the trick. Like a caricature of a satire on Kafka's *The Trial,* leaving everything favorable out and doctoring the unfavorable that was left in, the extent of bias is mind boggling. Shall we say that boys will be boys, that admitted excesses must be tolerated to preserve a free media? Adler's achievement is to reach inside her readers so they find such easy rationalizations troubling.

An international news magazine and a national television network accuse two generals of complicity in mass murder directly, by suggesting revenge in Lebanon, and indirectly, by falsifying intelligence estimates in Vietnam. No small thing. What, in such circumstances, do we think ought to be the standard of evidence? Must we, before leveling such dreadful accusations, positively know that they are true? Or should a negative standard—not knowing they are false—prevail? I say "we" because Adler rightly wants us to think hard about what we, and not only the media involved, would do. The jury in the Sharon case evidently felt some such compunction because, after stating that there was no "clear and convincing evidence" of "actual malice," it asked permission to include this statement: "We found that certain *Time* employees, particularly correspondent David Halevy, acted negligently and carelessly in reporting and verifying the information which ultimately found its way into the published paragraph of interest in this case." The reaction of the attorney for *Time* was this: "We won, flat-out and going away." Won what?

Adler offers more excuses than she needs to for the printing of the Sharon story and the airing of the so-called documentary on West-moreland (an excellent CBS internal report found 11 major breaches of proper journalistic standards) in order to focus attention on the higher-ups who refused to admit their bias after they knew they didn't have the facts. When the correspondent on whom *Time* relied said that verification was in a secret Israeli document, and when his contention was shown to be false, he was asked to go back and verify his original information. The correspondent did so and reported that the same source he had used before stood by the story. Should *Time* have accepted an unknown source for a charge that involved killing women and children? (Would you?) Similarly, when CBS learned how its program had been put (or spliced) together, should it have withdrawn the allegations on the grounds that they were far from demonstrably true, or adhered to them on the basis that they could not be proven in court to be demonstrably false? By this time, of course, *Time* and CBS were being sued for huge sums, hot trials were underway, and what was true or false factually, or right or wrong morally, got lost in self-defense.

Why, I ask, in view of my interest in understanding media bias, did these stories appear in the first place without a very strong evidentiary base? Or does anyone wish to argue that the public interest was served by making accusations of heinous deeds against public figures first and then deciding afterward whether they were true or, more accurately, could be proven false?

What, I ask, would the reporters have to believe to think that their stories would be believed by their organizations? Sharon and West-moreland were commanders of the armed forces of First World countries that fought wars in Third World countries, wars that were widely regarded at home as demoralizing losses. Who was to blame for these misfortunes? The movie *Platoon* would have us believe that these wars were not directed against an external enemy but at the evil within us, not within the foot soldiers who were driven by circumstance but in the system that sent them there. Westmoreland and Sharon serve as convenient symbols of governmental systems that oppress other peo-ple as they deceive their own—for the good citizens of these countries would never have killed others less fortunate than they, had they not deliberately been misled. Had "system blame" not been part of the ethos of *Time* and CBS, had these media organizations not been peopled by American egalitarians, I suggest, they would not have suspended their personal consciences and abandoned their professional standards either by making such charges, or defending them, or expecting that others like them would applaud such actions.

If blaming individual leaders is evidence of system blame, how do I account for the steady current of criticism—especially from egalitarians—that the media focus on individual personalities, thus letting "the system" off the hook? Guilty as charged, but not quite. There *is* an inordinate emphasis on personalities, and this emphasis does tend to overwhelm larger considerations. Taken together over periods of time, however, the incessant drumbeat of criticism surrounding those who occupy (or bid to occupy) high office is sufficient to suggest that the entire system of relationships is flawed.

Why Do Egalitarians Leak More?

"Overall," Martin Linsky concludes in *Impact,* "we found that the press and policymakers are engaged in a continuing struggle to control the view of reality that is presented to the American people."[3] Unfortunately, since the author has no hypothesis to test on this subject, we learn nothing about what these views might be, which ones are held by reporters and editors in the national media, and what difference it makes to their stories. We are told that the national media are important. Public officials who make active use of the media do better. Right. I fear for those who come to public office not knowing these things.

The author draws from a sample of high-ranking executive and legislative officials, ending up with 432 responses to his questionnaire. In addition, lengthy interviews were undertaken with 20 accomplished policymakers and 16 journalists. What they say makes sense; the difficulty is that they are asked to take the place of the author in coming up with conclusions or relationships that have to be built into the investigation in the first place. (Did you ever change a policy because of media pressure? No one would admit to it.) *Impact* is uniformly intelligent, well-informed, and reasonable in its accounts and advice. However, it lacks a theory of media–government relationships guiding the choice of questions and their interpretation and, therefore, lacks exactly what its title suggests. Nevertheless, it does speak to our concerns.

Officials who have been around for a long time told Linsky that reporters are much more critical than they used to be. And they agree with other evidence that journalists have much more control over the content of stories and are less answerable to their publishers than in the past. Self-designated liberals, compared to moderates or conservatives—Linsky tells us—were far more likely to initiate stories about themselves or their activities, to feel comfortable with media representatives, to spend more than five hours a week with them, and—by inference—to leak more data. The chapter on "Dispelling the Leak Mystique," which portrays officially unauthorized disclosures to the media as a cooperative game, is the best in the book. But who cooperates with whom? Self-identified liberals believe that leaking pays; they get more favorable stories in the press. These liberals, as I shall show, are egalitarians. Why, I ask, do American egalitarians leak more? Because leaking is an antiestablishment device. It is, as Cyrus Vance explained when asked why he did not leak, disloyal. Exactly.

In asking why egalitarians use the press more, we can turn to six case histories that are used throughout the book to illustrate media–governmental relationships. The reorganization of the Postal Service, which substitutes one governmental monopoly for another, involves restrictive job practices. The other five involve egalitarian opposition to existing authority. The resignation of Spiro Agnew as vice-president presumably reveals the system for which he stands as corrupt. The neutron bomb warhead portrays people in power who care more about property than lives. Reducing the rolls of beneficiaries from Social Security disability is about a helpless minority that is savaged by an unfeeling Reagan administration, whose insensitivity in this matter is exceeded only by its granting Bob Jones University a tax exemption despite the school's admissions policy favoring whites. Why, to go to the last of these cases, is Love Canal interpreted as an egalitarian issue? In the minds of those who think this way (actually not a single case of serious harm has been verified, but never mind), Love Canal shows that corporate capitalism causes cancer—that is, that established authority secretly imposes involuntary hazards on people, who suffer irreparable damage. A nice system wouldn't do that.

Egalitarian legislators use the media more—to better effect and with greater confidence than hierarchists and individualists—because the two world views intersect. Each believes in greater equality of condition. Each sees itself as battling against entrenched and unworthy authority. Stories that put authority in a bad light serve their preferences. Hierarchists, correspondingly, can expect to find less comfort when they seek to uphold authority or to maintain a traditional social policy on such an issue as abortion. And individualists who want to sell off public lands or to auction off "pollution rights" might not be greeted with open arms. Because they are not statist but egalitarian, members of the national media may be mobilized to support deregulation, as in airlines or in the post office, provided that the villains are overprivileged and people of lower income benefit. Differential use of media, therefore, may have less to do with ignorance of its importance than with a correct perception of what kinds of policies and politics are likely to receive a favorable reception.

Measuring the Media Elite

What is necessary in order to test theories of media bias directly are surveys of its members' political preferences and investigations of their stories. In this way, the relationship between their preferences and their reporting, if any, may be appraised.

The great virtues of S. Robert Lichter, Stanley Rothman, and Linda S. Lichter's *The Media Elite* are its seriousness of purpose, its diversity of methods and studies crisscrossing the same subject, and the authors' ability to relate media preferences to media performance.[4] The book is based on surveys of the social backgrounds and political attitudes of journalists at the New York *Times,* the *Wall Street Journal, Newsweek, Time,* the CBS, NBC, and ABC television networks, and National Public Television. Content analyses of three major issues— nuclear power, busing, and the energy crisis—reveal how the national media treated these issues. These analyses are based not only on media performance but on how other elites, such as nuclear engineers, viewed the same sort of events. In addition, the researchers asked journalists to interpret different kinds of stories and various types of pictures (using the Thematic Apperception Test, TAT). While ranging so far afield opens up the authors to charges of attempting to do too much, and questions can be raised—as always—about the appropriateness of their methods, weaknesses in one area are made up by strengths in others.

As is true of most elites, members of the national media have gone to school longer, make more money, and are markedly more secular than the rest of the population. More relevant to our purpose, 54 percent call themselves liberal while only 17 percent think of themselves as conservative. From 1964 through 1976 (in the authors' survey, and to this very day in other surveys), more than 80 percent of media members support Democratic presidential candidates. Johnson was preferred to Goldwater 94 percent to 6 percent.

The strongest views of the national media are on social issues. Ninety-seven percent think government should not regulate sex; 90 percent think women have a right to decide on abortion; 80 percent support affirmative action. On the governmental–institutional level, more than half believe that U.S. exploitation causes Third World poverty, that the goal of American foreign policy is to protect business, and that use of its resources abroad is immoral. Five out of six think the American legal system favors the rich, while 49 percent believe that the structure of society causes alienation. In regard to economic relationships, more than two-thirds of the national media think government should reduce gaps in income, just under half want government to guarantee jobs, but only 13 percent favor nationalized industry. An overwhelming proportion—86 percent—think that people with more ability should earn more.

It would be difficult to paint a portrait of people who more closely resemble egalitarians tinged with individualism than national press and television journalists. They want to reduce practically every social difference they can find. They blame the system for exploiting others and for alienating its own people. Part of this rejection of institutions is universal—28 percent believe that all political systems are repressive—with the rest reserved for American inequalities. Their economic policy stresses redistribution of income within a private ownership that retains income disparities based on ability.

Surely our national media are not socialist. Before congratulating ourselves on having learned this much, however, we should understand that their nonsocialist inclinations cut two ways: While media elites are opposed to nationalization and leveling, they are also opposed to existing authority. Coming from hierarchically organized political parties, believing that bigger is better if social welfare spending goes up, socialists demand and support greater governmental power. Our American egalitarians demand that government reduce inequalities, but they are opposed to increasing its authority.

What are the consequences of having national journalists with predominantly egalitarian views? We have seen they overwhelmingly adhere to the Democratic party. Lichter, Rothman, and Lichter show that media elites uniformly cite sources for their stories that have egalitarian proclivities. When shown pictures and told tales that could be interpreted in different ways, moreover, "they ruminate on racism,

poverty, exploitation and the ultimate failure of the downtrodden."
They also evidence anger at "establishment figures as slavishly pursuing personal profit or narrow self-interest at the public's expense." So
what? Why does it matter if vast majorities of nuclear scientists and
engineers favor nuclear power and if comparable majorities of science
writers who cover such stories are against nuclear power? The true
test is in the content of the media. A content analysis reveals that,
apart from a small pronuclear tilt in *U.S. News and World Report,*
stories in the major media were decidedly antinuclear.

Stories on busing began with an affirmative slant that declined
somewhat in 1973–74 as reports of "white flight" surfaced and climbed
to an even more favorable level thereafter. Violence was played down,
compliance played up. The findings from this content analysis are
important, the authors rightly inform us, because they

> argue against one fashionable interpretation of media coverage—the "bad
> news bias," or the notion that news coverage of any public policy issue
> will be predominantly critical, negative, or anti-establishment in tone. . . .
> The major media often dismissed or reinterpreted to so-called bad news
> about busing. In both the political arena and the classroom, they empha-
> sized order rather than disorder, established channels for protest rather
> than spontaneous outbursts, and the importance of the end goal (integra-
> tion) rather than the weakness of the means (busing).

The national media, in sum, are not opposed to established authority
per se but will support it when it is seen to uphold egalitarian values—
except nationalization of course. If one thinks of the bulk of its
members as affirming the desirability of diminishing inequalities, rather
than opposing authority no matter what, then their stories on busing
are not exceptions but are entirely consistent with their world view.

When oil companies make big money as their reserves are revalued
upward during OPEC price increases, the media play up their profits;
when profits plummet, the media either ignore the subject or say that
profits are too high. Analyses showing that profits in the oil industry
over time do not exceed those of industry in general are disregarded.
As usual, the telling question is this: Who is to blame for misfortune—
in this case, energy problems? If we combine the oil industry and
government as representing the establishment, and OPEC as outside
of American responsibility, interesting answers emerge. The New York
Times and *Time* magazine have blamed the establishment around three
times more than OPEC. The television networks blamed the establish-

ment almost five times more than OPEC (70 percent to 15 percent). Given a chance to externalize blame on a plausible target—namely OPEC—60 percent to 70 percent of these important segments of the media chose to blame established American institutions. Their profession may impel them to be critical and their competitive position may impel them to be sensational, but neither professional standards nor economic necessity tell the media who to be critical of or sensational about.

I am less inclined to credit the views of Lichter, Rothman, Lichter on the psychological dynamics of elite journalists: "We have argued that inner ambivalence toward power may be displaced outward as antagonism toward the seekers and holders of power." One reason is that I doubt the validity of probing collective psyches. Another reason is that I suspect most elites (including political scientists) would like to be powerful. My strongest reason is that power can be pursued in numerous ways. One could, after all, join the establishment as well as fight it.

To go back to the beginning of this chapter, it is not so much the fact of bias but rather identifying the kinds of bias under which the national media operate that will improve the quality of this debate. In analyzing the tendencies of journalists, Lichter, Rothman, and Lichter tell us,

> When their TAT stories contained socially relevant themes, figures of authority tended to evoke fantasies about the abuse of power in the form of greedy businessmen, deceitful lawyers, conniving politicians, intimidating policemen, and sadistic military superiors. Conversely, socially relevant stories tended to portray the average man as the victim of malevolent higher-ups or an uncaring social system.

This is an egalitarian bias.

Print and television journalists are adamant about their devotion to equal opportunity and not to equal results. No intelligent person, certainly no respectable journalist—they insist—believes in such ridiculous notions as that all people are or ought to be alike. So far as it goes, this statement of beliefs, which I have heard many times, is accurate. But that does not end the matter. For the self-same journalists also believe that there cannot be genuine equal opportunity without much greater equality of results. As Lawrence Joseph argues in an article on different views of equal opportunity, "compensatory equality of opportunity . . . can have quite radical implications, when carried to its logical conclusions." National media elites say "equal opportunity," but the evidence shows they mean much more equal results.

Knowing that they have not consciously worked out an ideology through which many conclusions flow from a few premises, television and print journalists are likely to deny the whole thing. Another idiot professor (who does not understand the constraints under which they work) has attributed to them concepts and connections that have never entered their minds. In that case, I ask, how come they sound so much alike?

Media journalists pride themselves on their individuality. They—so they tell themselves—value individual differences. After all, being unlike others is part of their stock-in-trade. They glorify the maverick, the nay-sayer, the whistle-blower. They identify with the outsider. But with the problems of established authorities, they show no empathy and little sympathy. Our national media support individuals who attack existing authority. These media elites do not recognize their own collective portrait, but it is there for all to see. Try for yourself classifying their stories as hierarchical, egalitarian, or individualistic and see how they come out.

Where Bias and Influence Meet

Of the three great questions about the influence of the major media on political opinion—Is there a systematic media bias? If so, in what direction does it flow? Is public opinion strongly influenced by the media?—the last is arguably the most important. For if opinion is not much influenced by the way the media report the news (or determine what is news), the prior questions about the extent and direction of bias are, in political life at least, irrelevant.

Shento Iyengar and Donald Kinder's *News That Matters* does matter, because it demonstrates conclusively that television newscasts powerfully affect opinion.[5] The ingenious way in which Iyengar and Kinder persuade us to accept their thesis makes their joint work the leading book in its field. All that follows, whether it supports, modifies, or challenges their conclusions, will have to begin with their work.

It is important to realize that until recently the prevailing wisdom was that television news has only a weak and fleeting influence on opinion. Television news was assumed to be too brief, too scattered, too visual (as opposed to cerebral) to influence opinion. Following on older studies of newspaper influence where editorials were reported to be unread and news stories too complex, there appeared little point in worrying about media that have trouble even holding people's atten-

tion, let alone persuading them to change their views. Forgotten were
Walter Lippmann's caution in the 1920s about the media's ability to
influence what people take to be important (which Iyengar and Kinder
call "priming") and Bernard Cohen's seminal *The Press and Foreign
Policy,* in which he argues that the press "is stunningly successful in
telling its readers what to think *about.*" But how, amid rival specula-
tions about whether television news affects public opinion, when each
hunch is plausible to its holders, is evidence to be brought to bear so
as to arrive at a persuasive conclusion?

Surveys of the general population and selected groups have their
uses. They can tell us about the kinds of people who hold certain views
and can test plausible guesses about why they hold them. The variety
of possible influences is so great, however, that it is difficult to establish
causality. It is not easy to say exactly how a person surveyed was
exposed to the stories in question, whether or not other factors
intervened, how changing the time or the person or the story's presentation would affect the result, or what to do if one wishes to study
television coverage of energy when television coverage is exclusively
about poverty. The conducting of experiments, the authors' chosen
method, overcomes these handicaps, by allowing for control over
exposure and exposee. We will not know how successful their method
is until critical studies have appeared.

Iyengar and Kinder's genius, as I see it, consists of figuring out how
to expose handpicked audiences to selected television news broadcasts
without permitting the viewers to know that the news was "cooked."
By going over news from the same channels on the same subjects they
wanted to cover from the past two years, they were able to splice their
own material carefully in without arousing suspicion. One more thing:
patience, energy, and frustration-tolerance play a vital part in their 14
experiments. They continually revised the experiments, inventing new
ways to learn about phenomena they later realized were important but
had not programmed in at the start. A willingness to accept the lack of
perfect foresight is needed by the compleat researcher. So is a willingness to supplement one's preferred method with others (the authors
use surveys where helpful), a good example of methodological pluralism. What have they found that is so important?

The first finding the authors rightly term "the *agenda-setting hypothesis: those problems that receive prominent attention on the national
news become the problems the viewing public regards as the nation's
most important.*" First, small groups of adult participants in New
Haven and Ann Arbor were selected and exposed to the experimentally

prepared television newscasts. Before and after this controlled exposure, their beliefs about the importance of national policy problems were measured. The social and economic status and demographic characteristics of the participants are shown to be equivalent. Table 6.1 is typical of the authors' results. Except for inflation (then raging at unheard-of levels), those issues given greater exposure on television news grew substantially in the importance that citizens ascribed to them. Indeed, in several experiments, "viewers' priorities were significantly affected by a *single* news story." And these influences on priorities were maintained over time.

Suppose, however, that television is tracking what viewers independently consider the most important problems so that the actual causal effect runs from the people to the media, and not vice versa. To my satisfaction (though the methods used, as reported in their appendix B, are too complex to be described here), the authors succeed in differentiating what opinion would have been with and without the pattern of television news. Thus actual current conditions pertaining to energy, from oil imports to oil and energy prices, had no prestudy impact on public concern, whereas this concern rose by 1 percent for every seven broadcast news stories. The public's memory, however, appears to be limited, for "when television news focuses on a problem, the public's priorities are altered, and altered again as television news moves on to something new."

Immediately, many common-sense hypotheses qualifying those con-

Table 6.1   Change in Problem Importance before and after Viewing
Experimental Newscast

Experiment	Problem	Percentage Naming Problem as One of Country's Most Serious		
		Before the Experiment	After the Experiment	Change: Pre- to Post-
2	Defense	33	53	20
	Inflation	100	100	00
	Pollution	0	14	14
8	Arms Control	35	65	30
	Civil Rights	0	10	10
	Unemployment	43	71	28
9	Unemployment	50	86	36

Source: Shento Iyengar and Donald R. Kinder, *News That Matters. Television and American Opinion* (Chicago: University of Chicago Press, 1987), p. 20.

clusions come to mind. One of the most obvious—vivid, emotional stories that might touch the heartstrings—have no discernible impact on agenda-setting. Another common-sense observation, by contrast, is important: Lead stories matter more; indeed, they matter most, since "virtually all of the change in the public's concern over energy, inflation, and unemployment that is produced by alterations in television coverage can be traced to lead story coverage."

It is not so easy to guess how personal experience affects the perceived importance of issues. On the one hand, the connection sometimes seems to be notable for its absence. Unemployment, the Vietnam War, and the energy crisis, for instance, did not generate more concern among those personally affected. On the other hand, one of Iyengar and Kinder's experiments reveals that black people rate civil rights far higher than do whites, and that the elderly rate Social Security higher than do others. When news first appears it engenders more interest among those who consider themselves personally affected; but if network coverage continues, those who do not yet see the importance of the problem begin to do so.

A second important finding involves priming: "*By calling attention to some matters while ignoring others, television news influences the standards by which governments, presidents, policies, and candidates for public office are judged.*" Two possible directions of causality have to be distinguished: Do people *project* their feelings about presidential performance onto specific issues? Or do their appraisals of how well presidents do on particular matters condition or *prime* the public's appraisal? As the authors explain,

> The political differences between priming and projection are enormous. If priming holds, then television news possesses the capacity to alter the standards by which a president is judged, and therefore the degree of public popularity a president enjoys and the power he can wield. If projection holds . . . that implies a sharply reduced role for television news as a molder of opinion.

Iyengar and Kinder demonstrate that, while projection and priming both exist, priming predominates: Increases in news coverage alone more than double the importance of an issue in determining presidential performance ratings. It follows, empirically as well as conceptually, that the more the media attribute responsibility for events to presidents, the more citizens evaluate their performance by that criterion.

Perhaps it is not only the media perspective but also the audience that matters. People who are politically active, it turns out, are better able to resist agenda-setting than are their opposites, but by the same tests, the politically involved are equally subject to political priming. Political groupies carry with them more of their own policy agenda, but their evaluations of political objects are still primed by the media.

Under what conditions would there be reason for concern about the political power of the major media? A two-by-two matrix (figure 6.1) captures the key considerations. At stage one, we find the previous conventional wisdom: If both media influence and media bias are weak, then concern about the subject is trivial. And while media bias by itself might be dangerous, efforts to exert power (stage two) would be futile.

Iyengar and Kinder have now taken us to stage three, where media influence is strong but its bias is weak. There is potential but not yet actual power over elections or policies. Were this power to be realized by being connected to systematic bias, the results would be troublesome (stage four). Read the authors' conclusions: "Our results suggest that by priming some considerations and ignoring others, television news can shift the grounds on which campaigns are contested. Priming may therefore determine who takes office—and with what mandate— and who is sent home. . . . Less clear . . . is whether this influence is necessarily undesirable." If creative research like theirs demonstrates, as I believe it will, that we are actually at stage four where strong

Figure 6.1 Stages of Media Power

Media Influence

		Weak	Strong
Media Bias	Weak	1) Trivial	3) Potential
	Strong	2) Futile	4) Troublesome

Source: Developed by the author using a Thompson–Tuden matrix; see J. Thompson and A. Tuden, "Strategies, Structures, and Processes of Organizational Decision," in J. Thompson, ed., *Comparative Studies in Administration* (Pittsburgh, Pa.: University of Pittsburgh Press, 1959), pp. 195–216.

media influence is matched by strong bias, then Iyengar and Kinder's query about desirability answers itself. Soon enough it will become apparent that we have reached the troublesome stage where media influence has to confront the fact of media bias.

7

Theories of Risk Perception:
Who Fears What and Why?

with Karl Dake

> How odd it is that anyone should not see that all observation must be for
> or against some view if it is to be of any service.
>
> Charles Darwin

In social science, rival theories seeking to answer the same questions
rarely confront one another. Indeed, a variety of perspectives have
been employed in research on public perception of risk, but alternative
formulations remain largely untested. Missing most of all is a focused
comparison of rival hypotheses.

One could hardly find many subjects that are better known or
considered more important to more people nowadays than the controversies over harm to the natural environment and the human body
attributed to modern technology, whether this be from chemical carcinogens or nuclear power or noxious products introduced by industry
into the land, sea, or air, or into water or food supplies. Thus we ask:
Why are products and practices once thought to be safe (or safe
enough) perceived increasingly as dangerous? Who (what sort of
people) view technology as largely benign, and who as mostly dangerous? To what degree are different people equally worried about the

---

This chapter first appeared as an article in *Daedalus* 119, no. 4 (Fall 1990), pp. 41–60.

same dangers, or to what extent do some perceive certain risks as great that others think of as small? And how do concerns across different kinds of risk—war, social deviance, economic troubles as well as technology—vary for given individuals? Only by comparisons across types of danger can we learn whether individuals have a general tendency to be risk averse or risk-taking, or whether their perceptions of danger depend on the meaning they give to objects of potential concern. The test we shall put to each theory of risk perception is its ability to predict and explain *what* kinds of people perceive *which* potential hazards to be *how* dangerous.[1]

The most widely held theory of risk perception we call *the knowledge theory*: the often implicit notion that people perceive technologies (and other things) to be dangerous because they know them to be dangerous. In a critical review of *Risk and Culture,* for instance, John Holdern's belief that perceivers are merely registering the actual extent of danger to themselves—the "of-course-people-are-worried-they-have-lots-to-worry-about" thesis—comes out clearly.

A much simpler description might suffice: people worry most about the risks that seem most directly to threaten their well-being at the moment; environmental concerns predominate only where and when people imagine the risks of violence and economic ruin to be under control. . . . What is wrong, after all, with the simple idea—paralleling Maslow's stages of wants—that worries about more subtle and complex threats will materialize if, and only if, the most direct and obvious threats are taken care of?[2]

If Holdern is correct, perception of danger should accord with what individuals know about the risk in question. But do risk perceptions and knowledge coincide?

Another commonly held cause of risk perception follows from *personality theory*. In conversations we frequently hear personality referred to as if individuals were without discrimination in their risk aversion or risk-taking propensities: Some individuals love risk-taking so they take many risks, while others are risk averse and seek to avoid as many risks as they can. We will test this common, if extreme, view. We will also examine a more moderate theory of personality: that stable individual differences among persons are systematically correlated with their perceptions of danger. Leaving aside the extraordinary Oblimov-like characters staying in bed all their lives, or the Evel Knievels breaking bones on too-daring feats, this version of personality theory suggests that individuals are so constituted as to take or reject risks in an enduring manner.[3] But do traditionally assessed attributes of personality such as intrapsychic dynamics and interpersonal traits relate to risk perceptions and preferences in predictable ways?

The third set of explanations for public perceptions of danger follow two versions of *economic theory*. In one, the rich are more willing to take risks stemming from technology because they benefit more and are somehow shielded from adverse consequences. The poor presumably feel just the opposite. In "postmaterialist" theory, the rationale is reversed, however: Precisely because living standards have improved, the new rich are less interested in what they have (affluence) and what got them there (capitalism) than in what they think they used to have (closer social relations) and what they would like to have (better health).[4] Is it true, though, that these newly affluent folk desire postmaterial values, such as interpersonal harmony, and hence fear environmental pollution and chemical contamination?

Other explanations for public reactions to potential hazards are based on *political theory*. These accounts view the controversies over risk as struggles over interests, such as holding office or party advantage. The view of politics as clashing interests would connect conflicts to different positions in society. The hope for explanatory power in such approaches to risk perception is thus placed on social and demographic characteristics such as gender, age, social class, liberal–conservative ratings, and/or adherence to political parties.[5]

Viewing individuals as the active organizers of their own perceptions, *cultural theorists* have proposed that individuals choose what to fear (and how much to fear it) in order to support their way of life.[6] In this perspective, one's selective attention to risk and one's preferences among different types of risk-taking (or avoiding) correspond to "cultural biases"—that is, to world views or ideologies entailing deeply held values and beliefs defending different patterns of social relations. "Social relations" are defined in cultural theory as a small number of distinctive patterns of interpersonal relationships: hierarchical, egalitarian, or individualistic.* No causal priority is given to cultural biases or social relations; they are always found together interacting in a

---

*Cultural theory delineates two additional cultures: fatalists and hermits. It also makes finer distinctions regarding nature, technology, and risk perception than are discussed here. Were it possible, we would prefer to measure cultural biases in their social context. Instead, we have taken the approach suggested by the survey data at our disposal. We assess biases as world views.

mutually reinforcing manner. Thus there are no relationship without cultural biases to justify them, and no biases without relations to uphold them.

Socially viable combinations of cultural biases and social relations are referred to in cultural theory as "ways of life" or "political cultures." More specifically, then, hierarchical, egalitarian, and individualist forms of social relations, together with the cultural biases that justify them, are each hypothesized to engender distinctive representations of what constitutes a hazard and what does not. Among all possible risks, those selected for worry or dismissal are functional in the sense that they strengthen one of these ways of life and weaken the others. This sort of explanation is at once more political (there being a political purpose to all of this perceiving—defending a way of life and attacking others) and less obvious: What has risk perception to do with ways of life?

Since cultural biases are forms of ideology, there should be high correlations between certain biases and corresponding ideologies (e.g., egalitarianism and political liberalism). When we vary the kinds of possible dangers to which people react, however, we should see that the left–right distinction captures the cultural bias of egalitarianism but fails to distinguish between hierarchy and individualism. Hence we expect cultural biases to predict a broad spectrum of risk perceptions better than political ideology does.

According to cultural theory, adherents of hierarchy perceive acts of social deviance to be dangerous because such behavior may disrupt their preferred (superior/subordinate) form of social relations. By contrast, advocates of greater equality of conditions abhor the role differentiation characteristic of hierarchy because ranked stations signify inequality. Egalitarians reject the prescriptions associated with hierarchy (i.e., who is allowed to do what and with whom), and thus show much less concern about social deviance.

Individualist cultures support self-regulation, including the freedom to bid and bargain. The labyrinth of normative constraints and controls on behavior that are valued in hierarchies are perceived as threats to the autonomy of the individualist, who prefers to negotiate for himself. Social deviance is a threat to individualist culture only when it limits freedom, or when it is disruptive of market relationships. Our expectation is that individualists should take a stance between hierarchists, to whom social deviance is a major risk, and egalitarians to whom it is a minor risk at most.

Egalitarians claim that nature is "fragile" in order to justify sharing the Earth's limited resources and to discomfort individualists, whose life of bidding and bargaining would be impossible if they had to worry too much about disturbing nature. On the contrary, individualists claim that nature is "cornucopian" so that if people are released from artificial constraints (like excessive environmental regulations) there will be no limits to the abundance for all, thereby more than compensating for any damage they do. Hierarchists have something in common with individualists: They approve of technological processes and products, provided their experts have given the appropriate safety certifications and the applicable rules and regulations are followed. In hierarchical culture, nature is "perverse or tolerant." Good comes if you follow their rules and experts, bad if you don't.

People who hold an egalitarian bias (who value strong equality in the sense of diminishing distinctions among people such as wealth, race, gender, authority, etc.) would perceive the dangers associated with technology to be great, and its attendant benefits as small. They believe that an inegalitarian society is likely to insult the environment just as it exploits poor people. Those who endorse egalitarianism would also rate the risks of social deviance to be relatively low. What right has an unconscionably inegalitarian system to make demands or to set standards? The perceived risks of war among egalitarians would be low to moderate: They are likely to mistrust the military (a prototypical hierarchy); they also believe that the threat of war abroad is exaggerated by the establishment coalition of hierarchy and individualism in order to justify an inegalitarian system at home.

Cultural theory's predictions for the individualist bias are just the opposite: Its adherents perceive the dangers of technology as minimal, in part because they trust that their institutions can control or compensate for the severity of untoward events. These same predictions hold for the cultural bias of hierarchy. How then do we distinguish between the world views of hierarchists and individualists? By varying the object of concern. A study of technological risks alone would leave these two cultures hopelessly confounded. Both are technologically optimistic, individualists because they see technology as a vehicle for unlimited individual enterprise—to them, risk is opportunity—and hierarchists because they believe that technology endorsed by their experts is bound to improve the quality of life.

Due to the emphasis placed on obedience to authority within hierarchy, its supporters scorn deviant behavior. In contrast, individualists, who prefer to substitute self-regulation for authority, are much more willing to permit behavior that is the product of agreement. And yet, here too, a distinction must be made. If the object of attention is personal behavior, such as sex between consenting adults, individualists will be against allowing government to intervene. But if the subject is crime or violence against established institutions, they will be more disposed to support a governmental crackdown. In other words, if "order" signifies support for the stability and legitimacy necessary for market relationships, individualists will support government action toward that end.

Economic troubles represent a different kind of risk than those of technology or social deviance, since almost everyone has a reason to worry about them—egalitarians because lower living standards are especially harmful to the poorest people, and adherents of hierarchy because it weakens the system they wish to defend. We would expect individualists to fear economic failure more than others, however, because the marketplace is the institution most central to their life of negotiated contracts.

Method

To test these rival theories—knowledge, personality, economic, political, and cultural—we drew on the risk-perception data archives established by Kenneth H. Craik, David Buss, and Karl Dake at the University of California's Institute of Personality Assessment and Research.[7] We used the "pro-risk" index of their Societal Risk Policy instrument to gauge the extent of an individual's endorsement of risk-taking versus risk aversion in regard to technology. This pro-risk index assesses whether risk-taking and risk management are viewed as presenting opportunities for advancement, or rather as an invitation to catastrophe at the societal level.

We assessed perceptions of risk associated with technology and the environment, war, social deviance, and economic troubles, using variables chosen from a list of 36 "concerns that people have about society today." Following procedures similar to those used in the most important pioneering study of risk perceptions, we selected average ratings of 25 technologies on risk and benefit.[8] These indexes enable us to compare public responses to different kinds of dangers. Now we turn to the factors that have been used to explain such responses.

Knowledge

One measure of knowledge we have used is the individual's self-report of how much he or she knows about specific technologies. Another measure is self-report of educational level. Self-ratings are the simplest and best way to address some psychological phenomena—who knows better than the individual how much dread a perceived hazard evokes for him?—while in regard to other phenomena they are notoriously poor. To avoid the potential pitfalls of relying only on self-reported knowledge, we developed a measure of perceptual accuracy based on differences between public and expert judgments of annual fatalities associated with eight technologies: contraceptives, nuclear power, diagnostic X rays, bicycles, lawn mowers, motor vehicles, home appliances, and commercial aviation.[9]

Personality

In order to explore the correlations among personality characteristics and risk perceptions, we have drawn on a broad set of traditional personality measures, including the Adjective Check List and the California Psychological Inventory.[10]

Political Orientation

To evaluate predictions of risk perceptions based on political variables, we utilize measures of political party membership and liberal–conservative ideology (both self-rated and calculated on the basis of 20 policy issue stances).[11]

Cultural Biases

To test the relations among perceptions of danger and the world views justifying hierarchy, individualism, and egalitarianism, we developed new measures to assess individual endorsement of three cultural biases.

Hierarchy

This index embodies support for patriotism ("I'm for my country, right or wrong"), law and order ("The police should have the right to listen in on private telephone conversations when investigating crime"), and strict ethical standards ("I think I am stricter about right and wrong than most people"). It also expresses concern about the lack of discipline in today's youth and supports the notion that centralization is "one of the things that makes this country great."[12]

Individualism

Our index for the cultural bias of individualism expresses support for continued economic growth as the key to quality of life, and private profit as the main motive for hard work. It espouses the view that democracy depends fundamentally on the existence of the free market, and argues that "the 'welfare state' tends to destroy individual initiative." The individualism scale also indicates support for less government regulation of business, and endorses private wealth as the just rewards of economic endeavor: "If a man has the vision and ability to acquire property, he ought to be allowed to enjoy it himself."[13]

Egalitarianism

Our measure of this world view is based on survey items written to assess attitudes toward equality of conditions. The egalitarianism scale centers on political solutions to inequality: "Much of the conflict in this world could be eliminated if we had more equal distribution of resources among nations," "I support federal efforts to eliminate poverty," and "I support a tax shift so that burden falls more heavily on corporations and persons with large incomes." The egalitarianism index also convers perceived abuses by the other political cultures: "Misuse of scientific and expert knowledge is a very serious problem," and "The human goals of sharing and brotherhood are being hindered by current big institutions."[14]

There are many theories that might account for the perceptions of risks, from those based on knowledge, personality, or economics, to those based on politics or culture. Our task is to discriminate among these rival theories by comparing their power to predict who fears what and why.

Cultural Biases Best Predict Risk-perception Findings

Knowledge

If it were true that the more people know about technological risk, or about technology in general, the more they worry about it, then it would follow that risk perception goes along with such knowledge. Using the measure of self-rated knowledge about technologies, and self-rated education, we see quite the opposite.

Our findings show that those who rate highly their self-knowledge of technologies also tend to perceive greater average benefits associated with technologies than those who are less confident about their knowledge.[15] Those who report higher levels of education tend to perceive less threat from the risks of war. Otherwise, self-rated knowledge and education bear only weak (i.e., statistically insignificant) relations to preferences for societal risk-taking or to perceived risks associated with technology and the environment, social deviance, and economic troubles.

The more an individual's annual fatality estimates correspond with expert estimates, in addition, the more likely that person is to rate other risks as small—at least compared to those who are less accurate. While on the whole those who are more in accord with expert mortality estimates perceive less risk, they are also less optimistic regarding the benefits of technology. Overall, the conclusion is compelling that self-rated knowledge and perceptual accuracy have a minimal relationship with risk perception.

Personality

We find that those who feel our society should definitely take technological risks can be described as patient, forbearing, conciliatory, and orderly (that is, the pro-risk measure is positively correlated with the personality traits "need for order," and "deference.")[16] Advocates of societal risk-taking tend not to be aggressive, or autonomous, or exhibitionistic, but are more likely to be cautious, shy, and seek stability rather than change. This pattern is suggestive of a technologically pro-risk personality, which emerges as an obedient and dutiful citizen, deferential to authority. Such a personality structure fits extremely well with the political culture of hierarchy.

By contrast, those citizens who perceive greater risk in regard to technology and the environment tend to turn up positive on exhibitionism, autonomy, and need for change, but negative on need for order, deference, and endurance—that is, just the opposite of those who score as favoring societal risk-taking. This technologically risk-averse pattern of personality traits also holds for those who endorse egalitarianism.

Those who endorse egalitarianism are also more likely to be personally risk-taking, but societally risk averse, while those who favor
hierarchy tend to be personally risk averse, but societally pro-risk with
respect to technology and the environment. Thus, we find no evidence
for a personality structure that is risk-taking or risk averse across the
board. Risk-taking and risk aversion are not all of a piece, but depend
on how people feel about the object of attention. Cultural theory would
predict, for example, that hierarchists would be risk averse when it
comes to taking risks with the body politic.

Political Orientation

Relative to conservatives, those who rate themselves as liberals tend
to be technologically risk averse at the societal level, are more likely
to rate the risks of technology and the environment as very great, and
are comparatively unconcerned about the risks of social deviance. As
the self-rating of liberal increases, the average ratings for the risks of
the 25 specific technologies increases, and the average ratings of their
benefits decreases.

Political party membership is less predictive of risk perceptions and
preferences than left–right ideology, especially on the Democratic side
(undoubtedly because Democrats are the more heterogeneous party).
When we ask what it is about thinking of oneself as a liberal or
conservative that makes such a big difference compared to thinking of
oneself as a Democrat or Republican, the findings are informative.
Whether by self-rating or policy designation, liberals have strong
tendencies to endorse egalitarianism ($r = 0.52$ and $r = 0.50$), and to
reject hierarchy ($r = -0.55$ and $r = -0.51$) and individualism ($r =
-0.37$ and $r = -0.31$). Likewise, membership in the Democratic
party is correlated with egalitarianism ($r = 0.30$), but is not predictive
of agreement or disagreement with the hierarchical or individualist
point of view. Republicans have a penchant toward individualist ($r =
0.31$) and hierarchical biases ($r = 0.40$), and an equally strong procliv-
ity for rejecting egalitarianism ($r = -0.45$). These correlations among
political party membership, left–right ideology, and cultural biases are
huge by the standards of survey research.

Cultural Biases

How does cultural theory compare with other approaches to perceived
risk? Cultural biases provide predictions of risk perceptions and risk-

taking preferences that are more powerful than measures of knowledge and personality and at least as predictive as political orientation. We find that egalitarianism is strongly related to the perception of technological and environmental risks as grave problems for our society ($r = 0.51$), and hence to strong risk aversion in this domain ($r = -0.42$). Egalitarianism is also related positively to the average perceived risks, and negatively to the average perceived benefits, of 25 technologies. One could hardly paint a worse picture of technology—little benefit, much risk, and the risks not worth taking.

Individualist and hierarchist biases, in contrast, are positively related to a preference for technological risk-taking ($r = 0.32$ and $r = 0.43$) and to average ratings of technological benefits ($r = 0.34$ and $r = 0.37$). Here the image is more sanguine: The benefits are great, and the risks small, so society should press on with risk-taking to get more of the good that progress brings with it.

Discussion

Whether measured by cultural biases or by political orientation, we have shown that perceptions of technology are predictable given the world view of the perceiver. But one should not conclude that the establishment cultures of individualism and hierarchy always favor risk-taking, or that egalitarians are always risk averse. Perception of danger is selective; it varies with the object of attention. For we find that, compared to advocates of egalitarianism, those in greater agreement with individualism perceive greater risk with respect to war ($r = 0.15$ versus $r = 0.40$, respectively). Likewise, it is the hierarchical bias that is most highly correlated with perceived threat of social deviance ($r = 0.35$ compared to $r = 0.15$ for egalitarianism). Nor is it always the adherents of establishment cultures versus those of egalitarianism. As predicted by cultural theory, it is not that devotees of individualism and hierarchy perceive no dangers in general, but that they disagree with those who favor egalitarianism about how dangers should be ranked. Just as technological and environmental risks are most worrisome to egalitarians, social deviance is deemed most dangerous to hierarchists, and threat of war (which disrupts markets and subjects people to severe controls) is most feared by individualists.

It is obvious that culture neither causes nor influences demographic characteristics such as gender or age (though it may influence their social meanings). Thus we do not argue that the weak correlations we find between cultural biases and personal attributes like income or social class reveal the influence of political culture on those variables. Whether we look at knowledge, personality, political orientation, or demographic variables, however, we find that cultural theory provides the best predictions of a broad range of perceived risks and an interpretive framework in which these findings cohere.

The importance of using a wide range of risks in studying how people perceive potential dangers should now be apparent. Employing only dangers from technology—while better than nothing—is far less powerful than considering a panoply of dangers from the threat of war to social deviance to economic collapse. Broadening the spectrum of related questions to be considered allows for more discriminating tests of rival theories. With perceived dangers from technology as the only issue, moreover, one cannot tell whether the level of concern registered by an individual comes from aversion to or acceptance of risk in general, or is evoked differentially by various risks. By observing whether there is a variegated pattern of risk perception (and now we know there is) and by ascertaining who rates each kind of risk in which way, we may study patterns of risk perception. Fitting these patterns to alternative explanations, we believe, is a superior test of competing theories.

Comparing rival theories—not just a single explanation—has similar advantages. Making the rival theories confront each other reduces the temptation to claim easy victories. It is not enough to show respectable correlations; it is also necessary to do better than the alternatives.

Viewed in this light, the cultural theory's greater power than alternative explanations is manifest in its ability to generate broader and finer predictions of who is likely to fear, not to fear, or to fear less different kinds of dangers. Having derived from cultural theory a number of explanations approximated in our findings, the next question is what this tells us about risk perception.

Our findings show that it is not knowledge of a technology that leads people to worry about its dangers. In the current sample, the difference between public and technical estimates of annual fatalities ranges up to several orders of magnitude in size. The enormous variation in these public perceptions is not accounted for by knowledge, leaving considerable room for other explanations. Indeed, if people have little knowledge about technologies and their risks, then public fears can hardly coincide with how dangerous various technologies have proved to be.

Wait a minute! Everyone knows that nuclear radiation and AIDS can kill. We agree. When these subjects become politicized, however, disagreement develops along the fault lines of policy differences, seizing upon whatever cracks of uncertainty now exist: What are the health consequences of prolonged exposure to low levels of radiation? Is there such a thing as an amount of radiation so small that exposure causes no harm? Can AIDS be passed along by social contact? Should sufferers from AIDS be quarantined? Should their sexual contacts be traced and informed?

Our findings on personality raise the question of why there are such interesting sets of correspondence among traditionally assessed traits and cultural biases. Part of the difficulty in interpreting these findings is that personality entails such a wide set of characteristics—from intrapsychic to interpersonal relations—that virtually no aspect of individual life is left out. Were there theories connecting particular aspects of personality to patterns of risk perception, interpretation would be easier, for then we could test these hypotheses. One possibility is that personal orientations may guide individuals to make commitments consistent with specific political cultures while, at the same time, cultures may select from among individuals those that support their way of life. Since there are no such theories, however, we are left to explore among personality characteristics to see what fits.

Assuming both personality and political culture are operative, which is more powerful in predicting perceptions of danger and preferences for risk-taking? Clearly, the closer one gets to asking questions about policy preferences, the better one's predictions of the selective perceptions of danger should be. Since our measures of cultural biases are closer to public policy than traditional measures of personality, we should expect them (other things being equal) to predict better. And they do. But if that were all there were to prediction—proximity of the explanation to the explained—then we would expect assessments of political ideology to predict risk preferences far better than cultural bias does. As we have shown, however, public policy stances and self-rated political orientation do not do as well as cultural biases in predicting risk preferences and perceptions—even though they are the most proximal to risk policy of all the variables we test.

How then do cultural biases, which are so remote from the evidence regarding risks, guide people in choosing what to fear? A detailed answer is presented in *Risk and Culture*. Here, we can say only that hierarchists favor technological risk-taking because they see this as supporting the institutions that they rely on to make good their promises, to wit: technology can promote a stronger society and a safer future provided that their rules (and stratified social relations) are maintained. Individualists also deem technology to be good. They hold that following market principles (and individually negotiated social relations) will allow technological innovation to triumph, conferring creative human value on otherwise inert resources. They also believe that the enormous benefits of technological innovation will convey their premise that unfettered bidding and bargaining leaves people better off. If they believed that free market institutions were intrinsically ruinous to nature, individualists could no longer defend a life of minimum restraints. By the same token, egalitarians are opposed to taking technological risks because they see them as supporting the inegalitarian markets and coercive hierarchies to which they are opposed.

By this time, readers are right to wonder, in view of the assertions we are making, whether other surveys support our claims. A recent one to come to our attention is supportive in many ways. Its subject is the irradiation of food as a preservative process, widely considered safe by scientists, but a topic of considerable worry to concerned consumers. The participants were 195 adult women chosen from Pennsylvania's women's groups of various kinds—religious, civic, professional, social, and political. The respondents were given a questionnaire to fill out, then were shown different kinds of information about food irradiation, then filled out another questionnaire, and finally were engaged in group discussion. The authors, Richard Bord and Robert O'Conner, find—as we do—that knowledge (based on the information given to participants) is inversely related to fear of a technology: "Having accurate knowledge about the food irradiation process translates into greater acceptance." They add significantly that

> whether respondents received a technical or nontechnical communication about the food irradiation process and whether they received a detailed discussion of the major arguments for and against food irradiation had no discernible effect on their judgments.

It is not knowledge per se, but confidence in institutions and the credibility of information that is at issue.

> Trust in business and industry in general, the food irradiation industry specifically, government regulators, and science as a provider of valid and useful knowledge is the major predictor of whether the respondent indicates she will or will not try irradiated food. . . . Learning that others

have used food irradiation safely and of its approval by prestigious professional organizations enhanced its acceptability. . . . People who oppose big government and big business express greater fear of radiation.

One of the main topics of group discussion

was the respondents' view that complex technology bears a burden of too much uncertainty, too much greed on the part of its sponsors, and too little effective governmental control. The point was frequently made that even if the scientific-technical plan was flawless the people executing the plan and managing the technology would inevitably create serious problems.[17]

It is not only that "the facts" cannot by themselves convince doubters, but that behind one set of facts are always others relating to whether business and government can be trusted.

If there are any people to whom knowledge about hazards should make the most difference, it would be those who are professionally employed in the analysis and management of risk. Yet a survey of risk professionals drawn from government, industry, environmental groups, and universities shows something dramatically different. Thomas Dietz and Robert Rycroft find that self-reported ideology

appears to have the strongest links to environmental attitudes and values of risk professionals. . . . For example, on the question of whether we are seeing only the tip of the iceberg with regard to technological risk, 88.5 percent of [the] very liberal . . . agreed . . . as did 74 percent of liberals. Only 25 percent of [the] very conservative and 36.4 percent of [the] conservative respondents agreed.[18]

The more perceptions of contested subjects are studied, we believe, the more they will reveal the strong influence of cultural biases. In this respect, Paul Sabatier and S. Hunter's recent study of causal perceptions in belief systems is especially useful because, like the present analysis, it focuses on perceptual biases from more than one cultural direction:

Environmentalists perceived water clarity to be getting worse, while those in favor of economic growth and property rights simply refused to believe the wealth of documented, and widely diffused, scientific evidence developed by one of the world's leading limnologists demonstrating statistically significant declines in water clarity over the previous 10–15 years. This

suggests that in high-conflict situations, perceptions on even relatively
straightforward technical issues can be heavily influenced by elites'
normative presuppositions.[19]

This position reaffirming the importance of world views is bolstered by
Gerald Gardner and his colleagues' study of "risk and benefit perceptions, acceptability judgments and self-reported actions toward nuclear
power." Their respondents were taken from environmental groups,
blue-collar workers, college students, business people, and technolo-
gists (scientists and engineers employed by a utility company). While
education, sex, gender, religion, and other sociodemographic variables
were not related to protests or other personal actions taken against
nuclear power, Gardner and his colleagues found that liberal–conservative ideology was predictive: "The most important correlate of reported action and 'acceptability' . . . appeared to represent a 'liberal/
public interest group vs. conservative/private enterprise' dimension."[20]

The power of the ideological explanation is strengthened further by
Stanley Rothman and S. Robert Lichter, who analyzed questionnaires
filled out by a sample of 1,203 congressional staff, civil servants,
television and print journalists, lawyers, officials of public interest
groups, moviemakers, military officers, energy and nuclear power
experts. The results vary widely by group membership, with 98.7
percent of nuclear energy experts thinking nuclear power plants are
safe, compared to only 6.4 percent of public interest officials, and 30.6
percent of journalists on television networks. Rothman and Lichter's
major finding is that—compared to a variety of demographic, social,
and economic variables—political ideology was by far their most
powerful predictor. "We hypothesize," they conclude, "that nuclear
energy is a surrogate issue for more fundamental criticism of U.S.
institutions."[21] This restates the thesis of *Risk and Culture* for nuclear
technology.

Whenever other studies present comparable findings, they reveal
that the most powerful factor for predicting risk perceptions is trust in
institutions or ideology, which is largely about which of society's
institutions can be trusted. Such findings show that, however concep-
tualized—whether as political ideology or cultural biases—world views
best account for patterns of risk perceptions.

In summary, the great struggles over the perceived dangers of
technology in our time are essentially about trust and distrust of
societal institutions—that is, about cultural conflict. Once we vary the
object of concern, we do indeed discover that egalitarians (who fear

social deviance less than hierarchists and individualists) fear technology a great deal—seeing in it, or so the cultural theory claims, the corporate greed they believe leads to inequality. Individualists, who believe in competition and who are exceedingly loathe to place restraints on what they consider to be mutually profitable relationships, deem technology to be good. In contrast, hierarchists, who fear disorder and erosion of status differences, are more worried about social deviance and less worried about technological dangers than egalitarians.

We have shown that other surveys—with different assumptions, methods, and sample populations—find, as we do, that risk perceptions and preferences are predictable given individual differences in cultural biases. It is the congruence of our analysis with others that gives us the most confidence in our findings. We would have preferred to ask more subtle and differentiated questions about knowledge; but the other surveys we cite do that, and they also show the importance of cultural biases. Above all, we would have preferred more elaborate statistical analysis than small samples permit.*

Knowing what sorts of perceptions come from which kinds of people may allow for practical applications of cultural theory in a variety of policy contexts. Risk communication programs, for instance, might profitably focus on the underlying causes of risk perception—such as confidence (or lack of trust) in institutions, or the credibility of hazard information—rather than only on the facts regarding possible harms. Since cultural theory generates clues as to the propensities of those with various world views to underestimate or overestimate specific kinds of risk, in addition, it can be used to tailor educational programs—say, cigarette and alcohol warnings—to the plural rationalities represented in the general public.

It has been two decades since Chauncy Starr's seminal essay on "social benefit versus technological risk" asked how much our society is willing to pay for safety.[22] Since then, a lively and spirited research community has grown up around the issues of technological risks.[23] We hope to have set the study of risk perception in the right direction by: (1) expanding the scope of the questions asked to include patterns

---

*Our findings call for multivariate statistical analysis of the interactions between cultural biases and the classes of predictors. We are fullly aware of the difficulties of regression or path analysis on small samples. We are also sensitive to the fact that correlations do not necessarily imply causation. Cultural theory makes causal attributions, however, and the correlations we do find are consistent with its predictions.

of risk perceptions (not only technological hazards, but also war, social deviance, economic decline, etc.); and (2) comparing rival explanations of public fears. As predicted by cultural theory, we find that individuals perceive a variety of risks in a manner that supports their way of life.

8

The Turtle Theory,
Or Why Has the Democratic Party Lost Five Out of the Last Six Presidential Elections, Yet Retained Strong Control of the House, Won Majorities in the Senate, and Kept Three-fifths of State Houses and Most Governorships?

Why has the Democratic party, which does so well in state, local, and congressional races, had such a hard time winning the presidency? Focus on the shortcomings of its candidates has detracted attention from the two most evident trends in the American presidency: the high proportion of failed presidencies (Johnson, Nixon, Carter), and the inability of the Democratic party to win the presidency. I think the two trends are related in that the aura of failure and Democratic party loss of the presidency are due to the same causes: the rise of egalitarianism.

Same Results but Contradictory Reasons

Before we come to the underlying forces that make it difficult for Democrats to win the presidency, it is necessary to go over the surface explanations offered for the defeats of Michael Dukakis in 1988 and Walter Mondale in 1984. Within the Democratic party, recriminations over the 1984 and 1988 presidential elections have served to focus attention on the alleged inadequacies of their candidates as campaigners.[1] Aside from taking attention away from trends over time that most need to be explained, a brief comparison of the reasons given during the two campaigns reveal their contradictory as well as unsatisfactory character. Walter Mondale, it was said, was dull compared to his flamboyant opponent, Ronald Reagan. The same was said about Michael Dukakis, except, of course, that he could not have been more dull than George Bush. Mondale was said to have given too much to the nefarious "special interests," but then Dukakis was accused of giving too little. Dukakis hid his liberalism, while Mondale showed it too much. Had these elections gone the other way, we would no doubt have heard that the voters appreciated Mondale's and Dukakis's calm and steady ways compared to the excitable Reagan and the indistinct Bush.

The one obvious flaw in Dukakis's presentation of self—his lack of experience, especially in foreign policy—was first of all shared by Ronald Reagan, who was also a two-term governor without Washington experience, but inapplicable in any way to Walter Mondale who nevertheless lost. Faults are attributed to the losers—the point is—because they lost, not because there was anything necessarily wrong with them or with their campaigns.

Negative Campaigning and the Absence of Issues

What about negative campaigning on the one hand, and the ostensible lack of issues on the other? What about Bush's better and Dukakis's worse use of the media? In regard to all three subjects, I shall argue that they reflect systematic rather than personal factors. No doubt Dukakis could have done better, so could all of us at critical junctures in our lives, but we act against a background of forces that have arisen independently of our will and that necessarily influence us more than we are able to influence them.

Whether or not a television commercial about furloughing a convicted murderer who did harm after his release constituted dirty or negative campaigning (we shall come to race later), the larger meaning of that message has been missed. If one were to choose a cross section of liberal Democratic activists compared to their Republican counterparts, and ask whether they served on prisoners' rights or victims' rights committees, I do not doubt that the former would have chosen prisoners and the latter victims. Given their egalitarian propensities, Democratic activists are far more likely than Republicans to believe that the system is to blame for crime, not the individual.[2] Consequently, in the midst of a pandemic of crime—arguably the worst deprivation most Americans face—the Democratic party soft-pedaled the issue, treating it often as a code word for racism. No one, to be sure, wants or supports crime. But one's public stance toward it also matters. In this respect, it is not Dukakis who let down the Democratic party, but rather the Democratic party that dragged him down. True, Dukakis resisted repeal of the furlough law by a Democratic state legislature. Living among his fellow liberals, he was unable to understand that many citizens wish their president to empathize with their fear.

When it is said, and reiterated, that there were no issues in the 1988 presidential campaign, my thoughts first go back to my parents. They were fervent New Deal Roosevelt Democrats. Their reason was fear of anti-Semitism. (As a boy of nine, my father had been beaten in a pogrom in the Ukraine, after which he spent nine months in the hospital.) They were particularly fond of Eleanor Roosevelt who appeared to attend every wedding, Berith (the circumcision ceremony), and bar mitzvah in Brooklyn. To them, she meant a friend in power— hence protection against future indignities. So they voted for her husband. Was that wrong of them? Was their feeling of safety not an issue in the same acceptable way as the minimum wage or the deficit? I object to some people telling other people that their feelings are unworthy. If voters feel safer with George Bush, that is a pretty important consideration in a choice of leaders.

My second reaction to the charge of "no issues" is that the real blame belongs to Ronald Reagan, who took the words out of the mouths of the campaigners. The pundits are so used to denigrating President Reagan, or so it seems to me, that they fail to see that his was the commanding (albeit less visible) presence during the campaign. For one thing, Reagan's nuclear weapons reduction policy—from the INF treaty to the START negotiations—took the peace issue away from the Democrats. By outradicaling the Democrats on disarmament, Reagan forced them into silence. Either they had to outradical him, which would have made them extreme in a manner to which he was not vulnerable, or call him soft on communism, which was absurd and they did not believe it. So they chose silence. Though Bush probably agreed with those who wanted large reductions in Soviet forces in Europe as a prerequisite for nuclear negotiations, he went along. The meaning of the fact that foreign policy was little debated in the campaign is not that it was issueless but, on the contrary, that President Reagan had forced an implicit agreement on its major outlines that neither of his possible successors was willing to oppose.

Domestic policy was dominated by the deficit. When Ronald Reagan pushed through the 23-percent cut in income taxes, and led the way to tax reform that reduced marginal tax rates from the 70 percent he inherited to a top of 33 percent, and refused to abandon these policies in the light of large deficits, he again rendered both presidential candidates speechless. Departing from the antideficit stand of the Republican moderates who favored stability above all, Bush paid for the support of his party's more individualistic faction by making his public pledge against an increase in taxes. No doubt a "no new tax" pledge garnered votes apart from those of the conservative individualists. It was they, however—fearful he would change his mind—who insisted on a public commitment. "Read my lips" is not a bad line for someone who has to accept a position he would rather not defend out loud.

And what could Dukakis do? Recalling the criticism vented on Walter Mondale for saying what virtually everyone in his party believed—namely, that substantial tax increases were essential to reduce the deficit and run the government—Dukakis said essentially that he would decide when he became president. Nothing stopped him or his party in its platform from saying what they believed. Again, the dog that didn't bark—the refusal to commit to tax increases—was the clue. The issue was there alright but, courtesy of Ronald Reagan, it had been decided more against than for tax hikes.

When I say that systemic forces were at work, I do not mean to denigrate anyone's personal influence but rather to observe that, insofar as the rival presidential candidates were concerned, they faced social facts—laws specifying tax cuts, sizable deficits, the INF treaty, the START negotiations, a distribution of public opinion either in favor of these things or unwilling to alter them—that they could not ignore. It was their adjustment to these facts, more than their personalities or their talents or their campaign staffs, I contend, that made an election so full of portent seem so issueless.

Media Influence and Media Bias

The questions of media influence and media bias withstand easy answers because the forces at work operate in conflicting directions.

Research has produced some starting points. After early doubts, it now seems clear that media (especially television) influence is considerable; favorable and unfavorable comments help and hurt presidents and presidential candidates alike, forming public perceptions of what is most important and how the politicians involved perform.[3] Here, as well as elsewhere, however—as we shall see—there are limits to media influence. (I refer to the elite media: the major newpapers—the New York *Times,* the Washington *Post,* the Los Angeles *Times*—the major networks, and *Newsweek* and *Time.*) If the media help shape perceptions of the state of the nation, which no one can see directly, only individuals are experts on how they themselves are doing. When, as in 1988, citizens are informed they are in trouble, they may choose their personal experience of lower inflation and higher employment as the better guide.

Media bias is contested. A good place to start is with the constants. If we ask who makes up the elite media, the answer is easy: Politically they are overwhelmingly liberal Democrats; culturally they are egalitarians. When one asks whether these known occupational biases translate into biased reporting, there is no scholarly agreement. Hence I give my opinion that biases do exist and do (as one might expect) flow in an ideological direction, but that nonetheless, under certain conditions—such as those prevailing in 1988—there are countervailing forces at work stemming from the media's existence as an institution. In short, there exist both biases and limits to the influence exercised by those biases. Let me explain by example.

Why, I ask, were the hostages held by Iran in 1979 an item in the news and on television prominently and incessantly day and night, yet since 1986 the hostages held in Lebanon have gotten only a bit of coverage. It cannot be a matter of human interest and tragedy, because that is the same in both instances. Indeed, the Lebanese captives have been held longer. My hypothesis is that the media converged on coverage of the hostage crisis in Iran because it served to discredit the government, this being part of the egalitarian rejection of authority. True to experience, a foreign crisis sharply increased public support for the president. But as the news focus continued while the hostages remained in captivity, Carter's popularity plummeted. Why, then, the change? The diminution of coverage occurred after the Iran–Contra episode in which President Reagan was pilloried (rightly, I believe) for exchanging arms for hostages. Quickly the media converged on the view, damaging to the president, that it was wrong to make concessions to terrorists as a reward for releasing hostages. Afterward, I observed that the hostages received much less publicity. Since their captivity could no longer be used to attack the president—the media having ruled out every mode of gaining their release as illegitimate—there was no point, I reason, in keeping the hostages before the public eye. (There was, to be sure, no conspiracy—only a coming together of like-minded people hostile to authority.)

The lesson I draw from these events is that, on matters the media make highly visible, they can go one way or another but not both ways at once. An important limitation on media influence is generated by the need to maintain minimal consistency in the midst of an audience it has taught one thing and might be expected to react negatively to a diametrical change of course.

A simpler episode—equally instructive—occurred when Republican presidential candidate George Bush did less well than rival Bob Dole in the Iowa primary. Subsequently, the media was full of damaging comments about Bush's inadequacies and ineptitudes. When Bush did well in the New Hampshire primary, however, the significance of his victory was amplified because the media had previously lessened expectations.

From such events we learn about another limit on media influence: If the effort to run down a public figure fails to defeat him, quite ordinary conduct may thereafter make him appear superior. It could be, as Michael Dukakis and his advisors stated in his acceptance speech, that the election contest was not about ideology but only about competence—a statement of position they believed because the media had taught them that their opponent was a Wimp. No, a veritable Wimp of a Wimp—so much of a nothing it was not necessary to make changes. All Bush had to do after his initial media treatment was to put two literate sentences together and he appeared to be a savant. And when he did alright, as in the debates, he appeared to be at least a super-Wimp, a candidate above the ordinary. Again, we see that putting candidates down can rebound if, by contrast, it makes them seem superior.

While presidents and candidates manifesting egalitarian tendencies should do better in the media than those who are socially hierarchical or economically conservative, there is an opposing tendency. Anti-authority bias works in all directions. It is easy to forget that Geraldine Ferraro was savaged when she ran as vice president in 1984, as well as Dan Quayle in 1988.

A pronounced feature of the media coverage of the 1988 election was its concentration on the mechanics—who is winning and how close are the candidates. Its preoccupation with making the campaign appear competitive (the "horse-race" theme) led to a focus on campaign tactics. Often there was less interest in the substance of what was being said than in whether a given move was successful in narrowing the gap between the candidates.

Along with the usual discussion of candidate and party positions, therefore, came another theme about the success or failure of campaign tactics. When these policy and tactical themes work against each other—as they did in 1988, with the Democratic candidate being favored on policy by the major media while the Republican candidate was favored on tactics—media biases effectively cancel themselves out. Should a time come when the media's biases toward candidates who are egalitarian and tactically successful reinforce one another, a Republican loss could well become a rout.

It will be useful here to give charges of unfair tactics their usual, pre-1988 definition: A negative campaign is one in which the wrong candidate loses. I do not mean to deny the use of smear tactics. The point is that the media get interested in these personal insults only when their favorites get hurt. Discovering to their surprise—given Dukakis's early lead in the polls and their denigration of Bush—that the wrong man was winning, the major media independently hit on a strategy that would maintain its reputation for nonpartisanship. By charging Bush with "negative campaigning," the media hoped to help Dukakis while avoiding the taint of pushing a candidate of its own. But it was too late.

In order for media party bias to be effective, in sum, it has to be (a) disguised and (b) unidirectional. This may not be an easy combination to manage. Blatant partisanship would be counterproductive; and biases going in opposite directions are self-canceling.

Republican presidential victories, taken together with Democratic success in congressional (especially the House of Representatives) elections, has provided a puzzle that no one yet has been able to unravel. Nor will I, entirely. But enough progress can be made to make the attempt worthwhile.

Does Size of Constituency Matter?

The path to understanding, I am persuaded, lies in better specification of what it is that we are trying to explain. What accounts for the seemingly unshakable grip Democrats have on the House, their small preponderance (occasionally reversed) in the Senate, and their frequent large losses of the presidency? Why is it that the larger the size of the constituency, the better the Republicans and the worse the Democrats do? When Elmer Schattschneider wrote in *The Semi-sovereign People* that expanding the constituency altered the outcome, he thought that would favor the worse off, not the better off.[4] Gerrymandering, we know—due to Democratic party preponderance in state legislatures—favors its candidates to the extent that Republicans must win 52–53 percent of the vote to break even. It is also true that parties and candidates have a greater ability to fit the fancies of the electorate the further down they go. There can be no movement of boundaries in senatorial or presidential elections. Given the huge advantage of incumbency nowadays—verified again in the 1990 elections despite talk of a rejection of incumbents—the mere fact that the Democratic party had an earlier advantage may carry over to our time.

Without pretending to offer anything definitive, I am inclined to say it could be that voters are looking for different things in different places. Presidents play more of a symbolic role. It may, therefore, seem right to look to presidents for symbolic identification—Is he one of us? Does she exemplify our values?—while looking to Congress to serve material interests. At the same time, incumbent representatives may be better able to gear their presentation of self to local perceptions than can senators or presidents with much longer and usually more diverse constituencies.

Another reason Democrats do better locally may be that their activists—being more interested in public office (not so strange for the party of government)—make better candidates. Keeping the government out of things is not likely to be as strong a motive for public service as getting it to do things for which one can gain credit.

The visibility of the candidates is greater the more national the contest. Hence voters may be able to better distinguish the candidates' policy positions from each other and from their own personal preferences. If this ascending issue-clarity argument is correct—and it appears plausible on the surface—one implication will be that voters are by and large closer to the Republican than to the Democratic party on national issues. If this is so, however, why would conservative voters keep returning liberal legislators?

Whether the well-known incumbency effect—far more than 97 percent of the representatives and most senators who run for reelection succeed themselves—is due to name recognition, constituency service, or free franking (mailing) privileges, the fact is that incumbents win.

Neither party seems to be advantaged there, except that there are more Democrats to begin with. It is still easier (though by no means easy) to defeat incumbent senators. Why?

Do Voters Intend to Split Control?

A host of commentators have suggested that Americans are so enamored of the separation of powers that they deliberately vote for one party for president and another for Congress. While there is evidence that voters approve of split government, there is none I am aware of suggesting they target their votes to achieve this deliberately. Aside from the lack of evidence to support such intentions, the separation of powers theory fails to explain why it is the Republicans who win the presidency and the Democrats who usually control the Congress.

Byron Shafer has an answer to that. Voters, he hypothesizes, have come to look to the presidency for national defense and for cultural (or social) policies such as prayer, abortion, crime, and patriotism, and to Congress for welfare programs.[5] This fits the facts. What is lacking, so far, is evidence of and explanation for this bifurcated vision.

Nonetheless, if we look at the gross outlines of public opinion, we do get an interesting clue. Majority opinion favors liberal social welfare programs and a strong defense (though how much spending defense requires varies with time), and takes a conservative line on social programs—crime, prayer, patriotism, and so on. Such a political vision should be familiar; it was held by the mainstream of the Democratic party from the 1930s through the mid-1960s, sometimes referred to as the party of Harry Truman, Hubert Humphrey, and Henry Jackson. Only it does not exist anymore. Nowadays activists in the Democratic party are preponderantly egalitarian. Their continuity is with welfare programs; their discontinuity is with opposition to defense as inegalitarian (i.e., taking from social welfare), disaffection with capitalism (seen as increasing instead of diminishing group differences in resources), and their support of state-sanctioned positive discrimination to increase equality of results.

Can this sea-change in the Democratic party have led to the loss of the presidency? The most salient electoral facts are that black people have become more Democratic, Jews have maintained their liberalism, and women are pretty evenly split though moving in a Democratic direction, while white, nonretired, Christian men have been voting overwhelmingly Republican in presidential elections. The latter account for almost all the difference between the parties. Why, then, have these white men who work become so Republican in presidential but not congressional elections? And why does being married—exit polls in 1984 and 1988 give a 9-percent Republican edge to married over single men and 10–12 percent for married over single women[6]—impel voters in a conservative direction? A sociocultural explanation is indicated.

The Revolt of the Turtles

A tale from India tells of how the world rests on a huge elephant. On being asked who holds the elephant up, an Indian man responds that the elephant stands on an even bigger turtle. And who, the questioning continues, holds up the turtle? "Why," the response goes, "it's turtles all the way down." My theory is that the Democratic party has lost five out of the last six presidential elections by a large margin because it made the white working male into the turtle of American political life.

Were the Democrats to ask nine-tenths of the working population to help support the other tenth—the more fortunate majority holding up the less fortunate minority—this activity might be considered a matter of honor and compassion. But that is not at all the way it is put.

What role does the Democratic party at its presidential nominating conventions, we may ask, ascribe to its turtles? They are to support all the other more deserving people. Since everyone else had apparently been "locked out" of the political system, white working males became the residuals who were "locked in"—the broad shoulders on which to hold up the rest of the population. They alone were not underprivileged.

The Democratic party expanded the category of the deprived so that it included a good two-thirds of the population. Begin with women, who constitute some 52 percent of the population. Add racial minorities, who comprise around one-fifth of the total. Put in the elderly, who make up another fifth. Of course, there is double counting. Cutting back the proportion of seniors and minorities by more than half, however, still leaves at least two-thirds of the population defined as deprived. Yet we have not considered poor people, the physically and mentally handicapped, and numerous others for whom a plausible case of having less and needing more could be made.

To the question of who should pay to provide for this elephantiasis of the deprived, the Democrats give the same answer: "turtles all the way down." The categories of people that make up the Democratic party's vision of the deprived are urged to protest that they have not gotten their due. They are told to organize, to mobilize, to make demands. In sum, the deprived have interests it is their duty to declare so that others can meet their obligations.

Turtles, however, have obligations but not, it seems, interests. The usual scenario reiterated during recent election campaigns called for a turtle to say why he would vote Republican. Democrats then met the answer "Because I'll be better off" with the rejoinder "That's selfish!" I heard this routine several times on public radio and television talk shows.

Egalitarian dominance among Democratic activists was made evident as they defined virtually all creatures (except turtles) as endangered. They overreached. Their shared vision of an America peopled by fatalists blinded them to the danger of losing the only significant category of voters who were not to be favored.

Eventually, even turtles get tired. Because the revolt of the turtles did not occur on a particular date, like the storming of the Bastille or the Declaration of Independence, but took place in hearts and minds over the past two decades, it has gone unnoticed. Now the election returns make it evident. Unless it wishes to expand this revolt, therefore, the Democratic party will have to confine the categories of the deprived to the poor or to radical minorities or to some manageable proportion of the population, so that a broader band of turtles can bear the weight.

The lesson is not that the Democratic party has to put up with candidates who lose, but that its candidates have to put up with a party that delegitimizes the nation's second largest constituency: white working Christian males. Unless the Democratic party allows the voice of the turtle to be heard once again in the land, one might extrapolate, its next presidential election is also likely to be a loss.

Turning the Turtle

Turtles have hard shells but soft underbellies. A harsh way of putting our turtles' response is to turn it upside down: It is not that these white men feel put upon, but that they wish to continue their past practice of putting down black folk (or minorities in general, or all women added to the lot). Seeing blacks and minorities and women so prominent in the Democratic party—this proposed explanation goes—white men have voted Republican in order to retain their past dominance. Nothing complicated about the election, in other words—only simple racism, sexism, and (for good measure) homophobia. The insecurity of masculinity in the face of feminine demands for equality, long a staple of egalitarian thought, merely receives a new form of expression as a generalized "ism"—race, gender, sex, age, and so on.

But is it true? They are male, they are white, they are Christian, they are working, and they do vote Republican in presidential elections. But that by itself presumably does not make them racist, nor would it explain why many of the very same people are voting Democratic in congressional races.

The publicity accorded Jesse Jackson, the evident necessity Dukakis faced in coming to terms with him—all in the full glare of television coverage—might have brought to the surface a measure of latent racism. But not necessarily. Paul Sniderman and his colleagues, using experiments as part of their survey methods, have shown that attitudes toward black people vary, policies aimed at helping blacks being supported when they are seen to be meritorious by the same criteria applied to whites.[7] Should this proposition hold up, the turtle theory—white working men feel discriminated against by Democrats—and not the turnover turtle theory—Republicanism as code word for racism—would be validated.

Some substantial proportion of white working men favor welfare programs but do not believe they should be the only ones to sacrifice for them. They might well favor economic redistribution and believe that too much is being spent on defense without necessarily opposing prayer in schools. As believers in equality of opportunity, these white working men are opposed to discrimination but in favor of merit-based procedures for employment and promotion. Hence, when they see minorities who work hard discriminated against, they object. But these white working men are not prone to blame the system for what they perceive as individual shortcomings. Observing the Democratic party as it presents itself at national conventions, presidential campaigns, and other visible events, our turtles feel rejected by the national Democratic party. It is not of them or for them.

The turtle theory suggests that, if only poor people were singled out for special consideration (thus covering many blacks and women and elderly but not by category), then public reaction—especially white working male reaction—would be quite different. This would also explain the greater success of the Democrats (for instance, Dukakis in 1988) when they stress "populist" themes.

Marriage, Religion, Race, Poverty, and Other Forms of Socialization

If I am correct in believing that the Republican party provides a haven for those working men unwittingly rejected by the Democratic party, why do these self-same citizens vote Democratic at the congressional level? The answer, I think, is that the immense publicity at the national level, together with the inability to differentiate appeals to various constituents, makes citizens acutely aware of the relation of the national parties to their conception of self. At the local, congressional level, by contrast, they are either less informed about their congressman's policy preferences or less concerned about them. It would be important to find out which inference is correct.

What is it, we may ask, that those people who voted most heavily Democratic in 1988 might have in common? This list includes African Americans, Mexican Americans, Jews, very poor people, single women (especially), and also single men. Again, my answer is that they share a belief in egalitarianism.

It is fairly evident that very poor people and radical minorities desire redistributive governmental policies. But what about Jews who are neither poor nor colored? Obviously, a special explanation is required for the continued high level of Jewish liberalism. I believe that historical experience in being discriminated against has not only led to identification with the underdog, which is standard, but has also been transmuted into fierce resistance to distinctiveness, to being singled out. If we think of conservative Republicans as being concerned with the maintenance of social and economic distinctions and of liberal Democrats as desiring to diminish distinctions (or levels or ranks) among people, most Jews worry about being too much rather than too little exposed. (The orthodox, by the way, who live by the 613 *mitzvot* or commandments, are much more hierarchical and therefore Republican.) Thus, even the support for Israel evidenced by fundamentalist Christians worries Jews, who thereby become more liberal.

And what is it about marriage that increases Republican voting in presidential elections? Perhaps, as the old saw has it, marriage increases a person's sense of responsibility. But this is too much like rephrasing the question. My hunch is that the institution of marriage has a conservatizing effect, especially when there are children, because it increases the sense of social differentiation as a source of stability among the people involved. From a study of women we learn that the further they go along the way back toward the traditional family—wife at home with children—the more Republican they are.[8] They may well identify with the husband, viewing their vote more as furthering the family unit than they did when single; the wife becomes a turtle by marriage. Not only has the husband to consider others by virtue of being a family man, but—acknowledged "head of family" or not—he is likely to approve of role differentiation.

Alternative Explanations

I have left for last the most obvious and quite possibly the two most correct explanations of recent Republican presidential victories: favorable economic conditions, and the political transformations of the South. Each time a Republican won, he has been in office during good times or taken over in bad times. For all we know, voters may figure that, if a Democratic Congress and a Republican president go with prosperity, they might as well keep the status quo. Nor is it easy for the Democratic party to win presidential elections when it starts by losing all or most of the South. The reasons for this change are fairly well known. One—which Nelson Polsby attributes to air conditioning—is that numerous Republicans moved into the South as part of its economic growth. At the same time, or perhaps earlier, many black people who generally vote Democratic moved out of the South (though there is now a bit of movement back). In addition to this shift of populations, there has been a conversion on the part of some conservative Democrats to the Republican party. The result is that the Democratic party candidate has to win most of the rest of the states—a difficult task. Still, I would maintain that the South has become Republican in presidential years not because the Democratic party became economically liberal (which it already was), but rather because it became culturally egalitarian.

Is the Democratic Party Likely to Become Less Egalitarian?

Other people give Democrats advice like being more centrist, speaking positively about defense, talking less about social issues, and perhaps waving the flag a bit more. Thus Stuart E. Eizenstat, President Jimmy Carter's top advisor on domestic politics, told his fellow Democrats that "we have perverted liberalism." In order to win, the party should adopt a program of "tough" liberalism: strong foreign policy and economic management, plus compassionate welfare programs modified by individual responsibility, plus affirmative action based on income rather than race.[9] This may work if tried, but I believe the domination of the Democratic party by egalitarian activists will rule out the approach. The booing of Diane Feinstein at the California State Democratic Convention for endorsing the death penalty (opposed by egalitarians as racist) is a bad sign.[10] I doubt whether Eizenstat's advice, whether supported by turtles or other political animals, is likely to be taken.

The mainstream of the Democratic party, I believe, is now more firmly egalitarian than they have been in the past, and than the Republicans are hierarchical or individualistic. The best studies we have, by Warren Miller and Kent Jennings, cover party activists who became delegates to national conventions from 1976 to 1984[11] (supplemented by various polls in 1988) and reveal this fact foremost: While Republicans are strongly economically individualistic and socially conservative, Democrats are even more egalitarian. Under these circumstances, considering that Democratic officeholders are largely chosen from among their party's activists, it is unlikely they will agree to give up their policy preferences in order for their party to secure national office. It is not that they settle on these preferences at random; rather they choose to expand the ranks of the deprived and to question the righteousness of existing institutions because these policies are part and parcel of a world view dedicated to securing justice by diminishing differences among people. Representative Barney Frank of Massachusetts, himself a liberal Democrat, has publicly asked his party to say things that are no longer fashionable among them—like that capitalism is better than other economic systems. I believe he will fail because many Democratic activists do not believe these things.

While Republicans are still the more socially homogeneous party, the division between their individualists and hierarchists are greater than those found among Democratic activists. In any event, were nominating conventions left to their old devices in which state conventions were decisive, the results today would likely mimic those in Michigan in 1988 where party activists were dominant, thus leading to victory by Jesse Jackson for Democrats and Pat Robertson for the Republicans because these two candidates mobilized more fervent followers than the other candidates. A concession Jackson won at the Democratic National Convention was a substantial reduction in the number of "superdelegates"—the governors, state legislators, and congressmen recently reintroduced into the convention process. Another concession reduced the proportion of votes a candidate required to qualify for delegates and did away with "winner-take-all" primaries. This rule change will encourage factionalism by making it worthwhile for candidates to stay in the race longer so as to amass a larger force of delegates. More factions and fewer coalitions, I am afraid, are in store. Thus the desire of party activists to adopt more egalitarian policies, or their inability to reject egalitarian mechanisms—take your pick—will give egalitarians a greater voice in conventions to come. Not every future Democratic presidential nominee need be strongly egalitarian, but no one obnoxious to egalitarians will get far.

III

Contra Egalitarianism

9

The Reverse Sequence in Civil Liberties

For a number of years I belonged to the American Civil Liberties Union. To me this membership was part of a commitment to perfecting American democracy. I became a political scientist for the same reason. The two commitments—American patriotism and democratic values—went together. By improving the one (the procedures for participation in political life through protection of individual liberty) the other (America as a force for freedom at home and in the world) would also be enhanced. The combination of a strong national defense, social welfare programs, and civil liberties, as exemplified in the 1940s and 1950s by the New York State Liberal Party in whose youth division I was active seemed mutually reinforcing. But that combination, however comforting it seemed in the Eisenhower years, was not to last long.

In the early 1960s, while teaching politics at Oberlin College in Ohio, I served for a couple of years on the executive committee of the local ACLU. It was not easy, given our interest in procedures per se, to find violations of proper practice in a liberal arts college town. By moving a few miles away, however, we could come up with a couple of cases of unreasonable search or a few days of possibly unlawful detention. In retrospect, it was an innocent time and I know now, from having read William A. Donahue's *The Politics of the ACLU* that it was, for me at least, a time of naivete as well.

This chapter is a revised version of the introduction to William A. Donahue's *The Politics of the ACLU* (New Brunswick, N.J.: Transaction, Press, 1984). It appeared separately in *Public Interest,* no. 78 (1985). Further slight changes have been made for this volume.

The ACLU was never what I thought it was: an organization standing up for people whose civil liberties were threatened by the passions of the time. The ACLU has always been what Donahue says it is: an organization committed to a shifting agenda of substantive policy change as dictated by the political perspectives of its most active members.

Nor was the ACLU what its "purist" members thought: referring back to its name, a union of people concerned primarily with civil liberties. Whether it was support for unions in the 1920s and 1930s, the New Deal/Fair Deal social welfare agenda of the 1940s and 1950s, or its devotion to equal outcomes since the 1960s, the ACLU has viewed civil liberties—so Donahue shows—as instrumental to other purposes.

Starting somewhere in the mid-1960s, it became apparent to me that I was out of sympathy with the ACLU. Either it had changed (as I then thought), or I had changed, or both. Saddened by the loss of a sympathetic association and even, to an extent, a source of identity, I wondered what had happened to it or to me.

To say that organizations must adapt to a changing environment is a cliché. The ACLU is anomalous only in that it is such a classic example of the very spirit—absorption into the dominant values of the time—that the naive like myself once thought it was supposed to counter in favor of eternal verities.

When a group organizes to make demands on government to support the group's economic self-interest, no one is surprised that organizational doctrines change as a means of securing the substantive end of increasing its income. That large oil companies should favor market forces when these produce high prices, and governmental allocation when gluts produce low prices, raises few eyebrows. That an organization like the March of Dimes would seek new diseases to conquer after polio declined has been a subject of mild amusement. That the ACLU has radically reoriented its position on fundamental issues decade by decade, so that there is little relationship between what it said 50 years ago and what it says today, is more surprising. Yet this is exactly what has happened.

Quotas—anathema in the past—now have become desirable as a form of positive discrimination. (Who remembers when the ACLU taught that the Constitution is color blind?) Balancing competing values—order in society with the rights of the accused—has given way to attacks on authority. ("Lawlessness," the ACLU now says, "is a direct consequence of the failure of the community.") In briefest compass, the ACLU, once devoted to achieving individual freedom from government restraint, has become a convert to advocacy of governmental compulsion to achieve equality of condition. From defense of individual differences against government, the ACLU has moved to diminish differences among people—white and black, rich and poor, young and old, authority and citizen, parent and child. The list grows all the time.

Just as the ACLU identified itself with industrial unionization in earlier times, it has in recent years become part of the civil rights movement, the feminist movement, the movement against "ageism," and all the other movements devoted to diminishing inequalities in American life. There has been no conspiracy. No one pushed me out to put the present participants in. Two things happened concurrently: Activists in these other movements moved into the ACLU, and people discomforted by this trend toward support of equal results moved out. The process is self-reinforcing: New policies attract more like-minded adherents. No one has to tell the ACLU membership what to do. They can guess what equality of condition requires, and trial and error tells them what catches on with the people who flock to their cause. What is behind this reversal of values and practices?

The Original Sequence

Americans are able to agree about the desirability of "equality" because they mean different things by it. Equality before the law (or equal rights) signifies that people in similar positions will have similar legal standing, so that administrative and judicial decisions will be uniform and predictable. Equality of opportunity signifies the ability to enter contests of various kinds and to keep the proceeds, providing only that one does not prevent others from trying. Equality of condition (or outcome, or result) means that the resources possessed by individuals and groups in society should be roughly equivalent. Rights, opportunity, and outcome are worlds apart—so distant in practice that it has proved expedient for many to deny the full extent of the differences.

The much-remarked un-ideological (or better still, a-ideological) character of American political history may be attributed to the denial of these differences. Rather than admit that more of one means less of another, it has been the special bent of American political thought to claim just the opposite: More of one kind of equality would also lead to more of another. Equality before the law, secured by such devices as extension of the franchise and a Bill of Rights providing procedural guarantees, would help secure opportunity to participate in political and economic life. And genuine equality of opportunity, by preventing government from introducing unnatural inequalities into American life, would produce as much equality of condition as is compatible with the innate or behavioral differences among people or as is necessary to preserve republican government.

Observe the initial sequence of relationships among ideas about equality. They run from equality before the law, to equality of opportunity, and only then to equality of results. Of course, the prospects for republican government were originally related to the relative equality of condition fostered by American circumstances. America was blessed. In order, as the Declaration put it, to secure these blessings for posterity, this God-given equality was not to be decreased by the kind of distant central executive against which the colonies had so recently rebelled.

Insofar as inequality of condition resulted from differences in the faculty of individuals (but *only* to this extent, and no further), this was tolerable, expected, and natural, if not entirely desirable. In no way did the varying aptitudes for acquiring property (then considered an attribute or extension of the individual person) seem to threaten self-government. The battles of the party-of-the-country against the party-of-the-king in England were appropriated by the American branch of the British Whig opposition. Without an American equivalent of the king's men in Parliament—the hated placemen put there by royal patronage, including the venal sale of offices—neither the English monarch nor his American successors could maintain their preponderance of power. Once these special privileges (and the anti-federalists especially feared holders of national debt) were removed, equality before the law would help secure the equality of opportunity that kept sufficient equality of condition so that republican government could thrive.

The historic source of inequality was found in central governments ruled by strong central executives. Absent such an inegalitarian center, the United States of America and its Constitution became the exemplar of good (i.e., reasonably egalitarian) social relations. The flag—and hence the social relations for which it stood—was worth defending. Satisfaction with the circumstances of American life reinforced the original sequence. Inequality of condition could be bracketed-off and accepted, provided that legal and political equality were achieved. In this way a separate and protected preserve for civil liberties could be carved out. Of course there was nothing like universal agreement on civil liberties, but those who thought of themselves as civil libertarians could reflect a simultaneous satisfaction with conditions in general and dissatisfaction with flat-out violations of legal and political rights.

The Sequence Reversed

But the original sequence—in which equality before the law helps secure equality of opportunity and both, taken together, prevent such gross disparities of condition as to render republican government suspect—was based on assumptions subject to the ravages of time. The rise of corporate capitalism after the Civil War strained the social fabric. Yet populists could not quite bring themselves to turn against their Jeffersonian and Jacksonian forebears by embracing big government as the antidote to big corporations. Eventually populists merged into the progressive movement, which sought regulation to restore equality of opportunity to the conditions of competition in the face of inequalities fostered by giant capital. It took the Great Depression and the civil rights movement to raise (and, for some, to answer affirmatively) the question of whether the original sequence needed reversal.

It is the *reverse sequence* (to use a dramatic term from a quite different field) that has characterized the ACLU world view. Increasingly, unceasingly, equality of condition has been viewed as a precondition of equality of opportunity.

Driving home the proposition that the most widely espoused principles—equality before the law and equality of opportunity—were being denied to black citizens (i.e., that the powers-that-be had not followed their own announced beliefs), the civil rights movement legitimated much that it touched, including a focus on group as distinct from individual rights. When a number of the movement's leaders came to believe that equal opportunity would, in their circumstances, lead inexorably to inequality of results, they began to seek policies enforcing equality of condition on a group basis. Their position deserves elucidation.

Under their formulation, equal opportunity may promote inequality of outcomes for individuals, but not for groups. Their objective is not to alter the range of inequality of results among individuals, they say, but to assure that the same distribution of inequality of results obtains across all relevant groups—whatever that range may be. Therefore, to them, a rough group parity of outcomes is a reasonable measure of the actual degree of equality of opportunity that exists. Thus they argue that no group as such (because it is *that* group) should be denied significant shares of equal opportunity, measured by equal outcomes compared to other groups. Whether those who hold these views would—once group differences narrowed—accept unequal outcomes for individuals within the groups, I cannot say.

For others, the present range of unequal outcomes (among both groups and individuals) is too high, and their goal is to narrow the range. It is this view, embodied in the reverse sequence, that I believe currently characterizes ACLU action. Without equality of resources, it was argued, competition for the good things of life is prejudged in favor of those who have more and against those who have less. In order to do better, one must be pre-endowed with the results of already having done better. Hence positive discrimination. What is more, without this substantive equality, the lack of equal opportunity would mean a denial of equality before the law. The opportunities that equal rights had been thought essential to maintain (for those who had them) or achieve (for those who didn't) instead become the prerequisite. Civil liberties have been turned upside down. The causes—equal rights and equal opportunity—become the consequences of equal results. What had been widely agreed—the indispensability of equal rights as a precondition of equal opportunity—is replaced in importance by what had been problematic: securing equal outcomes.

Liberalism and Civil Liberties

To this very day, the profound consequences of adopting the reverse sequence remain for those who regard themselves as civil libertarians. The spoken premise had always been that people who disagreed about policy outcomes could still agree on process and procedure. The American political system was legitimated by agreement that its processes must accord with equality before the law, which nurtures equality of political opportunity. Even if mass attitudes did not always favor the Bill of Rights, elites—despite policy differences—would rally around these procedural guarantees. Exceptions, such as denial of the franchise to black people, were numbered among faults to be corrected; and they were thought to be exceptions, not the rule. Had this not been so, it would not have been possible to distinguish civil libertarians from other people who differed about the role of government or the kinds of policies it should pursue but whose agreements on civil liberties were more important to them than their disagreements on other matters of public policy. Believers in the reverse sequence, however, not only seek to diminish differences among Americans in general; they have also obliterated the rationale for distinguishing a particular kind of American, a civil libertarian, from any other political actor. The seriousness of the consequences—those supposedly carrying the creed now laying it down in the name of the higher good of equality—has yet to be widely understood.

Now we know from casual observation, as William Donahue has shown in detail, that most members of the ACLU are and have been politically liberal as well. In the era after World War II, this meant that they (I would then have said "we") favored governmental action to improve the economic conditions of poor people and the political opportunities of racial minorities. Insofar as the reverse sequence meant adopting the liberal welfare program, it may have been uncomfortable for economic conservatives, but not for those who agreed with the substance. (Allowing substance to mask principle was a mistake, but it is not easy for people to see a threat lurking behind those who agree with them on policy.) If the ACLU was becoming more liberal, it must be because liberals cared more than conservatives about the people being hurt—or so I thought in the early 1960s.

In the 1970s, another consequence of adopting the reverse sequence emerged—this one harder to deny. The very government that was urged to achieve greater equality of results was also, by virtue of being in authority, responsible for keeping the deprived down. What else but the system (i.e., established authority) denied poor people, racial minorities, and women the equal rights and opportunity that could be enjoyed only by first achieving equality of condition? The disposition to blame the system led to an antiauthority position. This explains why, amid an epidemic of strong-arm crime, the ACLU fought to make arrest, detention, and conviction more difficult. If the system were to blame for crime, why punish the criminal?

At one and the same time, therefore, the ACLU—responding to the reverse sequence—favored stronger governmental action to reduce inequality while simultaneously attacking government's authority. A long-overdue appreciation of this no-win situation—government in America damned if it does and damned if it doesn't—led to my unwillingness to renew my membership.

I do not mean to say that those of us who were out of sympathy did not change at all, and that the ACLU did all the changing. We have less reason to cry foul than I once thought. For one thing, those who joined the organization in the 1950s became active during an aberrant period. The patriotism fostered by the war against fascism created common ground that gave way when the enemy stood for something other than gross racial, religious, political, and economic inequality. During the conservative Eisenhower era, widespread antipathy to communism and the Communist party made it unsafe to leap to their defense. Faced with a bipartisan consensus on security matters, the ACLU ducked difficult issues, not least by bargaining with J. Edgar Hoover, head of the Federal Bureau of Investigation. Of this, the membership knew nothing. What it *did* know was that in those days the ACLU concentrated almost entirely on procedural rights. Criticism and patriotism still seemed compatible. But the decades before and after this period when, by default, means were more important than ends, were times in which the reverse was more nearly true: Policy ends mattered more than procedural means.

Those of us who felt aggrieved at having our ACLU taken from us were too self-satisfied by far. Since we believed in the pure civil liberties project, and those who displaced us did not, we identified ourselves as the long-suffering adherents of the original creed. So far as it went, that was true enough. But we did not understand at that time (certainly *I* did not) that the original sequence reflected a set of preferences about how American society should be organized. We were (and are) no more neutral in our views than current ACLU adherents; the difference (and it is profound) is that what they take for granted—the desirability of equal results, even at some sacrifice of equal rights—is problematic for us, and what we assume—the desirability of equal rights and opportunity, even if inequalities do not thereby decline—has become problematic for them. The separation of legal rights from the maelstrom of social life, which in our own eyes makes us true-blue civil libertarians, makes us in their eyes apologists for unconscionable inequalities. And that (leaving out the "unconscionable") is what is in dispute.

Guilty as charged! Some of us discover that we approve of many aspects of traditional morality and, therefore, of the social hierarchy from which it stems. Acceptance of a modicum of hierarchy, moreover, includes respect for authority as well as other forms of inequality. Others among us 1940s and 1950s civil libertarians discovered that if we wanted the creativity and spontaneity of market forces, we had to accept the inequality (as well as the vulgarity) that goes with it. Had we believed that the combination of hierarchy and market relationships that constitutes whatever established authority remains in American life is vicious—leading to cumulative inequalities threatening American democracy along with its civil liberties—then we, too, might have considered equality before the law as an epiphenomenon and equality of condition as all that is worth fighting for.

When the ACLU accepted the reverse sequence (some time in the late 1960s or mid-1970s), it also rejected the insulation of law and opportunity from condition. From then on, equality of condition was primary and equality before the law secondary.

The ACLU's Future

The ACLU has become an adjunct of movements to attack existing authority in the name of equality. If these movements weaken, the ACLU—if its past is any guide to its future—will abandon the reverse sequence and retreat to delineating a privileged position for legal rights. Should these egalitarian movements grow stronger, the ACLU may well become absorbed into them, making manifest what is now latent—namely, its service as their legal arm. Whatever happens, the experience of the ACLU will have taught us something about the conditions for treating civil liberties as an end in itself.

One such condition occurs when civil libertarians are numerous enough to band together, but still so weak as a group as to require tolerance from dominant social forces. Rather than fight losing battles over the substance of policy, this civil liberties group seeks to separate itself and its issues from substantive outcomes. The stance is tactical: The emphasis is on procedures because the group is sure to lose on policy. Once the group is strong enough to enter contests over policy, civil liberties become the means to more important ends. Those who disagree on substance leave the organization; gradually, the end goals overwhelm the former (and expedient) concentration on the means, and the initial sequence gives way to the reverse sequence.

Are there, then, no social conditions that would sustain disagreement over substance in the midst of agreement over procedures? Yes, but these conditions are delicate in that they require a certain kind of balance among forces. There must be people favoring hierarchy, for without hierarchy there is no place for legal rights, universalistic rules, adjudication of who has the right to do what, or predictable responses from government. And to some degree there must be promarket forces. Without them there would be no one who believed in competition for its own sake. And without people to safeguard the right to switch support, there could be no change in political office. Egalitarians are needed, also, to keep differences—including those between authority and citizen—from growing too large. Otherwise, hierarchies might seek to throttle competition and capitalists to control markets, making it difficult for newcomers to enter. Should any of these social orders grow too powerful (the danger of which Aristotle was well aware), procedural rights would be nullified. Hierarchy might stifle alteration in office and the criticism that goes with it; market forces might create inequalities; and an egalitarian social order might deny liberties on the grounds that they would interfere with equality. What the proper balance should be has, to be sure, eluded all of us. No doubt those who promote the reverse sequence would argue there is so little equality of condition that American society could stand for a great deal more before it becomes unbalanced. No doubt others will say that the pendulum has swung too far toward seeking equal conditions. I believe that the reverse sequence, by making civil liberties hostage to prior conditions, will weaken liberty without achieving equality.

To see why this is so—why equal conditions drive out equal rights rather than fully achieve them, as is commonly asserted—consider the coercive qualities required to maintain the reverse sequence. How can it be guaranteed that no citizen or group will acquire an unfair (in contemporary discourse, read "unequal") command over resources? Acknowledging that perfect equality of condition is unobtainable and may even be undesirable, attempting nevertheless to attain it justifies regulation of virtually every aspect of life that tends toward substantive inequality—that is, most everything. So long as every deviation from equal conditions is regarded as unfair, undemocratic, and therefore illegitimate, governmental intervention in all the interstices of social life is mandated. In so sweeping a conception of democracy, equality before the law—except for instantaneous votes at the moment of achieving equality of resources—is a fatal impediment.

A different view of democracy, not heard from much in recent times, is that people get together to find common grounds on which to secure the blessings of liberty. The initial sequence—the procedural rights they can agree on—matters mightily precisely because people do not agree on substantive ends. They expect to come in with different degrees of interest and information; they expect to be unequal in some respects because they want to be taken as they are; and they think that established positions should give way only slowly, since this resistance to change will dampen their proclivity to do whatever they decide to do. By foreclosing the end—or, rather, by making the end of equal condition the only legitimate beginning of political life—there is no room for a democracy of learning what to prefer. There can only be a democracy of enforcing prior preferences. And that, ironically, renders civil liberties useless, because there are no preferences to be changed. The reverse sequence and the original sequence are antithetic to each other; if you have one, despite what the song says, you can't have the other.

10

A Review of *The New American Dilemma: Liberal Democracy and School Desegregation*

But some see racism as anomalous: the dilemma of Americans is our continued weakness in . . . weeding out our shame so that our true creed may flourish. Once we bring ourselves to pull the weeds, American idealism will bloom all the better. Others see racism as symbiotic: the American garden is rooted in and nurtured by blacks' second-class status. To eradicate it, we must be willing and able to change the whole shape and ecology of the American landscape. Only then can the American creed blossom. . . .

Anomaly theorists argue . . . that a garden can be rejuvenated by pulling one weed at a time. Symbiosis theorists argue that it cannot—if the soil and layout of a garden are unsuited to their intended crops, pulling a few weeds does no good and actually does harm by deluding us into false perceptions of progress. . . .

Anomaly theorists argue . . . that all Americans . . . would prefer a garden blooming with racial equity to one choking in the weeds of discrimination. Symbiosis theorists argue that we do not—that whites (and perhaps some blacks) benefit from a landscape that includes racial discrimination and will resist the bulldozing needed to reshape it.

Jennifer L. Hochschild, The New American Dilemma

We have no right to look upon future citizens as if we were master

This review originally appeared in *Constitutional Commentary* 3 (1986); slight editorial changes have been made. The author wishes to thank John Ogbu and Paul Sniderman for most helpful discussions.

181

gardeners who can tell the difference between a pernicious weed and a
beautiful flower.

B. Ackerman, *Social Justice in a Liberal State*

In her tough-minded, trenchant marshalling of evidence, Jennifer
Hochschild argues in *The New American Dilemma*[1] that, since racial
desegregation and political democracy are at odds, representativeness
should give way to results, equal rights to equal outcomes. Though
Americans claim they oppose racial segregation in schools, she contends, in fact we are unwilling to adopt the necessary remedies. She
claims further that incremental change actually makes things worse for
white and black alike. Hochschild recommends "bulldozing"—a
quick, comprehensive, and coercive policy drawing in all children in
entire metropolitan areas. Her analysis and her proposal are procrus-
tean: The policy fits all circumstances and all sizes of student populations. This is a bravura performance, relentless and compelling. But is
it wise?

Just as pollution is defined as misplaced dirt, so the practical
definition of a weed is a flower in the wrong place. If everything has to
be changed ("the whole shape and ecology of the American landscape") to change anything ("one weed at a time"), it is no wonder
that Hochschild fears for progress. Where she spies foul weeds parad-
ing as fragrant flowers—are we now and have we ever been believers
in the liberal creed?—I detect a confusion of classification. Where she
suggests a Rousseauist vision within which the American creed might
blossom, I see Robespierre weeding out undesirables.

Portraying herself as "a child of the 1960s" who shared "its mistrust
of and distaste for cautious middle-class-oriented change in the face of
serious, even desperate, problems,"[2] Hochschild begins by contrasting
racism and liberalism. Under liberalism, she writes, "all citizens have
an equal right to express their political wishes and equal opportunity
to act politically." By racism, however, she does "not mean personal
dislike or denigration of another race or ethnic group" but rather
"institutional racism," whether or not intended.[3]

Although, generally, Hochschild is commendably candid, her definition of equal opportunity turns out to be one of equal results. For
her, racism is any pattern of actions that result in different racial
outcomes—"actions," as she says, "that usually elevate whites and
subordinate blacks."[4] If the measure of equal outcomes is used, of
course, then the game is over before it starts, because we all know,
without inquiring about equality of opportunity, that outcomes in

America are far from equal. Indeed, by the time she is finished, Hochschild has adopted Alan Freeman's view that racism can be ended only by reverse discrimination—that is, as she puts it, "that blacks be given disproportionate resources, power, and status until race would no longer affect people's life chances." In her view, "the great risk is that such a massive disruption of normal patterns of reward and mobility would reveal the underlying class structure, and destroy the belief in equal opportunity that is the lynchpin of American society."[5] That is why she concludes—inexorably, according to her logic—that "if whites cannot bring themselves to give up the advantages that America's racial and class practices give them, they must permit elites to make that choice for them."[6] So much for democracy.

Having altered the conventional definition of liberalism from equal opportunity to equal results, Hochschild not surprisingly concludes that liberalism is incompatible with racism. She earlier defined racism as contrary to liberalism because "it uses ascriptive characteristics, not achieved character, to determine people's fate, and it proclaims that some groups should not partake of liberalism's promises."[7] Thus "racism" is now to be remedied by treating the majority of the population by their ascriptive characteristics—that is, by denying them equal opportunity.

This summary treatment of Hochschild's position does not do justice to the flair and distinction with which she buttresses her position. She makes use of a wide variety of data on black–white differences. She is aware that the overall position of blacks is improving but that by some measures things are getting worse. She is dismayed by the evidence that whites think things are getting better for blacks and blacks think they are getting worse. Her discussion of the evidence on busing is broad, fair, and persuasive. Even when concluding that the more drastic busing produces better public acceptance and, insofar as may be determined, academic performance, she provides counterinterpretations of the evidence.

The strongest part of this book—a book with which all later writers will have to contend—is its discussion of the evidence on desegregation. Instead of the view that all is peaches and cream or that all is rotten, Hochschild makes a good case for the marginally positive effects of desegregation. She is also ingenious in trying to show that incremental change does not lead to outcomes as good as radical change.

Nevertheless, I find her position, despite its force and verve, wanting. It is not so much what Hochschild puts in her admirable book but what she leaves out that is troublesome. As a citizen and a political scientist, I never (literally, never) think of any matter of political importance without asking myself about its consequences for race relations. For the future of American democracy may well depend on whether and to what extent racial reconciliation takes place. Would Hochschild's recommendations, I ask, take us closer to or further from that goal? In analyzing that question, I will begin with a closer look at her attack on incrementalism, and will then consider some broader issues relating to busing.

Incrementalism and Resistance

Hochschild uses the doctrine of incrementalism as a metaphor for conservative (small, slow, partial) as opposed to radical (large, speedy, fundamental) change. Let us consider this doctrine in historical perspective. A famous version of incrementalism, Sir Karl Popper's "piecemeal social engineering," was deliberately designed as a counterweight to dictatorial political systems whose leaders thought they had the knowledge ("scientific socialism") or the intuition (*"Meinkampf"*) to achieve grand objectives without taking into account popular preferences. In response, Popper sought to outline a far less ambitious approach that would conserve consent and understanding. The now-classical formalization of incrementalism is due to Charles E. Lindblom's seminal work.[8] In his hands, disjointed incrementalism—with its serial, remedial, small-scale attacks on problems—became a formal rival to synoptic or comprehensive decision making. The emphasis was on the use of the plural character of interests in society as aids to calculation. Instead of being viewed as a defect of democracy, as the unfortunate irrationality of the citizenry, Lindblom converted the desirability of consent into a positive asset.[9]

At this point it is important to observe what incrementalism was *not*. As Simon put it, decision makers "satisficed" because they had not the wit to maximize. When you thought you knew better, you tried to do better. In Lindblom's socially oriented approach, incrementalism was always a doctrine of the second best. When ends were substantially agreed and knowledge of means was strong, that was first best. Where those conditions did not obtain, amid the usual doubts about causality and disagreement about objectives, incremental methods were appropriate substitutes.

Although this facet has been insufficiently appreciated, incrementalism was also part of the doctrine of the positive state. Were incrementalism designed to justify inaction, the doctrine would have stressed the unacceptability—not the desirability—of trying out small moves. Given the increasing size and scope of government, one possible response to those who argued that intervention was interference because no one knew enough to assure desirable consequences was to say that there was an evolutionary sequence of small steps that would enable government to learn (perhaps quite rapidly) how to do better.

As incrementalism changed from a challenge to comprehensive means–ends analysis into something like the received wisdom, it became the object of numerous critiques. On the side of calculation, it became clear that decision makers might be more dependent on theory—if only to distinguish the effects of one marginal move from many others taking place at the same time—than was once thought.[10] In regard to agreement, the pluralist underpinnings of incrementalism—all interests would receive adequate representation in the political process—came under attack.[11] My impression is that as various authors began to doubt the rightness of American political life, especially as they felt its institutions were too inegalitarian, the acceptability of incrementalism declined.[12]

If we think of conservatism not as an innate psychological disposition but as a judgment about how far a system's outcomes are from one's own preferences, the charge that incrementalism is conservative makes sense. Willingness to accept small departures from the status quo does depend on how acceptable the point of departure is in the first place. For example, today antinuclear and other similar groups composed largely of leftists[13] oppose incremental technological change.[14] Thus the same sort of people, with similar political views, who regard incrementalism in social policies such as busing as unconscionably conservative, regard a similar approach to technology as murderously radical.

Incrementalism also has implications regarding public consent. In this regard, the difference between voting and busing as civil rights measures is illuminating. The legislative provisions in regard to voting took a long time amid repeated struggles to enact. Once passed into law, however, the voting provisions were quickly implemented. There may be a tradeoff, therefore, between the slowness of legislation, in which disagreements are either resolved or accepted with resignation (reasonable opportunity to decide otherwise having been exhausted) and the speed of implementation. Conversely, judge-made laws—quickly enacted—may leave so many questions unresolved, and so many voices unheard, that they spawn endless resistance in the process of implementation.[15]

Hochschild's view is quite the contrary. Her view, briefly, is this: What is decisive in school desegregation—what determines whether it succeeds or not—is decisiveness itself. Limit the scope of desegregation, or leave some aspects of it open to discussion, and you buy trouble. For you give opponents a reason to fight, to resist. Decide the issue, therefore, unambiguously, authoritatively, once and for all—making sure to leave no loopholes. Then people will accept desegregation and busing and do the best they can to make it work, either because they are (or will shortly become) persuaded that busing is desirable, or because they have been persuaded that it is inevitable.

How convincing is this *blitzkrieg* view of social change? It is not implausible at first blush, especially if courts can compel consent. But coordinating a unified national attack on the segregated schools would present grave difficulties. It is one thing for one judge to pick on a city, like Boston, and take over the local school system. It would be quite another to do this on a regional—even a national—scale, running across city and suburban (and state?) jurisdictions as Hochschild wants.

More generally, whether the courts are up to accomplishing desegregation depends in part on what doing so entails. Desegregation could mean seeing to it that blacks and whites go to school together, or at any rate making sure that blacks are not prevented by public officials from going to schools with whites. But that is not really what Hochschild has in mind—certainly, not all that she has in mind. School desegregation in her view is a quite open-ended objective: to eliminate any practices, or habits of thought, within the school that are disadvantageous to blacks. As Hochschild tells her readers,

> Full and complete desegregation would call into question parents' rights to send their children to private schools, teachers' seniority rights, the sanctity of city/suburb school district lines, and local financing and control of schools, to mention only a few sacred cows. Not only poor but also rich whites would have to give up precious components of their class position for desegregation to be complete.
>
> Desegregation's indirect attack on the class structure—its revelation of the hollowness of the equal opportunity ideal—is most dangerous to all. A demand for full and complete desegregation, and the responses to such a demand, unmask the role of schools in perpetuating rather than mitigating the class structure and the structure itself. Desegregation demands expose unwarranted tracking within schools, disparities in resources,

expectations, and curriculum between schools, and the strong connections among family background, academic achievement, race, and occupational success. The more blacks focus on results rather than opportunities and on institutional biases rather than individual acts, the more the liberal values of opportunity and individualism appear fraudulent or at best weak. Once these values are questioned, the whole social structure is called into question; once that occurs, the class structure becomes visible and therefore a subject of contention.[16]

Guaranteeing equal results from schooling is something, so far as I know, that no nation has done.

And if I am right in this—not right in supposing that things must miscarry, only that they may—then the key limitation of Hochschild's analysis stands out: She spends scarcely any time worrying about what happens if things go wrong. Is it all that obvious that we could not be worse off, following the policy she advances? Is it reasonable to suppose, for example, that white attitudes toward blacks must continue to improve? Hochschild argues that racism is built into American society; yet her recommendation makes sense only on the supposition that America has goodwill toward blacks, perhaps more so than other societies. So much so, in her own view, that Americans are willing to undertake in their behalf what no other society has. I see no reason to suppose that racial prejudice has had its day, that bigotry cannot make a comeback. It has before; it could again. Nor would I have supposed that the place of the courts—or more generally, the role of the law— was so secure as to require no concern whatever. It may be that American institutions seem so stable that instability and its consequences for the worst off, who often suffer most, need not be taken into account. Or it could be that existing inequalities are considered so unconscionable that nothing could be worse. Either way, political consent is evidently not considered a scarce resource.

The problem of implementation seems to me severe because I think Hochschild, otherwise so acute, has in one critical respect quite misunderstood the view of those she calls "anomaly" theorists—above all Gunnar Myrdal. The anomaly thesis, as I understand it, comes to this: Americans have (or had) one set of ideas and convictions about liberty and equality and fairness for whites, another for blacks. Their views regarding blacks are (or were), literally, anomalous: different from, and at odds with, their views generally—which is the reason for Myrdal's (relative) optimism. But the dilemma that interests Hochschild is quite different. The great obstacle from Hochschild's point of view is precisely the source of optimism from Myrdal's. For Myrdal supposes that it is only necessary for Americans to change their opinions about blacks, whereas Hochschild supposes that they must change their basic values. Where Myrdal's dilemma is one of classification—that is, whites placing blacks in the category where enlightened rules apply—Hochschild wants to change the rules. From Hochschild's point of view, the real obstacles are not a set of attitudes brought into play only or chiefly on racial issues. Many citizens object to a range of policies to assist blacks; but—and this seems an important point—they object to such policies whoever they are intended to help. They take the same position on policies designed to help women (e.g., comparable worth) or Mexican Americans (e.g., affirmative action). Myrdal's dilemma could be resolved in favor of racial equality (as he conceived it) because the weight of American values favored resolution; it is much less obvious that Hochschild's dilemma can be resolved in favor of racial equality (as she conceives it) because the weight of American values opposes it. Simply put, it asks whites to give a kind of assistance to blacks they would oppose even for whites. Movement toward equality of condition, as Hochschild prefers, is not at all the same as equality of opportunity or equality before the law, which most Americans now support. Starting with the older dilemma—when black people were denied equal rights—Hochschild has slipped in a dilemma that is real for her and for those who share her views, but not for most Americans.

What Box Are We In?

Incrementalism is intended to deal with situations in which we either lack consensus about goals or knowledge about means. Recourse to a version of the justly renowned Thompson–Tuden matrix, relating knowledge to agreement, will tell us that in regard to busing we disagree not only about what to do, but even about which box we are in[17] (See Figure 10.1.)

Everyone agrees that we are not in box one, where there is nearly total agreement on objectives and nearly complete understanding of means. There are those, against whom Hochschild directs her argument, who say that there is much agreement on the objective of improving education through integrated schools but little understanding of whether busing is a good way of securing integration and whether integration will improve education. They view themselves as being in

Figure 10.1 Degrees of Consensus on Busing

Knowledge	*Agreement* Much	Little
Much	1) Computation	3) Bargaining
Little	2) Search	4) ?

Source: Developed by the author using a Thompson–Tuden matrix; see J. Thompson and A. Tuden, "Strategies, Structures, and Processes of Organizational Decision," in J. Thompson, ed., *Comparative Studies in Administration* (Pittsburgh, Pa.: University of Pittsburgh Press, 1959), pp. 195–216.

box two, searching for better solutions. Hochschild, however, places them in box three: These whites know how to achieve integration and make it serve education, but they do not want to give up their privileges. Hence they bargain for less onerous forms, such as voluntary busing, limitations to older students, busing into white schools— in sum, the very provisions that Hochschild contends weaken its positive educational effects. Recent work by Arthur L. Stinchcombe and D. Garth Taylor suggests another explanation for resistance to busing.[18] They find that

> busing attitudes are only weakly related to the traditional, psychological measure of racism or prejudice. . . . National data and our own analyses show the same for Boston during the time of the court order. Busing attitudes *are,* however, related to people's perceptions that the new costs of integration by busing are inequitably allocated, illegitimately arrived at (illegitimately decided by the courts and the establishment), and pose personal threats to the personal well-being and academic achievement of one's children. For instance, people's attitudes about what will happen to test scores predicts very strongly how much opposition they will show to the court order.[19]

According to Hochschild, "Americans must choose between standard, apparently desirable modes of policy choice and enactment, and the goal of eradicating racism. If whites cannot bring themselves to give up the advantages that America's racial and class practices give them, they must permit elites to make that choice for them."[20] That last (previously quoted) phrase—elites to make choices for Americans—is a dagger aimed at democracy.[21] Before adopting the thesis that majorities have to be deprived of the right to effective representation in order to facilitate a gain in achievement by minorities, we ought, at a minimum, to be pretty well convinced that the remedy—desegregation by busing—will work. Otherwise, public policy will leave whites and blacks angry at institutions that do not live up either to their procedural or substantive promises. The possible explanation I am about to suggest, building on the work of others, is at once comforting (differences in ability are not at issue) and despairing (the factor at fault may be much more difficult to change).

The usual factors in discussion of differences in racial achievement—racism, social and economic class, educational resources, family background, school expectations, language difficulties, prior ceilings on jobs, culturally biased organizations—all have a place, but they are readily subject to discount in the context of the experience of different racial and ethnic groups. A recent example that will have to stand for many others, because the literature is far too extensive to be summarized here, concerns the effects of poor health. On average, black children are less healthy than their white counterparts. But one of the unhealthiest groups in the country—carrying a legacy of disease from Southeast Asia—is the Vietnamese population. Yet their educational motivation and achievement, despite this evident handicap and despite language and cultural differences, has been considerable, soon placing them above many whites—all without evident abandonment of their home culture.

Let us consider, instead, another variable: time spent in school and doing homework. If blacks spend considerably less time in school and do less homework, then no one need be surprised that they do less well in the measurable aspects of educational achievement. And that apparently is exactly the situation. Even blacks with higher educational aspirations study a lot less.[22] Yet a positive attitude toward education, manifested by spending more time getting educated, would seem entirely compatible with ethnic and racial identity and with individual integrity. If schools, parents, and peers all reinforced respect for education, one would expect a gradual reduction of black–white differences in achievement within the context of improvement for all. Simple, isn't it? Then why doesn't it happen?

When blacks were ready and willing to accept educational integration—not only in the sense of sitting next to white skins, but of accepting similar education standards—they were denied that opportunity. When many whites were willing to sit in the same classrooms, provided that educational standards were shared, many blacks were no longer willing. The legacy of racism somehow turned in on itself. Educational standards, once used to put blacks down, had themselves become tainted just as these self-same standards were about to bring them up. Any white club willing to have them—as the great Groucho would have put it—was not worth joining. If it is not any innate individual difference but this acquired cultural difference that distinguishes the black experience from that of other ethnic and racial groups who share many of the same initial handicaps, the American dilemma is bigger than we thought.

A recent paper by Harry Eckstein raises the right issue. Do the groups under consideration want to be treated like others or are they deliberately rejecting the mainstream culture, including its modes of learning for educational achievement?[23] Building on Mary Metz's seminal study of schools as moral orders,[24] Eckstein probes the deep implications of self-exclusion. Here, for the purpose of this review, it is sufficient to consider the implications of self-exclusion for Hochschild's thesis.

It is hard to see how the promise of American life—that combination of cultural diversity and material abundance—can be even partially fulfilled without both racial integration and educational achievement. Certainly, Hochschild's version of our common dilemma is that it is not to be solved by giving up one for the other—achievement for integration—but by maintaining that these goals are (or can be made to be) mutually supportive. In this optimism, she reveals her quintessentially American character. But how?

It is possible that the small positive effects observed from racial integration in classrooms occur because of the moral influence in favor of achievement. Coercion can bring these students into closer proximity; but it can also breed hostility if the value of education is in dispute. When it is recognized that the criteria of achievement in the larger, white society—criteria that Hochschild accepts—have yet to be accepted by many blacks, the limits on coercion become apparent.

Another alternative is suggested by anthropologist John Ogbu:

The academic performance of Black children can be increased (a) by having Black children adopt more serious attitudes toward their schoolwork and (b) by increasing their efforts and perseverance at their schoolwork. . . .

One prerequisite for finding a "solution" to the "community" dimension of the problem of persistent disproportionate academic lag of Black students is to recognize that this aspect of the problem exists. Blacks and similar minorities have generally expressed a kind of institutional discrimination perspective or "blaming the system" perspective. . . . This needs to be balanced with a recognition that some of their own responses to the "institutionalized discrimination" or to the dominant Whites' exploitation also contribute to the academic difficulties of Black children. From this point of view, my analysis is addressed largely to people in the Black community. I believe that given the oppositional theme underlying the problem, Black children are more likely to change their attitudes and behaviors if encouraged to do so from within the Black community.

Current awareness programs for Black students and similar minorities tend to emphasize discovering racial and ethnic identities and pride. This is fine but not enough. It is not enough to discover who they are or that they have their own racial or ethnic culture, especially if that reinforces equating school learning with acculturation into White middle-class culture. . . .

Blacks and similar castelike minorities tend to have what is essentially an acculturation or assimilation view of schooling. That is, they view schooling as learning White culture and identity or changing into White culturally and cognitively. Given that Blacks maintain oppositional identity . . . there is . . . ambivalence toward learning in school or "acting White." The dilemma is that the individual Black student has to choose between academic success or school success and being Black.[25]

Around the nation a variety of schools and school districts[26] are implicitly following Ogbu's advice in setting, monitoring, and enforcing high academic standards for all pupils. Tests are taken seriously, not as examples of cultural imperialism. Pupils are held back when they don't measure up. Excellence is color blind. It ought to work. If not, America faces the prospect of declining performance together with ever more bitter struggles over the political allocation of material goods. Only a single outcome is certain: The America the victors inherit won't be worth having. And that is the most un-American dilemma I can think of.

My own sense of the fitness of things (having grown up in Brooklyn where, despite calumnies, far more than a single tree grows) is based on a city boy's marvel at nature the trickster. Especially at her sweetest. On my fence in Oakland I have growing a lush vine, *clematis armandii,* which, besides producing a bevy of white flowers, is suffused with a sweet fragrance. It perfumes the air and is otherwise a delight. It is also easy to handle. One can snip off segments easily with little damage to appearance or odor. Should our vine entwine itself around another flower, however, it will keep tightening itself in such a loving embrace that soon friendly, welcoming, luscious clematis chokes the life out of its host. The wise—the adage goes—should protect against the damage done by the merely good.

11

The Crime of Inequality:
The Bork Nomination

Whereas other failed nominations to the Supreme Court sink quickly from public view, the debate over Judge Robert Bork maintained its intensity as if the state of the nation—and not merely the fate of an individual jurist—were at issue. Far from settling the matter, the Senate's rejection of President Reagan's first choice for the seat vacated by Lewis Powell spurred renewed efforts both to justify and to condemn what was done.

The case of Bork versus the U.S. Senate reflects our struggle over the meaning of America: Will these United States continue to be exceptional in believing that liberty and equality are compatible, or will the American people join the people of other Western nations in the ideological wars that pit equality of opportunity against equality of condition? Are we witnessing the end of American exceptionalism—with race, gender, and economic class coming to be seen as fundamental objects of division—or will we, the people, reaffirm our original convictions?

Whose Mainstream?

In recent decades it had been customary for the Senate to approve the president's choices for the Supreme Court as long as they were

This chapter first appeared as an article in *The Public Interest,* no. 98 (Winter 1990), pp. 98–117, under the title, "Robert Bork and the Crime of Inequality." Slight editorial changes have been made.

qualified individuals and of good character. It had also been customary not to inquire closely into nominees' views on constitutional interpretation, so as not to give any appearance of prejudice in cases that might come before the Court; Senator Edward Kennedy, for instance, used this rationale in defending the appointment of Thurgood Marshall. Such customs, however, require the political parties to be sufficiently close together that expertise matters more than ideology. The first thing that we learn from the Bork episode, therefore, is that consensus has been replaced by division; the two sides are too far apart to accept either presidential prerogative or neutral competence as a criterion for making decisions. Bork was attacked not on grounds of knowledge— where his opponents could hardly have bested him—nor on grounds of personal integrity, but on grounds of policy. Not he but his ideas were attacked as indecent.

One could hardly blame the senators had they simply done what comes naturally to them and voted their policy preferences. But the rhetorical stakes were much higher in the battle over Bork. Bork's philosophy was labeled not just undesirable, but immoral. The passion of these attacks reflected the unwillingness of Bork's antagonists to permit their egalitarian dogma to be questioned. Debate over equality was ruled illegitimate.

Consider, for example, the charge that Judge Bork was somehow "outside the mainstream" of judicial thought. Its preposterous quality was part of its charm: How could a superb legal craftsman be outside the mainstream when he was one of the leaders in determining what constituted excellence in legal reasoning? How could a judge who had written some 150 opinions, and had never been reversed by a higher court, be outside the mainstream? Why weren't America's political institutions, which Bork had devoted his life to protecting, in the mainstream that his opponents were accusing him of polluting?

Precisely because the charge of extremism was so unfounded, Judge Bork did not at first take it seriously. When he did, he discovered that the beauty of absurd charges is that the person who responds to them is made to look sillier still. For Bork to try to prove that he was not outside the mainstream is like your trying to explain that you're not really a vampire: Even repeating the allegation lends it more credence than it deserves.

If Bork was truly an extremist, after all, there was no reason to fear him. His weapon was the pen, not the sword. How could a self-evident extremist persuade a single justice of the Supreme Court—let alone enough to constitute a majority—to adopt views at once far out, destructive, and rejected by a large majority of the citizenry? No, the fear of Bork was grounded in the much more accurate perception that he would persuade his colleagues to uphold legislative majorities and the views of the Framers against those who would substitute their own values. Bork's opponents thought that he alone among contemporary conservatives was capable not only of crafting a coherent doctrine of constitutional interpretation, but of convincing others—his fellow justices, legal scholars, the political stratum—of the need to alter gradually but decisively the pattern of decisions. As Bruce Ackerman observed, Bork was the one possible nominee who had "the transformative vision and the legal ability needed to spearhead a radical judicial break with the past."[1]

"Mainstream," as the term was used against Judge Bork, was a code word for supporting equality of condition. Bork was being accused of fostering inequality. When one disentangles the charges against him, they are all variations on this theme: antiwoman, antiblack, antigay, antipoor. Listen to the testimony of those who spoke against him:

- Professor Burke Marshall: "adamantly opposed to protecting . . . disadvantaged and unpopular minority groups."
- Professor Philip Kurland: "directed to a diminution of minority and individual rights."
- Lawyer Vilma Martinez: "would provide less equal protection to racial minorities and to women than they currently enjoy."
- William T. Coleman, former chair of the NAACP Legal Defense Fund: "would turn back [the clock to a time when there were no judicial measures] removing the vestiges of slavery, of 350 years of legally enforced racial discrimination, and of centuries of irrational discrimination against women."
- National Coalition for Women and Girls in Education: "devastating impact on individual rights . . . Unprecedented hostility to . . . individual rights . . . Judge Bork would enable employers to dictate the parameter of female employees' 'reproductive freedoms.' "
- National Conference of Black Lawyers: "pernicious to everyone but those who comprise the majority."
- National Council of Churches of Christ: "It is victimized individuals, minorities, and the unrecognized public good that need the protection of the courts. . . . Bork's conception of 'judicial restraint' would deny them. [Bork would] shield the powerful against the weak."

In his defense, Bork claimed that his private views are not necessarily the same as his interpretations of the law; however he might personally feel about these matters, his duty as a judge would forbid him from reflexively finding that women or homosexuals or chiropodists have rights that are neither mentioned in the Constitution nor known to those who wrote, debated, and passed the provisions in question. But Bork's opponents denied any difference between the personal and the political: Judges who refuse to recognize a right because it is not stated in the law are no different from those who personally reject (and personally desire to reject) the right. Just as a dietitian might say that "you are what you eat," so Bork's adversaries equated intention (upholding the law) and outcome (denying a right): In their view, you are what they think you cause. To be a "racist," in this lexicon, one need not be racially prejudiced; it is enough if one's words and deeds tend to bring about results adverse to blacks. In the meaning of the 1930s expression, Bork had become "objectively" inegalitarian.

If Bork replied that he was trying to follow the original understanding of the Constitution wherever he could discern it, his adversaries made his argument into a prima facie case of moral defect. Instead of offering a forthright defense of his inegalitarian views—his adversaries charged—Bork added duplicity to inequality by denying that his personal political views determined his interpretations of the law.

Whose Record?

Nikki Heidepriem—a media specialist within the progressive community—communicating with her kind, put her finger on the nature of the anti-Bork campaign: "Whereas in election campaigns issues are legitimate, here, your issue agenda has to be a demonstration of why his philosophy is unacceptable." As the progressive community's focus-group report put it, "the overall sense that he is an extremist is a more powerful argument against him than his stand on any single issue."

Still, particular issues do help to show what Bork was up against. Thus Bork ran into difficulties when senators learned that he did not believe in the egalitarian commandment "one person, one vote"—that each person's vote is to count the same as everyone else's—either as an inviolable preference or as a "right" enshrined in the Constitution. State governments, Bork argued, could have adopted the principle if they chose, but they had not done so before the Supreme Court spoke;

all but one state have bicameral legislatures in which representation is based on districts' areas as well as their populations. And there are, after all, two U.S. senators from each state, a blatant violation of the egalitarian commandment. That most of these senators are hardly aware of the contradiction became apparent during the Bork hearings. It is also clear that, if compelled to decide today, they could not think of an argument that would justify the U.S. Senate. How extraordinary for a branch of the legislature to turn down a nominee on the grounds that he was determined to be guided by their will, as well as by the will of prior deliberative bodies back down to the constitutional ratifying conventions and the Framers.

Like everything else, "privacy" was also converted into an issue of equality. It is rich people's access to "safe abortions" that makes it unconstitutional, in liberal eyes, not to provide funds for abortions for poor women. Much depends on how the matter is put. A constitutional right to abortion might not get as much public support as a presumed right to the privacy of one's bedroom, which is not to say that abusing a child in private is constitutionally protected. As Michael Pertschuk and Wendy Schaetzel show,[2] the progressive (read "egalitarian") forces opposed to Bork were skillful at getting their version of privacy to be the one discussed in the media and inquired about in the Senate. Had the focus changed to the tax returns of governmental officials, Bork's antagonists might well have preferred a lot less privacy than Bork.

Or take the charge that Bork favored corporations. In a different context such a complaint might appear peculiar because the nation depends on business for prosperity. "Favoring business," moreover, is the explicit object of various programs designed to increase competitiveness. To egalitarians and their allies, however, favoring corporations means giving more to those who already have more than they deserve while depriving those who have less of the little they have. If not exactly a violation of the statutory law, it is at least a moral lapse.

How did his opponents prove that Judge Bork was partial to "the corporations"? One Bork decision favored a union, and Ralph Nader's Public Citizen group said that unions were in the "business of representing workers"; Bork was therefore probusiness. Then there was the case of a rancher who Bork decided could collect damages because government action had rendered part of his land unusable. Ranchers are in business, right?

Far worse than this stretching of the record was the method used: citing only cases in which there were dissents on Bork's D.C. Circuit

Court of Appeals—56 out of more than 500. Actually, as Ethan Bronner shows in his fair-minded and enlightening book on the nomination,[3] Bork's panels were unanimous 90 percent of the time, and Bork was in the majority 95 percent of the time. Had these larger numbers been used, of course, Bork's record could not have been made to appear deviant.

Whose Understanding?

The dispute over egalitarianism sheds light on the flap over the jurisprudence of "original understanding." Egalitarians do not believe that present inequalities can be justified by reference to the past. Regarding authority as a way to institutionalize inequality, they—like the appropriately named literary deconstructionists—seek to deny the authority of the constitutional text when they believe that it is used to perpetuate inequalities. It would not be going too far to say that Robert Bork's doctrine of original understanding or intent is accurately perceived by his adversaries as the major intellectual obstacle to the realization of their desires.

Developing and defending a doctrine of original understanding is not easy, nor can it (or any other formula applied to diverse conditions) be entirely consistent. However hard one tries to leave out the effects of contemporary social forces in favor of discovering and applying original understanding, these effects are bound to create inconsistencies. Suppose that the original understanding of the guarantee of freedom of speech is murky, yet a consensus has grown up around certain interpretations. How does one distinguish this consensual, evolutionary adaptation from the changes urged by those who substitute their own notions for the original understanding? Suppose, as Bork does, that one also values stability and order; then long-held and deeply entrenched interpretations, even if they depart from original understanding, may be acceptable. Thus Bork has to qualify his doctrine by saying that he would not disrupt the economy if, say, the existence of paper money ran counter to original understandings.

A similar problem is that in order to reestablish a narrower and stricter doctrine of judicial interpretation, recent rulings would have to be overturned. Maintaining the law by reversing precedent sat uneasily with the doctrine's adherents. Bork's ambivalence, even in his book,[4] between overturning decisions that have no evident constitutional warrant and merely restricting their future applicability by adopting

tests of disruption, reasonableness, community sentiment, and the like
was not—as his adversaries claim—an underhanded way of gaining
confirmation by suggesting that he was not so dangerous, but rather an
honest expression of the fundamental dilemma facing conservatives
caught between the principle of stare decisis and the flaws of recent
decisions.

Bork does about as well as might be expected in grappling with these
inherent difficulties—fairly well, but not entirely well. For he has more
than a formula in mind. According to Bork, a judge interpreting the
Constitution should begin with original understanding, supplement it
with a belief in the maintenance of the existing order through elected
representatives, and touch it off with a dose of common sense based
on the tacit consensus among judges about good legal craftsmanship.
This is not something that can generate decisions by computer, but it
provides both direction and flexibility. True, judges applying original
understanding might sometimes disagree, but they would disagree far
more with those applying a different standard. The other side of the
flexibility of Bork's doctrine of original understanding—the side feared
by his critics—is that a flesh-and-blood judge, confronting new circumstances, could actually apply it.

If one were to reverse field and ask Bork's enemies (noting that
opponents become enemies when they deny each other legitimacy,
whether by charges of racism or of authoritarianism) to justify their
damn-the-founders-full-equality-ahead approach, they would have a
great deal more difficulty. Few, after all, are prepared to say that the
Constitution does not matter. In practice, however, they do have a
counterpart to original understanding: The legacy of the Warren and
Burger Courts, it might be called "egalitarian understanding." It is
this egalitarian understanding—justified by prior judicial decision, but
not yet ratified in the court of public opinion—that leads them to say
that Bork is outside their mainstream.

Bork argues that the consequence of saying that the Constitution is
whatever judges want to make of it is judicial tyranny. Hence, in his
book, he gets back at his opponents by saying he would not support
aspiring judges unless they adhered to original understanding. He
scores points by observing that this is exactly what the Taney Court
did in the *Dred Scott* case before the Civil War, when it discovered a
new right to own slaves in its version of substantive due process. When
Bork says that those who read new rights into the Constitution are
"authoritarian," he means that they do not allow the political process
to work its will.

His assertion that egalitarians disregard democracy when they regard its outcome as inegalitarian rings true. Nowhere is this more evident than in regard to the death penalty, which—as Bork notes—the Constitution mentions as a possible punishment three times, going so far as to hedge it about with procedural restrictions. Public opinion supports the death penalty for heinous crimes. Rather than fight the matter out in public, however, efforts are made to put it beyond the reach of legislative and executive politics by claiming, as Justice William Brennan did, that it constitutes "cruel and unusual punishment." To Brennan and his allies, original understanding is at odds with equality of condition, for it is claimed that black people suffer disproportionately from application of the death penalty. In short, judicial activism is used to make up for inegalitarian opinion.

It takes two to dissent though. If Bork's opponents wanted him rejected because his judicial philosophy of original intent is outside their mainstream of egalitarian intent, he responded by writing his book to persuade Americans that "no person should be nominated or confirmed who does not display both a grasp of and devotion to the philosophy of original understanding."

Whose Politics?

Debates can turn on the struggle over whose way is deemed natural. Thus conservatives claim that the egalitarian tendencies of the Warren and Burger Courts are unnatural departures from the essential nature of the Constitution, so that radical rejection of recent precedents is required. When liberals see themselves as stalwarts of the existing order while conservatives consciously try to overturn it, something important is afoot.

Among the many contributions that the Bork affair can make to our education is the recognition that the dividing line between conservatives and liberals is not, as so often claimed, that the former hate change and the latter love it. Once we identify the values at stake—equality of condition for progressive American liberals, economic individualism for conservatives—we can see that a more straightforward proposition is correct: People like what they like and dislike what they dislike. Egalitarian liberals were defending the status quo in constitutional interpretation; indeed, the very point of declaring Bork outside the mainstream was to make sure that their beliefs were recognized as the status quo so that they could accuse conservatives of threatening to take away hard-won gains. If greater equality of condition was not merely a proposal but a right, it was more fundamental and hence more valuable than more temporary preferences. After all, if they had the rights, their opponents would be stuck with the wrongs.

As Bork accuses his opponents of politicizing the judiciary by inventing new constitutional rights, while they respond that he is doing the same by restricting rights that minorities already enjoy, we become aware that when values are in conflict there is no way to avoid playing politics. For there is always some expansion or constriction that would do better or worse for some interest or value than the alternative. Indeed, "what ought to be political?" is a political question. "What sort of politics is most desirable?" would be a better question.

Those favoring greater equality of condition seek to enshrine their dominant value as the law of the land. In doing so they follow the time-honored tradition of seeking that point of access to decision making that is most amenable to their views. The difficulty for egalitarians, who believe that decisions can be legitimated only by personal participation, is that the judiciary is by far the least participatory branch. When Pertschuk and Schaetzel entitle their account of the Bork battle *The People Rising,* they obscure the difference between the progressive community's activists, who did indeed rise to the occasion, and the citizenry that did not (unless one counts focus groups whose reactions were used for purposes of manipulation).

Bork's opponents were right to worry. Bork did want to "drop the entire notion of group entitlements. That meant an end to racial, ethnic, and sexual quotas." My guess is that if this proposition were put to a referendum it would win by a big margin. But to Senator Kennedy, like other egalitarians, there is something wrong with neutral principles "if the result is that Congress and the courts must be neutral in the face of discrimination." Here is equality of results writ large. Bork's fault, Kennedy continued, was that "he would allow majorities to write laws that give greater weight to some people's vote than others and that is the opposite of democracy." How extraordinary that an important democratically elected official should criticize "allow[ing] majorities to write laws."

The Supreme Court, of course, is part of a larger political process. Its members are nominated by presidents and confirmed or rejected by senators elected by the people. Over time, therefore, we would expect the Court, as Mr. Dooley put it, to follow the election returns. (Observe, however, the approbation Bork's opponents give to the current Court's octogenarians for their effort to outlive the people's choice of Republican presidents.) It is also true that political value judgments are inherent in cases the Court decides. But does this ineradicable political element mean that the Court is political in the same sense as a political party or a legislature or an elected executive? If there is no difference, why not subject the justices to democratic electoral responsibilities? If there is no difference, or only a little difference, why accept the verdicts of courts as anything more than partisan judgments, or the Constitution as anything more than the latest party manifesto?

Though Bork failed to wean liberal legislators from their dependence on judge-made law for their liberties, the nation owes him an enduring debt for his insistence (to the point of courting the defeat of a worthy lifetime ambition to serve on the highest court in the land) that it is the people and their elected representatives who must defend our liberties if they are to be successfully preserved. The view that the Supreme Court, or any court, or indeed any guardian elite could preserve the liberties of a nation is ludicrous. Even to state the proposition baldly is to reveal its nonsense: When the Court is most needed to preserve liberty—that is, when intense majorities are determined to act against it—it is least useful. The case of the forced relocation of citizens of Japanese descent during World War II, often referred to by senators as the kind of thing that they want future justices to prevent, is proof positive that the senators' hope is misplaced. Everyone now is certain that the relocation was unnecessary as well as abhorrent, but this hindsight does not reflect the passions of wartime 1942 when so many feared invasion and invoked "the law of necessity" in taking no risk (or so they thought) by denying liberty to Japanese Americans.

We the people, Professor Bork keeps trying to teach us, are the only possible guarantors of our liberties. "The tempting of America" mentioned in his book's title refers to the belief that the courts can substitute for the political process as a whole. How comforting to a generation of law students to imagine that they have in their hands (or their briefs) an Archimedean lever of change whereby a lowly but valiant lawyer sitting in a library cubicle writes a brief to another lawyer called a judge, who issues orders righting the injustices of this world. Absent from this vision, unfortunately, are ordinary people attempting to persuade one another of the virtues and vices of important policies arousing strong emotions—like the death penalty or affirmative action. Had there been debates on these issues, we might have reached a consensus; at least we would have had the chance to influence others in a deliberative process culminating in majority rule. But there have been no such debates, which is why these issues never seem to be resolved; they have not in fact been dealt with.

In the last third of the twentieth century, egalitarian movements have tried to reduce what their adherents believe are unwarranted distinctions: the power differences between men and women, blacks and whites, gays and straights, adults and children, old and young, experts and laymen, animals and people, and more. The degree to which such differences are considered proper is a product of negotiation among contending social forces, and therefore it changes over time. No one—certainly not Bork—claims that the Constitution froze the power differences that existed in 1789 or 1865 or 1898 forever into the fabric of American life. Judge Bork wants conflicts other than those memorialized in the Constitution to be carried on in the political arena, not primarily through the courts. Believing that those who have fewer resources than others face insuperable disadvantages in the political arena, by contrast, egalitarians wish to right the wrongs—to remedy the inequalities—by reading the Constitution to guarantee greater equality of condition.

This desire to right wrongs explains the rooting of egalitarian rhetoric in the language of rights, as in civil rights, women's rights, gay rights, and animal rights. Egalitarians have persuaded themselves that rights as they conceived them belong to the kinds of people they think need them. In their minds and hearts it follows that anyone who denies that greater equality of condition is enshrined in the Constitution is stealing it away from those who need it the most. Hence they convicted Bork of the most dastardly deed in their lexicon: the crime of inequality.

Whose Opinion?

But why, if public opinion and legislative majorities are not prepared to support a Constitution interpreted through the lens of egalitarian understanding, did the public not rise up against the new judicially created rights Bork opposes? Bork skirts this issue in his book. He is correct in saying that his views were distorted and that the major media opposed his nomination in their news stories as well as their editorials. That, however, does not explain enough. The Court really cannot get away with anything it chooses, but only with those ventures in which its opinions can attract significant support. What does the campaign against Bork show about support for the Warren and Burger Courts' egalitarian decisions?

If we were to look strictly at mass public opinion, we would cite popular sentiment to account for the Court's invention of a constitutional right of privacy, but not for the Court's discovery that the death penalty is unconstitutional. Indeed, though the abortion rights that flowed from the right of privacy have remained, the abolition of the death penalty has not stuck. Why? Many more people suffer from crimes of violence than from the absence or presence of abortion. It could be said that crime constitutes the most serious deprivation of liberty in the United States today. This accounts for the steep penalties imposed for repeated offenses. The oft-repeated line that the death penalty is antiblack, anti-Indian, antipoor (if this litany reminds the reader of the accusations against Bork, it should) is more difficult to drive home to those many citizens who consider themselves victims.*

Consider an incident that was recently reported in the New York *Times* concerning a New York City police officer, born in Puerto Rico but of Jamaican origins, who described himself as a Hispanic. When his 66.5 score on the sergeant's exam was above the cutoff for blacks (65) but below the cutoff for Hispanics (69) and Caucasians (75), he asked for reclassification as a black and was rebuffed by the state appellate court. As part of its news report, the *Times* wrote that "the department set different passing scores to insure that black and Hispanic members have the same opportunity as whites to pass the test." Has "opportunity" been redefined as "result"? I do not believe that most citizens would approve of setting different passing levels for different races. No doubt Bork had something like this in mind when he urged taking such matters out of the courts and into the more open arena of electoral politics.

In a way, however, affirmative action and related principles can be placed in the more participatory political arenas any time an elected representative thinks it worthwhile to bring them there. A sobering thought for the let-the-people-through-their-representatives-decide school is that the most conservative administration of our time, led by President Ronald Reagan—elected by huge majorities—had an opportunity to end affirmative action by executive order and did not take it.

---

*There is, to be sure, nothing inherent in death sentences that compels us to view them as inegalitarian. Criminals could be viewed as too strong and their victims too weak. Why it is that race or income is the dividing line, rather than the perpetration of murder, is of great interest in and of itself but would take us too far afield.

The president's advisors disagreed over whether the benefits of such an order would exceed the costs of the expected charges of racism.

Whose Strategy?

This brings us to the question of why Bork's enemies were able to mobilize so quickly and powerfully against him while his political friends were slow to organize and lacking in clout.

Judge Bork's intellectual position attracted enemies, but repelled friends—all but those few who knew him personally or were acquainted with his scholarship. Some say that Bork alienated his senatorial questioners by appearing to know more about constitutional law than they did, which is true on both counts: He did know more, and they were put off. It is only natural that in his book Bork wishes—knowing the outcome—that he had really told them off. Looking ahead instead of back, Bork softened his replies, giving his questioners more credit for coherence than they deserved and appearing more conflicted and contradictory than he was (e.g., that he was for original understanding, but not if it led to ridiculous results or contravened deeply held and widespread public preferences). Bork's effort to appear reasonable—as his political coaches told him he must—as well as his own disposition to admit of qualifying facets, left him exposed to the one line of attack to which he was vulnerable: Generalists might not know much about constitutional law, but they could talk knowingly about a contradiction they thought they heard in front of them.

The tone of the Bork hearings was so defensive as to suggest that if Bork were Bork he could not be approved. Seemingly endless testimony by his friends was devoted to explaining why his bite as a Supreme Court justice would not be nearly so bad as his bark as a professor. Thus his defenders told the Senate Judiciary Committee that as a professor seeking to establish new theory—as he had in the antitrust field—his tone had been combative; but it would be appropriately conciliatory if he were a justice. Very often he was defended by analogies to noted instances in which justices who were thought to be on one side ended up on another. His defenders seized on the times when Bork indicated that he might expand his views on the scope of free speech or of privacy to show that he could indeed change. Yet if his initial views were insupportable, why nominate him?

The irony is that Bork's personal policy preferences did not comport with those of many conservatives, while his efforts to disengage

himself from the strict consequences of original understanding by
saying he personally did not desire them fell on deaf liberal ears. By
the time the egalitarian onslaught reached the ears of conservatives—
that is, when conservatives were finally persuaded by egalitarian
arguments that Bork's theory of constitutional interpretation favored
them—it was too late. Bork's defense was at once too much for his
opponents and too little to attract those who would have been supporters.

The difference between constitutional interpretation and personal
preference also alienated libertarian individualists from Bork. They
feared the imposition of eighteenth- and nineteenth-century restrictive
norms on their personal behavior.

The "success of the anti-Bork forces in controlling the terms of the
struggle," as Bronner aptly puts it, "was found in the behavior of the
pollsters." They so loaded the questions to which the public was asked
to respond against Bork—"turn back the clock, limit the rights of
women and blacks, and make abortion illegal"—that such positive
phrases as "eminent and experienced jurist" likely had no effect. That
was how Southern senators learned that 51 percent of their constituents opposed Bork and only 31 percent favored him—a result that was,
in Bronner's words, "enormously influential." Had the various pollsters not been inclined to an egalitarian ideology, they would have
seen that they were prefiguring the outcome against him.

Other types of bias, now taken for granted, also operated against
Bork. Observe how balanced (by race, gender, and ethnicity) committees for almost every purpose have become. Members of these group-
ings are not chosen at random but from ideologically attuned activists.
Thus "balance" is achieved by adding people of egalitarian preferences. This explains why the American Bar Association's Standing
Committee on the Federal Judiciary, which gives advice on federal
nominees, had a liberal bias and why, therefore, the Reagan administration eventually refused to deal with it. The informal balance requirement, expanded to include "political balance," also explains why four
members of a 15-person committee (one voted not opposed) of the
American Bar Association voted that Bork was unqualified because he
lacked "judicial temperament."

Look through the eyes of Pertschuk and Schaetzel (who have written
the best account of movement mobilization that I know) at the diverse
groups opposed to Bork: the Leadership Conference on Civil Rights,
the National Abortion Rights Action League, the National Association
for the Advancement of Colored People, Public Citizen, the National

Education Association, People for the American Way, and many more. How did they come to believe that the Bork nomination posed a threat to their interests or their constituencies? According to Pertschuk and Schaetzel, Nan Aron of the Alliance for Justice persuaded Leonard Rubenstein of the Mental Health Law Project that Bork posed a severe threat to the rights of the disabled, upon which Rubenstein persuaded some 30 organizations concerned with mental health and disability, including the Epilepsy Foundation and the National Mental Health Association, to oppose Bork. After all, if Bork failed to find certain other rights in the Constitution, he might fail to find theirs. Together with Ralph Nader and others, Aron persuaded Brock Evans of the National Audubon Society that "Bork seemed to come up four-square for business or anti-environmental interests every time he had a chance." They said Bork would deny standing to those who could prove no evident harm. Although the Audubon Society did not take a formal stand, Evans recalls, "we [the staff] were all certainly there in spirit and talked it up." Thus Evans advised Senator Durenburger to "forget about the Arctic National Wildlife Refuge. [Bork is] the environmental issue that we really want you to work on."

The members of the anti-Bork coalition knew each other from prior struggles over civil rights. When they did not immediately recognize one another, "Ralph Neas puzzled some Steering Committee members by taking up precious time . . . by patiently asking each person in the room to identify himself or herself and his or her organization." The reason, Pertschuk and Schaetzel tell us, "soon became clear: the roll call was both a socialization process and a security check." It turned out that the suspiciously "clean-cut looking" men were from the Americans United for the Separation of Church and State. As Mrs. Thatcher might have put it, they were "one of us." Had Bork thought to follow a similar procedure when giving a talk to the Federalist Society, he would have found one of his opponents' staff there taking notes for future use against him.

The anti-Bork coalition was both centrally directed and run locally. General direction, such as suggestions about the type of appeals to make or what to avoid (the abortion issue), came centrally. Local groups could decide differently, but if they went too far they faced moral pressure—you're harming the cause of equality—from the center. What made it all fit together, since no one could compel anyone else, was a shared belief: Bork threatened to halt or reverse egalitarian advances. This was coordination by ideology, and it worked.

A crucial decision of the anti-Bork forces—reached not without internal dissent—was that no one who identified with the progressive community should testify. They did this to prevent charges of their extremism from becoming the center of the hearings. Instead, they chose to make Bork the extremist, characterizing him, in Bronner's words, as being in favor of "birth control police, poll taxes and literacy tests" for voting.

The anti-Bork forces worked hard to win over the media. They did exhaustive research, answered questions, fed their views to all who would take them. In this they were helped by the expectation (though not the certainty) of a favorable reception. In all the major media, they had people who were part of what they called the progressive community.

Not to take chances, the anti-Bork forces used focus groups to decide what appeal they might make to whom. Most anti-Bork messages inspired only boredom. But two were resonant: invasion of people's bedrooms (a worry to men), and control over their bodies (a worry to women). Nothing for it, then, but to accuse Bork of bringing about whatever these unsuspecting citizens feared most.

For all practical purposes, as Fred Wertheimer of Common Cause noted, "it was simply a question of who won the battle for the Southerners, and it would be won by blacks in the South." Why should senators accept the taint of racism for a nominee whose views on judicial interpretation they could hardly understand? Why not get another conservative justice without the taint? In politics, after all, it is not only the truth of an allegation but how intensely its partisans feel that matters. If constituents say they would interpret a vote for Bork as a vote against them, that is a political fact. In politics, unlike logic, the frequency with which a statement is made helps determine whether it is received as true.

And what if the mass of citizens wishes neither to support group entitlements nor to disturb them where they exist? In this way they do not have to choose between accepting a bad principle or openly denying that certain groups deserve special assistance.

Neither the senators nor their Southern constituents wanted to reignite the civil rights struggles of the 1960s. They may have agreed with Bork in private, but they were not prepared to take the consequences of supporting such views in public. They wanted those unhappy days behind them. If organizations with credibility among their black constituents said a nominee was racist, therefore, they were not going to look behind that. Being accused of racism is like being accused of child abuse: Even after acquittal, the charge is so vile that some of the stain always sticks. Whatever he said or did, Bork could not overcome the stigma of inequality.

Whose Cause?

It is not often that a person's ideological trajectory becomes an open matter for public discussion. Since Bork had not always believed what he believed when he was nominated, he was at pains to explain his transformation. In 1963 he wrote in opposition to the pending Civil Rights Act because, as a libertarian, he saw it as substituting coercion by governmental regulation for what should have been unforced individual consent to desegregation. As he became socially more conservative, Bork shaded his views toward community norms rather than unrestricted privacy or free speech. At the same time he retained a libertarian perspective on market transactions (hence his fairly successful advocacy of consumer benefit as a guiding criterion in antitrust cases). When a person is an economic individualist and a social conservative in regard to different aspects of life, it is not easy for him to demonstrate logical rather than cultural consistency.

It is said that Bork harmed his own case at the hearings by not making his own appeal to the emotions of his audience, and there is a certain truth to this claim. Even when senators on his side set him up with "fat pitches," he steadfastly refused to hit home runs. When an Arlen Spector advocated no limits to free speech, for instance, Bork could have replied that a community like Skokie had the right to prevent Nazis and Klansmen, with firearms under their sheets, from proclaiming their murderous ways. No Ollie North, Bork passed up these invitations to score for the home team.

More than three decades before, watching on television, I mentally berated Joseph Welch, the attorney in the Army–McCarthy hearings, for not opposing Senator McCarthy's grossly inadequate knowledge of communism. Far wiser than I, Welch understood that this was not an intellectual debate but a contest for the sympathy of the American people. But Welch was not on trial; Bork was. Nor was Welch trying to live up to a self-image in which grace under pressure meant adhering to a strict personal code.

Sometimes, when Bork refused a helping hand, he did so to indicate that his argument did not need help. At other times his inner fastidiousness rebelled against being tempted to come up with a mawkish, heart-on-his-sleeve line. Even as an opposition senator blundered into accusing him of making too much money from outside fees when he was a professor at Yale (as if making money were immoral), Bork viscerally recoiled at bringing out that this was a time of heavy medical bills as his wife was dying of cancer. What, exactly, was he unwilling to tell the Senate? What the next justice to sit on the Supreme Court said.

At his confirmation hearings, Judge Anthony M. Kennedy was asked whether he practiced that vicious, depraved, and disgusting thing: doctrine. No, said Kennedy (wise to the ways of this new world), he would never have any principle so unprincipled as doctrine. Kennedy then proceeded to tell his interlocutors that he would decide each case on its merits. Imagine: a person who has spent a lifetime on the bench has to deny that he sees connections among cases!

Asked why he had until recently belonged to clubs that excluded women and minorities (no privacy there?), Kennedy replied, "Over the years I have tried to become more sensitive to the existence of subtle barriers to the advancement of women and minorities in society." The Judiciary Committee questionnaire included a query about the qualities a Supreme Court justice ought to have (something like being asked to write about your summer vacation): Kennedy began with "compassion, warmth, sensitivity, and an unyielding insistence on justice." Here you have it: Bork would neither repeat back the egalitarian code words—compassion, sensitivity, let alone the "touchy-feely" warmth—nor would he keep repeating the word on which he had spent his life and to which his record as a man and a lawyer and judge spoke. If, by the time a judge was nominated for the Supreme Court, he still had to proffer his belief in justice, something was wrong. If public sentimentality was in, Bork was evidently out.

In addition to confronting multiple audiences—senators, legal colleagues, the general public, and himself—Bork was hurt by conflicting advice. Stick to principle; no, it won't hurt to bend a little. Show up the senators' ignorance of constitutional law; no, stroke them a little. It's hard to be a happy warrior when you're not happy with yourself. To show that he was fighting back, for instance, Bork presented Supreme Court briefs in which he participated as solicitor general supporting the rights of minorities and women. No doubt this was supposed to rebut charges of racism and sexism. By the very act of countering such charges, however, Bork gave them legitimacy. If it wasn't proper to look at results by race and gender rather than at relevant constitutional provisions, why were the Bork forces doing it?

Possibly, Bork might have asked himself why he had to shoot off his mouth (I use the locution of one doubting his own judgment) on cases like *Griswold v. Connecticut,* in which the constitutional right to privacy was created. Who asked me—he might have muttered to himself—to speak and write about an idiotic law forbidding the sale of contraceptives, which would have collapsed amid either laughter or horror the first time it was enforced? *Griswold* was a good case, though, to make the larger point that it was not a judge's business to prevent governmental idiocy unless he had a warrant in a constitutional provision. Had Bork refrained from expressing himself when he had no duty to do so, he might well be on the Court today; still, though he might have been richer in title (as such things are counted in this world), the nation would have been poorer.

Nonetheless, constitutional discussion has been noticeably cooler since the Bork example: If you want to be a judge when you're older, don't talk so much when you're younger. A chill has come over the process of discussion through which ideas are encouraged, deliberated, winnowed, and otherwise treated to the free-for-all hurly-burly of public airing. It is not only Bork but all we political groupies, including his adversaries like Pertschuk, who will be disqualified because we are so foolish as to voice our ideas in public. It is sad to see members of the political stratum use their commitment to participation to deny the inevitable concomitants of that activity: ideas that other people do not like, or ideas that on more mature consideration or the accumulation of more evidence do not appear as attractive as they once did.

Whose Ideology?

"Our most divisive political battles," Bork declares, "reflect the war in our culture about what should be the evolving morality of our tradition." Whatever that morality might be in the United States, it always comes out as a dispute over different visions of equality—whether this be equality before the law, equality of opportunity, or equality of condition.

We all revere the Constitution, because we read it differently. Thus not only does the Constitution reach out to us, but we reach into it, maintaining or altering the original understandings to support our preferred vision of equality. Believing as we all do that the Constitution supports our values, we come to believe that they must have been there all along.

Judge Bork was accused of favoring inegalitarian outcomes. This accusation was both true and false. Bork did not take sides; it would be repugnant to him to favor the wealthy or wellborn. Yet it is true that Bork was prepared to *accept* inegalitarian outcomes. Accepting the desirability of competition and therefore the unequal outcomes that often accompany competition, Bork was evidently not shocked or scandalized by inequality. His conscience might be more tender toward those whose exceptional talents were thwarted by regulation and redistribution than by those who wanted more than their meager talents could justify. Worse (from his adversaries' standpoint), he believed that people of talent could rise even if they initially had to enter competition with far fewer resources than those already well-established. Bork's crime was not only that he believed in the values that had once made America exceptional, but that he also built a doctrine of constitutional interpretation around them.

What we learn from the Bork nomination is that we can no longer count on common values among contending politicians to soften political disputes. Our inability to derive joy from the triumph of democratic capitalism abroad is explained by the rise of ideological warfare over equality at home.

12

Groucho's Law,
Or If Anything Americans Can
Accomplish Isn't Worth Doing, Why
Bother Trying to Remedy Problems of
Race or Poverty or Aging or . . .

When pollsters ask Americans how they are doing, they get largely favorable responses. But when they ask about how the United States is doing, people's answers turn negative. Individuals are the best experts on their own feelings. But for a sense of society's well-being, most of us must rely on discussion in the public sphere. And today anyone who listens, looks, and reads is left in little doubt that things are getting worse.

Those who believe that current prosperity and liberty cannot last forever have history on their side. But this does not explain either the widespread unwillingness to celebrate our accomplishments or the grim foreboding about the future that are staples of everyday public discourse.

So many good things have happened—some of them even due to our own efforts—that it raises the obvious question: Why is there so much unrelieved doomsaying? Certainly, serious difficulties exist: crime, drug addiction, persistent poverty, incomplete access to medical care,

This chapter appeared as an article under the title of "Dispelling America's Gloom: Why Bother?" in *The American Enterprise* (March/April 1990), pp. 26–31.

AIDS, and more. But why not grapple with these problems? One answer may be that if the United States is uncompetitive, foolishly living beyond its means, its people incapable, its politicians corrupt, why bother? The unasked question is this: If Americans cannot stand prosperity, if we cannot stand progress, why should we try to alleviate suffering, reduce poverty, or eliminate drug addiction? To the reported decline in our mathematical competence should be added the inability of Americans to count their blessings.

Containment (Remarkably) Contains

Another look at America's accomplishments is in order. One success has been the policy of containment. Severe internal weaknesses in the Soviet system are growing more obvious every day. Whether *glasnost* and *perestroika* are a response to containment or not, they are a direct challenge to the Stalinism that once confronted us. Yet who, as recently as a decade ago, would have predicted that while the U.S. president was praising capitalism, the first secretary of the Soviet Communist party would be criticizing socialism?

Along the way, there have been doubts and errors: How could we know change for the better would ever take place? Would containment merely reinforce hostile behavior on the other side? Where containment required military force, public opinion gradually turned against it (in Korea) or became positively hostile (in Vietnam). The less successful aspects of containment can now be viewed in perspective; errors are a necessary part of a series of trials that as a whole have left democracy triumphant at what seems, in retrospect, a small cost.

Events have shown, moreover, that the great Tocqueville was wrong about at least one thing: It is not dictatorships but democracies that are best able to conduct foreign policy over long periods of time. Let us just say that the Soviets outblundered us.

Capitalism Works Sometimes, Socialism Never

Connected to the defense of democracy is the peaceful victory of capitalism over socialism. To be fair, the evidence does not show that capitalist economies always succeed. But it does demonstrate—without a single exception—that, if socialism is defined traditionally as nationalization of private property combined with a centrally controlled, nonmarket economy, no such nation has maintained economic growth. When Fredrich von Hayek debated the Polish economist Oscar Lange at the end of the 1930s and early 1940s on the effects of socialism, Hayek maintained an extreme position: No socialist economy could grow because its antimarket principle was flawed. Yet history has vindicated his view of capitalism as the only engine of economic growth. When Hayek made his arguments, the laboratory of the world had not set up a host of natural experiments. Why should the North Koreans who live under communism have such a poor economy compared to the far more capitalist (and rapidly richer) South Koreans? Why do the Vietnamese—who fought so well against the United States, whose people are as smart and tough as Americans (or maybe smarter and tougher)—bemoan their inability to maintain a minimally satisfactory economy? Why did Poland lose a fifth of its GNP in two decades, and why has Eastern Europe and the Soviet Union stagnated or declined when no capitalist country has suffered anything worse than a temporary downturn? Why have health rates in the Soviet Union and parts of Eastern Europe gotten worse when every Western nation has evidenced continuous improvement? As people in those countries are discovering, there is not much point in stressing more equal distribution when it is poverty and sickness that are being shared out.

Evidence in favor of the comparative competence of the major institutions of the West—capitalism and democracy—abounds. How does one guarantee that a people will choose democracy and capitalism? We have seen it before our very eyes. Just inoculate them with a quarter-century of Polish socialism.

It is rare to have historic validation of basic regime values in one's own time. Peoples who practice democratic capitalism should be proud. Why aren't we?

The Bad News Is in Us, Not in Events

For one thing, we feel overwhelmed by problems. We worry that the United States is losing its preeminent power position in the world. Why should we worry about this? I, for one, am relieved. The United States doesn't want an empire, and we have not succumbed to the worst forms of superpowerism. There is, thank goodness, no Pax Americana. Who wants the United States to lord it over others? As long as the United States keeps growing moderately so that our living standards rise, why should we object to the Brazilians and the Koreans improving their lot even more dramatically? More power to them is the only sensible (as well as humane) response.

Wait a minute. Reports of American decline are exaggerated. Our economy is by far the largest in the world. This means we have a large say in international economic arrangements. Our military force and our capabilities are still the greatest. With an economy four times larger than in 1950, our defense capability is greater than ever. Meanwhile our main military rival—the Soviet Union—is in a state of disintegration. More important, the American regime values of democracy and capitalism are on the ascendant.

Economic growth is bound to increase the political power of other democracies. At the same time, Soviet–American arms negotiations reduce the influence of the two superpowers. Splendid. Let our allies do more and have more say. If a greater chance of conventional war is a price that has to be paid for reducing the probability of nuclear war among the large nations, it is a price well worth paying.

We worry too that the United States is losing its competitive edge. True, international competition opens up the possibility of loss and the necessity of change, and this may be cause for concern. But the results so far are pretty good. While American manufacturing has not grown, neither has it diminished much, and there continues to be considerable restructuring to meet new conditions. Is the glass of competitiveness, then, half empty or half full?

The pessimistic evaluation lies in us, not in external circumstances. It is not true that productivity has become negative in the United States. It slowed, but it has picked up recently. Over the past two decades, the United States has produced far more jobs proportionately than Japan, Scandinavia, or Europe; but instead of giving credit for this door to opportunity, people complain about "dead-end" jobs (as though work were bad for people) or complain about the burdens that two-earner families bear (as though women were not breaking down doors to be admitted to the world of work). If consumption is down, fear of depression rises; if consumption is up and saving is down, we hear about profligate behavior. Foreigners are buying more stakes in America than they used to, yet is it not better to live in a country in which people want to invest rather than one in which there is capital flight? Our economy has been getting a bum rap.

In the past year, major reports have rejected or cast grave doubts on essential aspects of the charges made that grave damage is being done to the physical environment and human health. From the beginning of these charges in the 1960s, it was known but not noticed that accident rates were going down while life expectancy continued to climb. Now we know that the scare over asbestos in the classroom, home, and office is entirely false. The risk is zero. Yet the relevant facts were known long ago. Green-purple asbestos is deadly; fortunately we have little here. Brown asbestos is best avoided; only a little is exposed. The vast bulk of asbestos in homes, schools, and offices is white. Unless white asbestos is absorbed in huge amounts, coupled with heavy smoking, it does not produce injury. After all, asbestos is a naturally occurring mineral; all of us ingest something like a million fibers a year without injury.[1]

Rain is naturally acidic. Coal and other exhaust emissions have made it more so. Now the National Acid Precipitation Assessment Program (NAPAP) report shows that, while not benign, acid rain does little or no damage to forests and only a small amount to lakes.[2] A special committee of scientists set up to review evidence of harm to American veterans from a defoliant called Agent Orange has found none. Sailors on ships offshore had higher rates of the diseases supposed to be caused by Agent Orange than did soldiers exposed to its use on land.[3]

Finally, a group of scientists at the 1990 meetings of the American Association for the Advancement of Science, led by toxicologist Robert Scheuplein of the Food and Drug Administration Center for Food Safety, sought to bring attention to the vast implications of the fact that "ordinary food contains an abundance of carcinogenic initiators that in totality appear to dwarf all synthetic sources." This means that human health is exceedingly unlikely to be affected by food additives or pesticide residues unless ingested in improbably huge amounts. Ellen Robinson-Haynes reported the reaction to Scheuplein's announcement: "While his audience was filled with experts on nutrition and disease, neither he nor the other speakers received any scientifically based opposition to their revolutionary stand."[4] These facts support biochemist Bruce Ames's claim that the amount of carcinogenic material in ordinary food per day by weight and potency is ten thousand times plus (yes, 10,000X+) greater than synthetic agents from industry entering the food chain.[5] These findings signify that alarm over this or that additive or pesticide is likely to be misplaced.

So, too, with our record on the environment. The environment is going to hell, we are told. In part, this allegation is false: Not only are people in the Western industrial democracies the richest and the healthiest in history, but the physical environments in which they live today are also the most benign.

Won't global warming—the "greenhouse effect"—get us for our sins? Leaving aside the possibility that the Earth or parts thereof may actually be getting colder, let us imagine that global warming is occurring. What would be the negative consequences? Among the foremost might be food shortages. Advances in biotechnology are capable of more than making up for such losses. Burning fossil fuel is said to be a major contributor to global warming. An alternative fuel— nuclear power—produces no carbon dioxide, the main (though not the only) active agent presumed to be operative. Good news amid the gloom? It could be, if the benefits of a particular technology were allowed to offset its detriments. But so far that has not been the case. When the same sort of people who want the nation to undertake drastic measures to alleviate the effects of global warming simultaneously reject the best alternatives, they are in essence causing—not merely predicting—catastrophe.

But then, catastrophe or crisis is what preoccupies us. Johnny can't read, Jane doesn't want to add, television is stultifying their minds, crack is destroying their bodies, and the family is going to pot. It is normal to have problems; what is abnormal is to feel overwhelmed by them, especially when the situation calls at least for a guarded optimism.

My favorite bit of bad-mouthing the American economy comes from the Washington *Post*'s January 21, 1990, "Economic Outlook for the 1990s." I will just list the headlines:

"IS IT ALL DOWNHILL FROM HERE? THE CASE OF THE
   MISSING PRODUCTIVITY" (p. H1)
"POLITICS OF PARALYSIS" (p. H4)
"FISCAL POLICIES LACK BOLDNESS" (p. H5)
"JAPAN, THE SEEMINGLY UNSTOPPABLE GIANT"
"SERIOUS SLUMP . . ." (p. H10)
"LABOR SHORTAGES" (p. H10)
"CHRONIC LABOR SHORTAGES" (p. H13)
"PRODUCTIVITY: GAINS REMAIN ELUSIVE" (p. H16)
"SHORT TERM TACTICS CAUSE ALARM" (p. H17)
"BRACING FOR AN INVESTOR BACKLASH" (p. H18)

Were it possible to talk the economy down, it would have disappeared below ground level long ago.

There is a certain disingenuousness to the largely true claim that many Americans are feeling bad about the future of their country when this claim is made by people who are observing the consequences of their own actions. The Sunday, July 8, 1990, San Francisco *Examiner* tells the whole story in miniature. For purposes of comparison, let us look at what kind of reports would make people feel good. For that we have to turn to the business section where we read Alexander Malchick, who migrated from Leningrad to Big Fork, Montana, in 1973, and now uses the knowledge gained in acquiring his master's degree in electronics to interpret technology between Soviets and Americans. Malchick recalls the hard times he experienced when he first came to this country; but his belief that America would afford him a chance has been fortified not only by his own experience, but by the fact that his daughter now attends Princeton University.[6] Other than this high note, however, in the Sunday paper, it's all downhill, especially in the first section. There, on page one, we read a story headlined "AMERICA'S CRISIS OF SPIRIT." Based on a variety of surveys, the story reports "a lack of confidence in the future, and in one another among Americans." "Large segments of the nation," the front page continues, "have lost the will to excel."

Now, in all innocence, why might Americans be losing faith in the future or in each other or in their will to excel? On page A-17, Christopher Matthews, the *Examiner*'s bureau chief in Washington, D.C., writes that "we're selling off our land to meet current expenses," that we have "created a class of overseas creditors with an appetite for priceless European art and prime North American land," that both Germany and Japan spent half again as much as the United States on domestic research and development, and that—to top it all off—"while we deploy the MX missile on Amtrak, the Japanese have gotten comfortable with high-speed 'bullet trains.' " Why be gloomy? "The good news," Matthews concludes, "is that the Third World War is being fought economically; the bad news is we're losing."[7]

The same information could be put in rather different form. The United States has spent a great deal of money running one of history's most successful foreign policies; peace is worth a lot. The fact that the two nations the United States defeated in World War II are now coming up economically is one of the greatest triumphs imaginable—compared, say, to the immense destructiveness of a defeated and angry Germany after World War I. That past successes often lead to future problems is well known; that it would be better to have had past failures is extremely doubtful. That there is a zero-sum relationship between the United States on one side and Germany on the other—so that more for them means less for us—is nonsense. The greatest trade occurs between those who have the strongest economies.

On the same page an *Examiner* columnist, Stephanie Salter, knows how to warm our hearts:

> Over the past five years the complexity of homelessness, its refusal to respond to our haphazard and shortsighted "cures," has transformed liberals into neofascists and Christians into people who have forgotten one of Jesus's main points: how you treat "the least of my brethren" is how you treat Christ.[8]

The column is full of angst and accusation.

Another part of the scene is painted by columnist Rob Morse:

> This may seem just another bit of San Francisco lunacy. A white guy and an Asian buy a gay bar and are called racist by a white employee, whereupon out-of-town gays at a gay activists' school try to shut down the bar (chanting, "Sweater faggots!" at the bar's young professional clientele) while the cops look on, concerned not to violate gay's rights. It's a freaking joke.[9]

But who is the joke on? As Morse says, "The worst thing you can call someone in San Francisco is a 'racist.' You have no appeal to the Supreme Court, no way to cop a plea, no night school course in correct attitudes. Somebody sticks you with the label 'racist,' and you are pronounced guilty with no chance of being proved innocent." Here we have a clue to the decline in national morale. Those who hold up greater equality of condition as a norm and find that the country is not quite there yet are feeling bad. Those who feel differences are appropriate are disappointed because these differences are being derided. Not too many appear to be satisfied just where they are now.

Sociologist David Reisman of Harvard and linguistic professor Noam Chomsky of MIT separately report similar findings that working people even in the depth of the Depression of the 1930s were more optimistic about the future of their country than they are today. But there is considerable difference in their explanations. Today, Reisman says, we are constantly reminded of everything that is amiss and problematic, and it is harder to have hope for the future. Chomsky has his sights set elsewhere, however: He thinks there may have been services for youth available in the Depression that are not available today. And he

suspects, possibly rightly, that slums are worse today. But actually
Chomsky does not have to look so far away to find another cause: If
Chomsky read Chomsky about America, would he have hope for its
future?

Accentuating the negative is not confined to California, then. Who
has failed to hear how badly schooled are the young people in the
United States? The basis for this endlessly repeated complaint was a
report by the New York Telephone Company that 84 percent of the
applicants for jobs it advertised had failed its math and literacy tests.
No one noticed then that the jobs were at the lowest level of pay with
no benefits. "When the American Telephone and Telegraph Company," the New York *Times* reported, "gives a similar test to applicants for full-time clerical or operator jobs, positions that include
health and pension benefits, the rate of passing is much higher."
AT&T's director of employee testing came up with a not-too-surprising
conclusion: "It has been our experience that when you offer a temporary job, it gets a lesser quality person." Moreover, when the number
of applicants is very large, the company intentionally fails more than
half so that it will end up with the best—that is, those who score above
average.[10] What this tells us is that there is a mechanism at work
selecting out the worst possible slant even when it is implausible on
face value.

Inequality Did It

The key to understanding the gloom may lie in the way problems have
been redefined to suggest society should be reproached for every ill.
Self-reproach suggests self-blame. For what? Blame is a relative concept. It takes on meaning only in regard to a norm from which one has
deviated. Of what violation, then, are the American people guilty?

The Catholic bishops, in their pastoral letter on the economy, define
poverty not in their church's traditional way—that is, in terms of
having insufficient economic resources—but in the new way of relative
deprivation, or having less than others. The Reverend Jesse Jackson,
without challenge so far as I know, speaks often of "economic violence," as though having a low income were equivalent to being put
down by physical force. Then-Mayor Ed Koch of New York City was
excoriated for ordering a mentally troubled woman taken off the street,
while Hollywood stars think it right to portray such street people as
individualists unfairly stigmatized for choosing to live differently from

others. Other examples abound. What they all have in common is the premise that inequality is evil. The pictures of the homeless, the right to redress economic grievances by force (or why else speak of economic violence?), the defining of poverty as inequality, all suggest that there is something terribly wrong with having more money or power or health than others. Once equality of condition is established as the guiding norm, no apparent accomplishment—such as making almost everyone better off—counts for much, since the distance between people is not narrowed.

To redress inequalities, an ever-larger and ever-stronger central authority is required. When such strong leadership does not appear, gloom and doom issue forth. Should strong leadership actually manifest itself, however, it would immediately be suspect as domineering. From the "wimp" to the "imperial" presidency is but a short distance.

Every time I look at how the figures purporting to show the United States at an economic disadvantage are calculated, they are biased against us. Is the United States sending more abroad in payments than it is receiving? Try valuing U.S. gold not at the present market price of $350 an ounce, but at the old official price of $35. Or value the foreign holdings that Americans acquired in the 1950s and 1960s and that those foreigners acquired here in the 1970s and 1980s at purchase price, thus selling the United States short by some $200 billion. Want to compare U.S. and Japanese investment? Try calling American spending on roads "ordinary outlays," while the Japanese call the spending "investment." Or say the United States is becoming a service economy— as if it were a disease—without noting that the Germans and the Japanese are moving even faster in the same direction. The mechanisms of deception differ, but the results are the same: The United States is made to look worse.

The prevailing sense of dread about American society is a result not of past failures or of insuperable future challenges, but of adopting a self-defeating standard. Equality of condition is the perfect reproach because it is always lacking in some respect. Americans may not succeed but, if they do, things are set up so they won't be able to enjoy it.

Groucho's Law

It is difficult to enjoy the fabled American trip from rags to riches when other people are busy making sure that your riches will turn back into rags. This is a reverse Cinderella syndrome of sorts. It is a product of generalizing from Groucho's Law: Anything Americans can achieve isn't worth accomplishing. Like all great magic, it is done in broad daylight so nobody notices. The trick is to create contradiction—the achievement and its negation—at the same time but in different places, or at the same place but at different times.

The historical method involves collective amnesia; it will work if everyone agrees to forget. Years ago, for instance—so far back it affected another generation—there were protests against the building of airports and highways. These terrible things seemed to involve rip-offs by rich developers against poor citizens, whose eardrums and communities, so it seemed, were being equally outraged. Soon enough, without our quite realizing it, airport and highway construction slowed. Now the complaint—often uttered by the protester of an earlier era— is that the skies are so crowded it is dangerous to fly. Here is the paradigmatic case of achievement (a mass flying public) turning into failure (overcrowded skies and underprotected passengers).

Perverse behavior is being honed into a fine art. Are you worried about the trade gap? Then refuse to drill for oil, which makes up about a third of that gap. With one hand, rent control is justified as an aid to poor people while, with the other, it is blamed for reducing the supply of housing. The same stars who brought us deinstitutionalization of the mentally ill now complain the most about the homeless.

Our Perverted Priorities

The United States must be the only place in the world that suffers simultaneously from a Social Security and a health-care crises, since people cannot be living longer and shorter at the same time. Gresham's Law has a variant in the worrywart United States: Smaller dangers drive larger ones out of our consciousness. The worry syndrome prevents us from setting priorities; because so many things are crises, without whose resolution it is alleged this nation cannot endure, everything must be done or nothing is worth doing.

The deficit provides another good example of a pseudocrisis. Every effort to correlate the size of the deficit with bad things, such as unemployment and inflation, has failed. By blowing up a modest problem into an insuperably difficult one, the entire public policy process is stymied. Causing a depression to prevent one—the usual proposal of the public-spirited is to raise taxes and cut expenditures substantially—is not promising. Taking Social Security out of the deficit calculations would require huge increases in taxes and cuts in welfare spending. And that is happening now. It is also foolish, for it assumes that high Social Security taxes play no part in people's willingness to pay other taxes. Why should this nation fight basic battles about taxes and spending when the likelihood is that the results—except for mutual exhaustion and exasperation—will be much the same as they are now? Instant budget balance and massive measures to avoid presumed global warming present the unusual spectacle of fanatical measures proposed by moderates. (A fanatic is one who proposes extreme remedies for distant problems that may not materialize.) The worst consequence of such counterproductive demands is that they forestall efforts to deal with social problems.

How can poverty be alleviated by disparaging the American economy? How can children be made strong by scaring them with tales about the grape monster and the applesauce witch? Where will the human and spiritual resources come from to overcome the racial anger that threatens our internal peace if Middle America, whose residents are among the richest, healthiest, and best-educated people who ever lived, is caricatured as sick, poor, and incompetent and, worse still, racist?

The extent and blatancy of system blame in the major media are extraordinary. Evidence comes from a report published by the Center for Media and Public Affairs in Washington, D.C., which studied 318 stories about race relations (204 broadcast on NBC, CBS, and ABC nighttime news, and 114 printed in *Newsweek, U.S. News and World Report,* and *Time*) run during 1989. Under the heading of "institutional bias," charges of racial discrimination outnumbered denials eight to one (89% to 11%). Charges against business amounted to 91 percent with 9 percent denial. Not only government but sports and religion were condemned. For example, the Reverend George Stallings was quoted as saying (without a counter), "The Catholic Church is a white racist institution." Are the American political and economic systems fair to all, or are they discriminatory? Ninety-two percent of those who addressed this question in the media spoke for institutional bias. (See Figure 12.1. A typical media statement justifying these findings is the following: "African Americans . . . have all been victims of an intellectual and cultural oppression that has characterized the culture and institutions of the United States . . . for centuries."[11]

Consider the question of drug abuse. It is spreading throughout the nation, at its worst in inner-city neighborhoods. In a manner of

Figure 12.1   Are Institutions Biased?

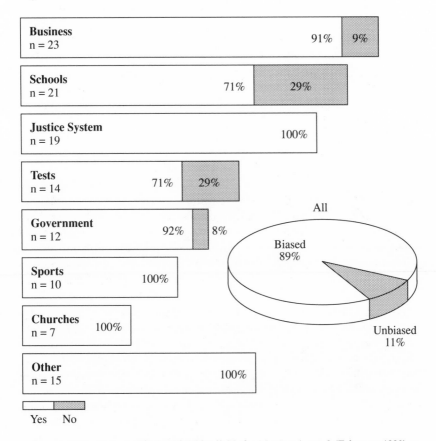

Source: "The News in Black and White," *Media Monitor* 4, no. 2 (February 1990), p.
5. (Published by the Center for Media and Public Affairs, Washington, D.C.)

speaking, two solutions have proven efficacious in the past: criminalization and legalization. Criminalization requires extreme force—essentially, executing pushers and users. This makes society healthier, but
(as Prohibition showed) government becomes sicker. Legalization
makes government healthier (far fewer crimes it cannot solve, fewer
bribes, and so forth), but society gets sicker as there are more addicts.
Legalization is not now acceptable to white or black America. Criminalization cannot work for the understandable reason that Americans
do not wish to give up life, liberty, and the pursuit of happiness. What

is left? Moral suasion. If our collective consciences are to provide guidance, with the individual accepting the norms of society, however, there must not only be a conscience but a collective authority whose norms are worth making one's own. Yet the messages are mixed: Don't use drugs, but the society and its public authorities are vicious and/or stupid, thus not worth obeying. Appeals to refuse drugs are less effective because those who ask us to just say no won't legitimize our collective authority—American Society—which is the only source from which individual consciences strong enough to deter danger as drugs can come.

In Whose Interest?

During the past 20 years, the United States has effectively doubled its gross national product. The numbers of educated citizens, from high school through graduate school, have vastly increased; our science and communications are superior by far to what they were, and our people are considerably healthier. As a whole, we are clearly more capable than we were. But one would never guess that from public commentary.

What do those who claim to speak for the poor hope to gain by impugning the capacities of government while at the same time urging new responsibilities upon it? What is their interest in purporting to show that the nation cannot afford to alleviate the difficulties of the poor? Is this, then, their idea of grand coalition? One side brings the blood and sweat of a confrontation, and the other side provides the tears of self-destruction? Convinced it is not doing well and will soon be doing worse, why should Middle America spend resources it doesn't have on people it is incompetent to assist, about whom it is not justified in levying demands for moral action? If Americans come to believe that any goal they can attain is not worth achieving, why should they try?

The essential purpose of this doomsaying in the media and the public realm generally is not to build a much stronger central authority, but to build political support for reducing inequalities. The decline in support for homeless people suggests, however, that such critics are much more likely to achieve what they don't than what they do want. Who will benefit from an America no one wants?

13

If Inequality Is an Abomination in the Sight of God, Why Should There Be Bishops or a Pope?

The centerpiece of the draft pastoral letter written by the U.S. Roman Catholic bishops on "Catholic Social Teaching and the U.S. Economy" is "the preferential option for the poor." On this moral vision it stands or falls.

Although at times the pastoral letter speaks of the preferential option as if it referred to minimum conditions of material life, for the most part—given the repeated references to powerlessness and marginalization, as well as the explicit condemnation of the existing distribution of income as unjust—poverty is equated with inequality of resources in general, not just income in particular. Hence a preferential option is one in which choices are made in favor of poor people by reducing income differentials in society.

If the most important moral merit of the nonpoor is to reduce their disparities with the poor, a double dehumanization takes place: The nonpoor are made into means for the ends of others, and the poor are converted from subjects into objects whose merit consists in how others treat them.

These remarks were occasioned by Bishop John S. Cummin's invitation to comment on the first draft of the pastoral letter on the American economy. Bishop Cummin is the ordinary of the Diocese of Oakland, California. I have added a number of paragraphs from a lecture at Loyola University in Chicago on March 14, 1985. Published under the title "Idolatry and 'the Poor,' " *Catholicism in Crisis* 3(1985), pp. 42–44.

227

Homogenizing the poor dehumanizes them. They are no more alike than are the rich or people of middle income. By depriving the poor of will—they are helpless, therefore others must act on them—irresponsibility is added to their other ills. Refusing to inquire into why individuals are poor on the grounds that comparisons are odious not only renders poor people faceless, but also deprives them of virtue. May they not have been improvident, as well as hard done by, mentally ill, as well as badly treated? Getting out of poverty can hardly deserve praise if there is nothing a poor person can do about it.

Collectivizing sin undermines the moral relationship between individual human beings. For if it is evil institutions—not good human nature—that brings bad into the world, the emphasis shifts from individual sin to oppressive (read "inegalitarian") forces. I had thought the church as an institution was necessary to help individuals improve their behavior. Do you suppose that, if people believe all hierarchical organizations are oppressive (because hierarchies institutionalize inequality), they will add a saving clause exempting the Catholic church (and its bishops) from these strictures? Authority is also a form of inequality, is it not?

The Preferential Option Implies Schism

The poor are not only homogenized, but politicized. In the draft pastoral letter, their lack is not only or primarily material resources, but political power. This explains the joining of "poverty and powerlessness," or "vulnerable and needy," or "defenseless and poor," as if the terms were equivalent. The salvation of the economically poor evidently lies in reducing disparities of power—that is, in using political power to wrest resources from others. If the main cause of poverty is institutional oppression—the doctrine that existing institutions kill quietly by maintaining and enlarging power differentials—the only remedy is to take it away. I hardly need add the usual phrase for justifying violence—"by any means necessary."

Since the preferential option is justified as virtue itself, it is only right to consider the implications (and early church history would be a good guide) of organizing life on the basis of equality of condition. How do groups behave who organize their lives according to purely voluntary principles with equality of condition as their sole value?

"Sects breed schism"—so H. Richard Niebuhr taught. Unwilling to accept institutional authority, egalitarian groups have only one way of solving differences of opinion: expulsions and splits. Fearing disintegration, they accuse established authority of bringing the world to destruction. While seeking state power to redistribute resources, they simultaneously reject it as unworthy. They denigrate economic growth as a source of hated distinction while urging redistribution of existing resources. Their vision of the world as divided between the nice egalitarian "us" and the nasty, predatory "them" justifies their unwillingness to compromise. The recent rise of egalitarian sects in the United States has been accompanied by the decline of every large-scale, hierarchical organization that attempts to go beyond single issues—the big churches, the political parties, the unions, the federal government. Why do the Catholic bishops advocate as a general principle for society a mode of organization that would make it impossible to govern any society (or, for that matter, church) of size or social complexity?

Institutions shape character; they are not only means but ends in that they embody values. The Catholic church is a hierarchical institution. (I grew up in Brooklyn near St. Jerome's, where the local Irish used to refer to their church as "the hierarchy.") As such, it is committed to the view, hammered out through centuries of conflict, that mankind requires institutional constraints to become better. To hold otherwise is to commit the heresy of believing that each individual has immediate access to God and is in need of no instruction by mediating institutions like the church.

I had hoped that the Catholic church would reassert and reinterpret its traditional values. These would, of course, include the sacrificial ethic of the hierarchy in which the parts are enjoined to sacrifice for the whole and the collective takes care of its weaker members. Instead, to my dismay, I see an effort to create another single-issue sect under the rubric of "the preferential option for the poor."

And that—church or sect—is *the* issue. It is not only that this unidirectional option will undermine the church (indeed denying the authority of any large-scale, integrative organization) for that is of concern mostly to its members, but that this preference will make the United States more difficult to govern.

Democracy is based on agreement to do what is agreed; thus there is ample room for disagreement. So long as proper procedures are observed, policy disagreements are tolerable. If Americans have to agree on egalitarian policies before they can accept governmental decisions as legitimate, however, how can democracy—based on consent among people who differ—be sustained?

On what grounds could equality of condition have first priority? Were there cumulative inequalities—so the rich got richer and the poor poorer—both political democracy and economic opportunity would be threatened. But this is not so. There is a lot of downward and upward mobility. A substantial proportion of the economically poor, as well as the politically influential, turn over with the passage of time. More than one resource—numbers, activity, knowledge, formal position, shared values, votes—is important in determining government decisions. The vast number of new businesses as well as the high rate of failure testify to the continued vitality of economic opportunity. Money is no more the root of all evil than its lack is the source of all that is good.

By viewing individuals as if they were isolated beings—apart from family, friends, neighborhood, church, fraternal organization, union, or political party—the egalitarian program makes them poorer than lack of financial resources ever could. It is impossible to imagine how the poor can do anything, from learning language to exercising citizenship, if they are all alone in the world except for their predators. Were this unmediated view of the world accepted, everyone would end as poor as where they began. It is one thing to complain forever about the lack of long-term horizons among some poor people, and another to specify the social structures that would imbed the principle of sacrificing in the present to improve the future. It is group experiences that inculcate such rules, rather than reliance on remonstration. Where family and church show that one generation can help another, and that different members play different roles—all valuable—the sense of a division of labor and of a time span of social support is taught better than in any text. And what better teacher of the virtues of institutional support than the Catholic church?

After a long period of struggle and—as I recall—not a little denigration (not least from Catholic smart Alecs and Alices), the virtues of Catholic schooling are becoming more widely accepted. And, as good fortune backed by centuries of experience would have it, none appreciate these virtues so much, or make such excellent use of its opportunities, as the economically poor. For, in Catholic schools, critical thought is taught against a background of respect for authority. Homework and homely discipline reinforce the notion that the school authorities care enough to make and enforce demands. Self-worth and self-discipline—even, dare I say it, modesty and gratitude, the two virtues in shortest supply nowadays—are taught with seriousness and commitment. Alas, as in Sherlock Holmes's famous clue of the dog that didn't bark, none of this—not a word—appears in the draft pastoral letter. Nary a hint is to be found of the combination of hierarchy, tempered by competition, that has served the church so well. Instead, we get a warmed-over version of a radical egalitarianism that disbelieves in economic growth, that rejects institutions, and that would, in the end, leave everyone worse off. Though we might share misery equally, however, there would be no church left to console us—for its authority would also be delegitimized, being a barrier to equalization.

Why has the church abandoned its permanent historical truths in favor of today's political slogans? If it is poverty and not the church that is to be diminished, the church knows more than those it imitates. The sons and daughters of the Catholic church have risen from poverty. They know not only in theory but in practice what it takes. They can testify to the power of solidarity that is reinforced by networks of information sharers, built on a solid education, and resting on a rock of established authority. If this rock be abandoned, what place for the church or, for that matter, for the poor who—more than others—need institutions to protect them?

The Preferential Option Is Destructive

To the extent that there is a class of permanently poor, and especially that it is disproportionately black, that is a cause for concern. Maintaining minimal levels of income commands widespread agreement. What government should do and how it should do it, beyond that, so that economic poverty becomes only a transient status, is a matter of much dispute. I fail to see in the pastoral letter any doctrine of Catholic social thought brought to bear on the improvement of economic conditions that is not found in contemporary political tracts. Of what, then, does its special vision consist?

The bishops say that "the poor have a special claim on our concern because they are particularly vulnerable and needy." Is there merit in this position? Yes, providing only that "special claim" is not the only claim, and that "concern" does not translate into a demand that differences in wealth and income be dramatically reduced even if in the process the vast bulk of society, which is not permanently poor, is coerced. There is no moral claim to equality of condition. Inequality is also variety. The homogeneous society has no claim on our consciences. There is nothing wrong with disparities unless they are permanent and cumulative. So long as people are able to live decently and to try to better themselves, disparities are a source of innovation and opportunity, not of condemnation.

We see what has happened: The condition of the worst off is being used to drive society as a whole in the direction of equality of condition. This, I maintain, is morally undesirable.

Equality of condition is at odds with other commonly accepted and important meanings of that term. Virtually all Americans agree on the desirability of "equality" in general because they attribute quite different meanings to it in particular. Were it the dominant value, equality of condition would become incompatible with equality before the law. Equal rights must give way when some people are deemed more equal or more entitled than or preferred to, others. Equality of opportunity, so people can be different, is evidently at odds with equality of reward, so people can end up with the same. When only some players are allowed to score more than others, the game hardly gives each player an equivalent opportunity. If most people are oppressed, it becomes difficult to single out the most needy for special help. If the vast majority are deprived, this is an indictment of America, not a proposal to help the poor.

All the bishops meant to say, you may reply, was that more needs to be done to alleviate the plight of the economically poorest people. Then they should have said so. What "the preferential option for the poor" does do—aside from failing to alleviate economic poverty—is justify hostility toward existing institutions.

It is not the welfare state but the welfare of the state that is in crisis. Our institutions for providing welfare are in danger, not our ability to support poor people. The two terms that are used so often together that they have fused in our minds as a single expression—welfare state—have now been turned against each other. One side says that the state does not provide welfare, the other side that welfare undermines the state. The same rationale that is used to build up welfare programs—the desirability of greater equality of condition—is also used to undermine the institutions that provide welfare on the grounds that they, too, are insufficiently egalitarian. Charged as they are with protecting their church, it is blindness to the destructive institutional implications of their policy prescriptions that is the most striking aspect of the Catholic bishops' views on poverty.

14

The Rise of Radical Egalitarianism and the Fall of Academic Standards

The American doctrine of freedom of expression is undergoing a profound reexamination on several fronts, legal scholars say, prompted by troubling and diverse questions like whether universities should punish students for making racist remarks and whether communities may ban sexually explicit rap music.

Even at traditional bastions of free speech, like the universities and the American Civil Liberties Union, there are strong new efforts to rethink the meaning of the First Amendment, as part of an intense debate over curbing offensive speech on campuses. . . .

Mary Ellen Gale, a professor at the Whittier College of Law in California and former president of the Southern California affiliate of the A.C.L.U. who helped draft a resolution approving such restrictions, said women and minorities are a special case when it comes to speech.

"The ideal is that everybody should have a chance to speak and everybody should be listened to," she said. "But racism, for example, has proved intransigent and we live in a real world, not an idealized marketplace of ideas."

When someone is a target of racist speech on campus, she said, that person is silenced, frightened and no longer able to participate fully in university life. . . .

Speech delivered at a symposium on "The Transformation of Academic Culture, 1964–1988" for the National Association of Scholars, held in New York City on November 12, 1988. The separated paragraphs at the beginning and end have been added. The speech itself was published in *Academic Questions* 2, no. 4 (Fall 1989), pp. 52–55.

"The social climate is suddenly less tolerant to free expression across a wide range of issues," said Geoffrey Stone, dean of the University of Chicago Law School. "One theme in all of these cases is that we can adjust our concept of free speech, slice off a few tiny corners and leave the core intact. But that's the argument that's always been used to justify restricting speech. . . .

Some university officials, outraged by a resurgence of racist incidents, have adopted codes punishing such speech. Stanford University, after a year of angry debate, last month became the latest to forbid verbal, written or symbolic attacks against individuals "on the basis of their sex, race, color, handicap, religion, sexual orientation or national or ethnic origin." . . .

To some, like Nadine Strossen, a professor at New York Law School and general counsel for the A.C.L.U., the argument has produced a lamentable conflict between civil liberties and civil rights.

Ms. Strossen said the new debate about free speech has also produced odd allies. "Now we have minorities and feminists and the left allied with fundamentalists who believe some communitarian values take precedence," she said. "To them, group rights are more important than individual rights." . . .

The universities have also become the setting for a resurgence of efforts to restrict pornography, not as obscene, but because it degrades women and violates their civil rights. . . .

"If there is a bedrock principle underlying the First Amendment, it is that Government may not prohibit the expression of an idea simply because society finds the idea itself offensive or disagreeable," Justice William J. Brennan Jr. wrote this month in the opinion striking down a law outlawing desecration of the flag.

Neil A. Lewis, "Friends of Free Speech Now Consider Its Limits,"
New York *Times,* June 29, 1990, p. B10

The speech I gave to the first meeting of the National Association of Scholars, made up mostly of academics who are worried about the trends described in the above New York *Times* story, seeks to explain why questions once believed settled are being reopened by the very same sort of liberals and radicals who were once the most vociferous defenders of the right to voice unpopular thoughts. Why has discrimination, which had heretofore been negative, all of a sudden become positive? Why has speech, which had heretofore been defended as free—especially when uttered against established authority—suddenly become restricted when advocates of those they judge underprivileged consider it offensive? Why have college courses, where the ideal had long been dispassionate analysis, suddenly become the opposite when concerned with issues from minorities to gender to foreign policy? What did these issues and the people advocating them have in common? Why is rhetoric about equality accompanied by such phenomena as the inflation of academic grades and the effort to validate general propositions by personal experience? Were one to ask about the ideological transformation of political parties, or the politicization of science, or the proliferation of groups proclaiming their rights, or the perpetual search for "authenticity," my answer would be the same: the rise of radical egalitarianism.

Let's begin, as is appropriate, with a sense of wonder. No one I know, including myself, at the end of the 1950s and the beginning of the 1960s anticipated *anything* like what has occurred. The period of McCarthyism was over. The restraints exerted by traditional boards at universities were being reduced. Jews and others previously excluded or limited were, in fact, entering the academy in increasing numbers. The idea that the threat to the academy could come from *within* was unthought of. Clearly this is what has now happened but, in the reading I've done, I can find nothing that even remotely recognizes the fact. This suggests that as academics our first task is to try to understand why.

Do not be frightened of the E word; say it out loud. The movement that disturbs you, and that I'm going to describe, is radical egalitarianism. It is all radical egalitarianism, and is nothing but radical egalitarianism. There is nothing else to it. There is nothing underneath it! There is nothing on top of it! There is nothing crouching behind it! There is nothing to the left or right of it! This may appear to be a too simple thesis, but it is this thing and this thing alone that is happening.

By radical egalitarianism I mean not only an approach to the distribution of economic resources but, in a sociological sense, the idea of a culture or a way of life devoted to diminishing differences among people. Whose life, for example, has not been affected by feminism— the effort to reduce power differences between men and women—or the civil rights movement seeking to narrow the differences between black and white, or gay rights, or children's rights? Who could have imagined during the Eisenhower era that the government would one day intervene in the family in this way? Animal rights is one of the newest egalitarian movements, the idea being to make human pain and animal pain equivalent. The evidence is there. All you need to do is ask the animal rights people what else they believe about a variety of subjects and their egalitarianism spills out. In the long interviews with

activists that appear in Susan Sperling's *The Animal Liberators,* all
but one make a direct connection between animal suffering and human
inequality. Some environmentalism is unexceptional; everybody's concerned with clean air. But much of it is an effort to show that corporate
capitalism causes cancer, that when you have a disgusting and despi-
cable and vile and unconscionable system with its horrible and excru-
ciating inequalities—the kind that when you get up in the morning
makes you think of America and want to puke!—Mother Nature is
raped along with everybody else.

It's happening everywhere. In the state courts a massive and con-
certed attack is being mounted against private property. When you
listen to these judges (and I could quote from them at length), their
justification for taking people's property is not on the grounds of
anything in the Constitution, but on the grounds that it would lead to a
more egalitarian result or that it would somehow be good for the
environment.

The question in the job market is no longer quality of work, but
equality of job distribution, as you can see in the case of a hospital
administrator recently recounted in the New York *Times.* Accused of
not having enough blacks on the staff, what does this administrator
say? She doesn't say it is wrong to have quotas. She says, "We're
trying awfully hard, there's just not a big enough pool."

Let's go to a question many of us deal with in the classroom: the
question of American exceptionalism. What makes this country so
different, without socialism and as big a welfare state as elsewhere, or
class warfare, or a national university? The essence of exceptionalism
as originally conceived was the belief among the Jeffersonians, and
later the Jacksonians, that equal opportunity under American conditions could be made compatible with equal results, provided the central
government did not add artificial inequalities.

Jefferson's and Jackson's parties and the anti-federalists were coalitions of radical egalitarians and competitive individualists. They came
together against the distant hierarch, George III, and they justified
their alliance, which lasted until the Civil War, on the grounds that if
the central government was unable to avail itself of artificial means to
promote inequality—banks, charters, franchises, and debt—the competitive conditions of American life would offer enough equality of
opportunity to ensure sufficient equality of overall result and thus
preserve republican government.

Today, however, the alliance of radical egalitarians and competitive
individualists that provided the basis for American exceptionalism has

been severed. Now our radical egalitarians believe that you can achieve genuine equality of opportunity only with much greater equality of condition. Therefore they refuse to legitimate established procedures. As in the case of the hospital administrator, they want to make sure that enough "unequals" are being hired. That is their test of democracy—not whether appropriate procedures have been followed, or qualifications met, or agreements reached but whether the desired more equal result has been attained. In their view, democracy is not about gaining agreement, but about obtaining a substantive result. No longer is it possible to believe that democracy is viable in our country because we do not have to agree on substantive policies as long as we agree on procedures for legitimating decisions. For egalitarians believe that we must first achieve greater equalization of resources before the decisions made by government can be considered legitimate.

How did this change come about? Originally, even the proponents of egalitarianism believed in a weak state. They were happy if central government did not coerce them. The abolitionists made a big mistake in this regard. Instead of asking for something that could never be granted—like perfect safety, to take a contemporary instance—they asked for something that could be had—namely, the abolition of slavery—and thus brought about their own eventual demise. Even in the 1930s radical egalitarianism was weak, as you can see if you read the pronouncements about race made by top Democratic party officials of that era.

By the 1960s things began to change. The big change, of course, was the civil rights movement. Our system refused to recognize basic rights. The realities of both equality before the law and equal opportunity for black people were persistently denied. The leaders of that movement—thus ennobled by standing for equal opportunity and equality before the law—became the leaders of feminism, children's rights, gay rights, and other egalitarian movements. They fanned out everywhere, with very strong self-selection into the media. Soon enough, national defense became an egalitarian issue, because it allegedly took from welfare; and abortion (a woman's power against forced procreation) and prayer in schools (against hierarchical power) were seen to be mostly about the same thing. (One might add to this the way in which the Vietnam War was interpreted so as also to delegitimate authority.) In any event, into the media and the academy came substantial numbers of people who believed more and more in greater equality of condition.

Does that reflect Marxism? You mustn't think that our radical egalitarians are mostly Marxists, or that they could on one foot—or eight feet—begin to explain the mysteries of historical materialism. What they do like about Marxism, however, is its critique of our institutions as unconscionable, insupportable—that is, inegalitarian. They therefore set out, quite atheoretically, to reduce every kind of inequality they can find, instituting a kind of endless affirmative action in spending on schools, hiring, firing, you name it.

When you have only a small proportion of egalitarians around, they can perform helpful services. As critics of hierarchical institutions, they'll be quick to tell you how the emperor has no clothes, that the establishment is lying; and this has not a little truth to it. When their proportions expand, however, they may try to coerce others into egalitarian ways. If you read Pin Yathay's tragic account of the Cambodian Khmer Rouge revolution (*L'utopie meurtrière*), you will understand, for you will learn how a soldier in the name of equality can justify murdering ten-year-olds.

When you are committed to egalitarianism as a way of life, you have certain problems. One problem is that you believe that human nature is good but is corrupted by evil institutions. That sounds very academic, but what it means is that you cannot countenance internal conflict. How could there be disagreement among good people? Their answer is that some people only pretended to be egalitarian and hence good. Thus, egalitarians engage in accusations of witchcraft against unseen enemies, conjuring up, for example, images of people called capitalists poisoning our insides with what we eat and breathe, making our fingers fall off and our stomachs fall out. Another big problem for egalitarians is "splits." They split all the time, partly because they're passionate, partly because they're without authority, and partly because, having just one major value (equality of result), they are reluctant to compromise it. Because egalitarians are so single-value-minded, they are also instrumental in their thought and action: Whatever they believe increases equality of result is good, and whatever doesn't is bad. That is why they have turned on academic values. Seeing that conventional criteria of intellectual quality did not improve equality of result, they seek to provide it by guaranteed—that is, administrative—means.

There are also strengths that go with these weaknesses. Egalitarians believe that the only way one can legitimate a system is to participate in every decision. That leads to miracles of participation, involving coming early and staying late and everything in between.

If you have a problem with splits, what can you do? I call it the

Armageddon complex. You bring all the dangers of the future into the present, hold them over the people, and say the most terrible things will happen unless your views are accepted. If we are not freezing to death from nuclear winter, for instance, then the greenhouse effect is going to fry us to a crisp. The solution, of course, will be local, state, national, international, and intergalactic regulation to prevent these awful things from happening. Only a centralized authority can create and maintain greater equality of condition.

What are we academics to do? First and foremost we must strengthen our own standards. The criterion of truth has become undervalued. Whether the claim is economic decline, environmental catastrophe, or—in a change of direction—that everything is hunky-dory, the query "But is it true?" deserves to be heard more often. Scholars especially need to take responsibility for evaluating the truth claims of their field, lest the de facto standard become (or, alas, remain) "anything goes." All research and all findings and all arguments must not be considered to be created equal. For then we would lose our intellectual and moral justification for professing anything. Hence we ought to develop much stronger justifications as to why inequality of results, both in academic life and outside it, is desirable. Let me put it another way: if equality of condition is the norm, then why shouldn't ideas or moral rules be equivalent? Any criterion of choice other than judgments of intellectual quality is bound to corrode educational values. What else should a university be about than intellectual excellence?

Faced with this massive onslaught of egalitarianism, in the society as well as the academy, the appropriate role for scholars is opposition. By that I mean *you must say it is wrong*. It's not that you can't do it; it's that you *ought not* to do it. It is fundamentally wrong to have quotas. Positive discrimination is fundamentally wrong. This is not easy; when inequality is considered a moral wrong (like stealing), it brings opprobrium on those who challenge it.

There is a wonderful piece by Nathan Glazer called "Remembering the Answers." We need to remember the arguments and use them against the application of nonintellectual criteria to the acquisition and teaching of knowledge.

Academics are not alone in this. The events that disturb us on our campuses are part and parcel of major changes in society at large. The political difference between the McCarthyism of the 1950s and the egalitarianism of the 1980s and now 1990s is that this time the enemies of free speech, dispassionate inquiry, and scholarly merit are within. Therefore, they are more difficult to recognize, more galling when recognized. That invasions of academic freedom take place in the name of social justice is not so surprising. We memorialize this very same thing when we speak of the horrors perpetuated in the name of liberty. Only now it is happening to us.

It is all too easy for professors to believe that they live (and ought to live) in enclaves especially protected against the turmoil of the society outside. This "sheltercove" view of colleges and universities easily shades into the belief that academic standards ought to and can remain inviolate even as the principles underlying these standards are violated. Viewing society as loosely coupled—the various parts imperfectly joined—has merit, but not, I think, this time. When a value and the social relationship it justifies (now equality of result) is adopted by strategic elites (a majority of Democratic party activists, reporters in the major media, and parts of student bodies, professors, and campus administrators), no sanctuary is possible. Academics by and large sat still while affirmative action was applied to labor unions. Maybe they deserve this treatment—the thought went—but we do not. A big mistake.

At one time I thought that, in the interests of increasing minority college graduates (which, by itself, is desirable), intellectual tests could be dispensed with. After all, tests and grades are far from perfect indicators of future performance. No doubt more would flunk out, but more would also graduate as previously unseen talent would emerge. True. It turned out, however, that it was considered unacceptable to have higher dropout rates. Now the same principle has been extended to the faculty and administrative levels. Perhaps minority and female graduate students would feel and do better if they saw professors of their own color and gender. That would mean it was not what you know but who (by race and gender) you are that matters. The story of the policeman born in Jamaica who claimed he was black not Hispanic, so he could pass a test for promotion with lower scores, speaks volumes. Authenticity is essential if you have to prove you belong to the right group.

The point is that there is no stopping point. Once the principle of equalizing results is accepted, the push is on to apply it everywhere. Hence I have concluded that the thing to do is what we believed all along—namely, to act on this principle: moral and intellectual discrimination, yes; discrimination on all other grounds, no.

Conditions now are such that nondiscrimination will likely be defeated. This gives no reason to quit or despair. By now we know the refrain when faced with substances or principles that are bad for us: Just say no.

Understanding radical egalitarianism enables us to explain the phenomenon of political correctness on college campuses. What is correct? Radical egalitarianism. Who decides? Radical egalitarians. How do they decide? By determining among themselves which actions support greater equality of condition and pressuring other campus constituencies to comply with their demands. Why do they succeed so often despite violating widely held norms of academic life? Because arguing against greater equality of condition subjects critics to charges of racism and sexism but also because arguing against equality in any form makes Americans uncomfortable. Yet exactly this—arguing against equality of condition as the most moral criterion of judgment— is what must be done if freedom of speech and inquiry are to be preserved in American colleges and universities. And not only there.

Notes

Introduction

1. See Mary Douglas and Aaron Wildavsky, *Risk and Culture: An Essay on the Selection of Technical and Environmental Dangers* (Berkeley: University of California Press, 1982); and Aaron Wildavsky, *Searching for Safety* (New Brunswick, N.J.: Transaction Press, 1988).

2. Wildavsky, *Searching for Safety*. Transaction Press, 1988).

3. Michael X. Delli Carpini and Bruce A. Williams, " 'Fictional' and 'Non-fictional' Television Celebrate Earth Day (Or, Politics Is Comedy plus Pretense)," paper prepared for delivery at the American Political Science Association Annual Meetings, San Francisco, August 29–September 2, 1990.

1   A Cultural Theory

1. The best statement of my position on political cultures is in Michael Thompson, Richard Ellis, and Aaron Wildavsky, *Cultural Theory* (Boulder, Colo.: Westview Press, 1990). This cultural perspective originated with Mary Douglas. See her *Natural Symbols: Explorations in Cosomology* (London: Barrie and Rockliff, 1970), and "Cultural Bias," in Mary Douglas, *In the Active Voice* (London: Routledge and Kegan Paul, 1982), pp. 183–254.

2. Michael Thompson and Michiel Schwarz, "Beyond the Politics of Interest," in *Divided We Stand* (Hertfordshire, England: Harvester Wheatsheaf, 1990), pp. 39–55.

3. Terrence Ball, "Interest Explanations," *Polity* 12, no. 2 (Winter 1979), pp. 187–201, quote on p. 199.

4. Mary Douglas, "How Identity Problems Disappear," in Anita Jacobson-Widding, ed., *Identity: Personal and Socio-cultural,* (Uppsala, Sweden: Uppsala Studies in Cultural Anthropology, papers from a symposium 1983), vol. 5, pp. 35–46.

5. See a perceptive paper by James March for a list of "the properties of tastes as they appear in standard prescriptive theories of choice." His list includes two properties of special interest: "Tastes are *relevant*. Normative theories of choice require that action be taken in terms of tastes." Yet, "Tastes are *exogenous*. Normative theories of choice presume that tastes, by whatever process they may be created, are not themselves affected by the choices they control." As March observes, "each of these features of tastes seem inconsistent with observations of choice behavior among individuals and social institutions." James G. March, "Bounded Rationality, Ambiguity, and the Engineering of Choice," *Bell Journal of Economics* 9, no. 2 (Autumn 1978), pp. 587–608. Keith Hartley's paper, "Exogenous Factors in Economic Theory: Neo-classical Economics," explains the general perspective: "Utility or preference functions are central to neo-classical economics and are assumed to be given." *Social Science Information* 24, no. 3 (1985), p. 470.

6. Charles E. Lindblom, "The Market as Prison," *Journal of Politics* 44 (May 1982), pp. 324–36, quote on p. 335.

7. "Fatalistic attitudes are discernible in many Romanian literary creations, indeed even in folklore. The most famous Romanian folk ballad is 'Miorita,' or 'The Lamb.' It is the moving, beautiful story of a Moldavian shepherd whose fellow shepherds plot to kill him and steal his flock. Learning of the plan from his 'wonder lamb,' the young shepherd makes no move to keep it from being carried out. He serenely accepts his fate, comforted by the thought that he will be reunited with nature." Michael Shafir, "Political Culture, Intellectual Dissent, and Intellectual Consent: The Case of Romania," *Orbis* 27, no. 1 (Spring 1983), pp. 393–420, quote on p. 405.

8. For further discussion of why left–right differences are inadequate, see Aaron Wildavsky, "Choosing Preferences by Constructing Institutions: A Cultural Theory of Preference Formation," *American Political Science Review* 81, no. 1 (March 1987), pp. 3–21; and Richard Ellis and Aaron Wildavsky, *Dilemmas of Presidential Leadership: From Washington through Lincoln* (New Brunswick, N.J.: Transaction Press, 1989).

9. Samuel Huntington, *American Politics: The Promise of Disharmony* (Cambridge, Mass.: Belknap Press of Harvard University Press, 1981), pp. 3–4.

10. See Richard Ellis and Aaron Wildavsky, "A Cultural Analysis of the Role of Abolitionists in the Coming of the Civil War," *Comparative Studies in Society and History* 31, no. 1 (Winter 1990), pp. 89–116.

11. Huntington, *American Politics,* pp. 39, 41.

12. Ibid., p. 237.

13. A test of cultural consistency is provided by what James March and J. Richard Harrison call "postdecision surprise." When things go badly, the excuses should fit the culture. The market-oriented should accept more personal responsibility than the members of a hierarchy; egalitarians should blame "the system." See J. Richard Harrison and James G. March, "Decision

Making and Postdecision Surprise,'' *Administrative Science Quarterly* 29 (March 1984), pp. 26–42.

14. Paul M. Sniderman, Michael G. Hagen, Philip E. Tetlock, and Henry E. Brady, ''Reasoning Chains: Causal Models of Policy Reasoning in Mass Publics,'' *British Journal of Political Science* 16 (1986), pp. 405–30.

15. Pamela Johnson Conover and Stanley Feldman, ''The Origins and Meaning of Liberal/Conservative Self-identifications,'' *American Journal of Political Science* 25 (1981), pp. 617–45, quote on p. 618.

16. Robert A. Dahl, *Who Governs?* (New Haven, Conn.: Yale University Press, 1961).

17. A more substantial analysis of leadership from this cultural perspective may be found in my ''A Cultural Theory of Leadership,'' in Bryan D. Jones, ed., *Leadership and Politics: New Perspectives in Political Science* (Lawrence: University Press of Kansas, 1989), pp. 87–113.

18. Mary Douglas and Aaron Wildavsky, *Risk and Culture: An Essay on the Selection of Technical and Environmental Dangers* (Berkeley: University of California Press, 1982).

19. Stanley Rothman and S. Robert Lichter, ''Elites in Conflict: Nuclear Energy, Ideology, and the Perception of Risk,'' *Journal of Contemporary Studies* 8 (1985), pp. 23–44.

20. Karl Dake and Aaron Wildavsky, ''Theories of Risk Perception: Who Fears What and Why?'' *Daedalus* 119, no. 4 (Fall 1990), pp. 41–60.

21. Kathy Bloomgarden, ''Managing the Environment: The Public's View,'' *Public Opinion* 6 (1983), pp. 47–51.

22. Joseph P. Kalt and Mark A. Zupan, ''Further Evidence on Capture and Ideology in the Economic Theory of Politics,'' *American Economic Review* 74 (1984), pp. 279–300.

23. Oakland *Tribune,* August 10, 1986, p. 2.

24. Owen Harries, ''Best-case Thinking,'' *Commentary* 77, no. 5 (May 1984), pp. 23–28, quote on p. 27.

2   Individualism and Egalitarianism

1. Theodore J. Lowi, ''Why Is There No Socialism in the United States? A Federal Analysis,'' in Robert T. Golembiewski and Aaron Wildavsky, eds., *The Costs of Federalism* (New Brunswick, N.J.: Transaction Books, 1984), pp. 37–54.

2. Samuel Huntington, *American Politics: The Promise of Disharmony* (Cambridge, Mass.: Belknap Press of Harvard University Press, 1981).

3. See Charles E. Lindblom's circularity hypothesis in his *Politics and Markets* (New York: Basic Books, 1977).

4. Karl D. Jackson, *Cambodia, 1975–1978: Rendezvous with Death* (Princeton, N.J.: Princeton University Press, 1989); and Pin Yathay, *L'utopie meurtrière* (Paris: Robert Laffont, 1980); and review article of this latter book by Ferenc Feher in *Telos,* no. 56 (Summer 1983), pp. 193–205.

5. Mary Douglas, *Natural Symbols, Explorations in Cosmology* (Harmondsworth, England: Penguin, 1970), and "Cultural Bias," in *In the Active Voice* (London: Routledge Kegan Paul, 1982); and Mary Douglas and Aaron Wildavsky, *Risk and Culture: An Essay on the Selection of Technical and Environmental Dangers* (Berkeley: University of California Press, 1982).

6. See my "Frames of Reference Come from Cultures: A Predictive Theory," in Morris Freilich, ed., *The Relevance of Culture* (New York: Bergin and Garvey, 1989), pp. 58–74.

7. See my "A Cultural Theory of Leadership," in Bryan D. Jones, ed., *Leadership and Politics: New Perspectives in Political Science* (Lawrence: University Press of Kansas, 1989), pp. 87–113.

8. See my "Change in Political Culture," *Politics,* journal of the Australian Political Science Association, 20, no. 2 (November 1985), pp. 95–102.

9. Adrienne Koch and Willilam Peder, *The Life and Selected Writings of Thomas Jefferson* (New York: Modern Library, 1944), p. 123.

10. Lance Banning, *The Jeffersonian Persuasion* (Ithaca, N.Y.: Cornell University Press, 1978), pp. 43, 56.

11. Ibid., p. 59.

12. Koch and Peder, *Life and Writings of Jefferson,* p. 126.

13. James Savage, *Balanced Budgets and American Politics* (Ithaca, N.Y.: Cornell University Press, 1988), p. 95.

14. Herbert J. Storring, *What the Anti-Federalists Were For* (Chicago: University of Chicago Press, 1981).

15. Joseph L. Blau, ed., *Social Theories of Jacksonian Democracy* (New York: Bobbs-Merrill, 1954), pp. 25–28.

16. Ibid., p. 227.

17. Ibid., p. 196.

18. Robert Remini, *Andrew Jackson and the Course of American Freedom,* vol. 2: *1822–1832* (New York: Harper & Row, 1981), p. 44.

19. Ibid., p. 34.

20. Ibid., p. 166.

21. Daniel Bell, "The End of American Exceptionalism," *Public Interest,* no. 41 (Fall 1975), pp. 193–224, quote on p. 197.

22. Ibid. Bell cites Daniel Boorstin, Alexis De Tocqueville, and Richard Hofstadter as contributing to this version of exceptionalism.

23. Robert A. Dahl, *Who Governs?* (New Haven, Conn.: Yale University Press, 1961).

24. See Martin Landau, "Redundancy, Rationality, and the Problem of Duplication and Overlap," *Public Administration Review* 29, no. 4 (July/August 1969), pp. 346–58.

25. See my "The Media's 'American Egalitarians,' " *Public Interest,* no. 88 (Summer 1987), pp. 94–104. It makes up part of Chapter 6 in the present volume.

26. See Chapter 13 of this volume.

27. See William Donahue's *The Politics of the ACLU* (New Brunswick, N.J.: Transaction Press, 1984); and Chapter 9 of this volume.

28. See my "The Three Cultures," *Public Interest,* no. 69 (Fall 1982), pp. 45–58; and Chapter 5 of this volume.

29. Warren Miller and Kent Jennings, with Barbara G. Farah, *Parties in Transition: A Longitudinal Study of Party Elites and Party Supporters* (New York: Russell Sage Foundation, 1986).

30. Jeffrey N. Berry, *Lobbying for the People: The Political Behavior of Public Interest Groups* (Princeton, N.J.: Princeton University Press, 1977); and Jack Walker, "The Origins and Maintenance of Interest Groups in America," *American Political Science Review* 77, no. 2 (June 1983), pp. 390–406.

31. See S. Robert Lichter, Stanley Rothman, and Linda S. Lichter, *The Media Elite: America's New Powerbrokers* (Bethesda, Md.: Adler & Adler, 1986); and Shanto Iyengar and Donald R. Kinder, *News That Matters: Television and American Opinion* (Chicago: University of Chicago Press, 1987).

32. Charles E. Lindblom, "The Market as Prison," *Journal of Politics* 44 (May 1982), pp. 324–36.

33. For evidence, see Sidney Verba and Gary R. Orren, *Equality in America: The View from the Top* (Cambridge, Mass.: Harvard University Press, 1985); and Miller and Jennings, *Parties in Transition.*

34. See Richard Ellis and Aaron Wildavsky, *Dilemmas of Presidential Leadership: From Washington through Lincoln* (New Brunswick, N.J.: Transaction Press, 1989).

3 The Major Political Parties

1. Warren E. Miller and M. Kent Jennings, with Barbara G. Farah, *Parties in Transition: A Longitudinal Study of Party Elites and Party Supporters* (New York: Russell Sage Foundation, 1986), pp. 163–64.

2. Ibid., p. 166.

3. Ibid., p. 166–67.

4. Ibid., p. 175–77.

5. Ibid., 187–88.

6. Ibid., pp. 203–5.

7. Ibid., pp. 218–19.

8. Center for Political Studies, Institute for Social Research, "Convention Delegate Study: Report to Respondents," University of Michigan, Ann Arbor, 1985.

9. Ibid., pp. 3–5.

10. M. Kent Jennings, "Women in Party Politics," report prepared for the Russell Sage Foundation Women in Twentieth-century American Politics Project, Beverly Hills, Calif., January 1987, pp. 28, 32.

11. Ibid., p. 30.

12. Barbara G. Farah, "Delegate Polls: 1944 to 1984," *Public Opinion* (August/September 1984), pp. 43–45.

13. Jennings, "Women in Politics," pp. 11–12.

14. Jo Freeman, "Who You Know versus Who You Represent," in Mary Fainsod Katzenstein and Carol McClurg Mueller, eds., *The Women's Movements of the United States and Western Europe: Consciousness, Political Opportunity, and Public Policy* (Philadelphia, 1987) pp. 231–32.

15. Ibid., p. 242.

16. The seminal work is Maurice Duverger, *Political Parties: Their Organization and Activity in the Modern State* (London: Methune, and New York: Wiley, 1954).

17. Peter Begans, "The ABC News/Washington *Post* Poll," surveys D122–D125, 1984, pp. 4–5.

18. Warren Miller, letter of April 23, 1987. Material to appear in *Without Consent: Mass–Elite Linkages in Presidential Politics* (Lexington, Ky.: University Press of Kentucky, 1988), ch. 2.

19. See Nelson W. Polsby, "The Democratic Nomination and the Evolution of the Party System," and Raymond E. Wolfinger, "Dealignment, Realignment, and Mandates in the 1984 Election," both in Austin Ranney, ed., *The American Elections of 1984* (Durham, N.C.: Duke University Press, 1985), p. 289, p. 38.

4 Egalitarianism on the Rise

1. Frank Levy, *Dollars and Dreams: The Changing American Income Distribution* (New York: Russell Sage Foundation, 1987).

2. Stanley Lebergott, *The American Economy: Income, Wealth, and Want* (Princeton, N.J.: Princeton University Press, 1976).

3. For the best account of the influence of business, see David Vogel, *Fluctuating Fortunes: The Political Power of American Business* (New York: Basic Books, 1989).

4. Washington *Post,* Sept. 23, 1989, p. E18.

5. Steve Wilstein, "Different Vacations Stroke with 'Global Exchange,' " Oakland *Tribune,* June 17, 1990, p. B-7.

6. See for instance S. Robert Lichter, Stanley Rothman, and Linda S. Lichter, *The Media Elite: America's New Powerbrokers* (Bethesda, Md.: Adler & Adler, 1986).

7. Susan Sperling, *Animal Liberators: Research and Morality* (Berkeley: University of California Press, 1988, p. 1.

8. Ibid., p. ix.

9. Ibid., p. 4.

10. Ibid., p. 2.

11. Ibid., p. 4.

12. Ibid., p. 128.

13. Ibid., p. 17.

14. Ibid., p. 202.

15. Ibid., p. 122.

16. Ibid., p. 123.

17. Ibid., p. 123.

18. Ibid., p. 15.

19. Ibid., p. 19.

20. Ibid., p. 17.

21. Ibid., p. 155.

22. Ibid., p. 17.

23. Ibid., p. 136.

24. Ibid., p. 121.

25. Ibid., p. 121.

26. Ibid., p. 22.

27. Ibid., p. 20.

28. Ibid., p. 121.

29. Ibid., 2–3.

30. Ibid., p. 203.

31. Ibid., p. 3.

32. Taken from a February 7, 1986, letter from Clair Brown, acting chair of the Academic Senate Committee on University Welfare, to Professor Milton Chernin, chairman of the Board of Directors of the Faculty Club, University of California, Berkeley.

33. Sperling, *Animal Liberators,* p. 116.

34. See Mary Douglas and Aaron Wildavsky, *Risk and Culture: An Essay on the Selection of Technical and Environmental Dangers* (Berkeley: University of California Press, 1982); and Karl Dake and Aaron Wildavsky, Chapter 7 of this volume.

35. *Greenpeace* (November/December 1989), p. 17.

36. Ibid.

37. *Time* (December 18, 1989), p. 71.

38. *Time* (February 12, 1990), p. 6.

39. *Time* (December 18, 1989), p. 68.

40. *Time* (April 23, 1990), p. 82.

41. *Time* (June 25, 1990), p. 44.

42. *Sierra* (November/December 1989), p. 15.

43. *Time* (April 23, 1990), p. 76.

44. *Time* (January 8, 1990), p. 51.

45. *Time* (October 2, 1989), p. 21.

46. *Time* (April 23, 1990), pp. 77, 82.

47. *Time* (June 25, 1990), p. 44.

48. *Time* (April 23, 1990), p. 76.

49. Katherine Riggs, "Anti-nuclear Groups: The Goals, Tactics, and Composition of the American Nuclear Movement," unpublished, 1980. The author relied on doctoral dissertations by Lynn Ellen Dwyer, "The Anti-nuclear Movement in Middle Tennessee," American University, 1977; Alan Barry Sharaf, "Local Citizen Opposition to Nuclear Power Plants and Oil Refiner-

ies," Clark University, 1978; and Judith Ann Hays Johnsrud, "A Political Geography of the Nuclear Power Controversy: The Peaceful Atom in Pennsylvania," Pennsylvania State University, 1977.

50. Anthony E. Ladd, Thomas C. Hood, and Kent D. Van Liere, "Ideological Themes in the Antinuclear Movement: Consensus and Diversity," publication information n.a. See also J. Ball-Rokeach, Sandra Tallman, and Irvin Tallman, "Social Movements as Moral Confrontations: With Special Reference to Civil Rights," in Milton Rokeach, ed., *Understanding Human Values* (New York: Free Press, 1979), pp. 82–94; Steven Barkan, "Strategic, Tactical and Organizational Dilemmas of the Protest Movement against Nuclear Power," *Social Problems* 27 (1979), pp. 19–37.

51. New York *Times,* June 23, 1990, front page.

52. *In Brief* (Spring 1990), p. 8.

53. *In Brief* (Winter 1989–90), p. 1.

54. *Time* (November 6, 1989), p. 16.

55. *Time* (October 16, 1989), p. 50.

56. *Time* (March 12, 1990), p. 54.

57. 336 A.2d at 724, as quoted in Dennis Coyle, "A Reluctant Revival: Landowner Constitutional Rights and Political Culture," Ph.D. dissertation, Department of Political Science, University of California, Berkeley, 1988, pp. 138–39.

58. Ibid., p. 130.

59. Ibid., p. 167.

60. Ibid., p. 168.

61. Ibid., p. 169.

62. 456 A.2d at 415, as quoted in Coyle, "Reluctant Revival," p. 176.

63. Ibid., p. 166.

64. Samuel Gorovitz, "Against Selling Bodily Parts," *Report from the Center for Philosophy & Public Policy,* University of Maryland, 4, no. 2 (Spring 1984), p. 11.

65. Dinesh D'Souza, "The Bishops as Pawns," *Policy Review,* no. 34 (Fall 1985), pp. 50–56, quote on p. 51.

66. Ibid., pp. 51–52.

67. Dale Mezzacappa, "Catholic Bishops Issue Broader Plan Linking Abortion to Other Concerns," Philadelphia *Inquirer,* November 15, 1985, p. 2-A.

68. *Wall Street Journal,* May 24, 1985, p. 1.

69. Ibid., p. 12.

70. Ibid.

71. Vince Bielski, "Sanctuary Movement 'Not Political,'" *Daily Californian,* November 14, 1985, pp. 1, 10, 15.

72. Sperling, *Animal Liberators,* p. 141.

73. *Wall Street Journal,* date n.a.

74. *Time* (May 7, 1990), p. 117.

75. Oakland *Tribune,* October 22, 1985, p. A6.

76. Anthony L. Leto,*"New York State Club Association v. City of New York:* Ending Gender-based Discrimination in Private Clubs—Are Associational Rights Still Protected?" *Hastings Constitutional Law Quarterly* 16, no. 4 (Summer 1989), pp. 623–37.

77. *Time* (April 16, 1990), pp. 64–65.

78. Oakland *Tribune,* July 1, 1990, p. 2.

79. *Newsweek* (June 11, 1990), p. 26.

80. *Wall Street Journal,* February 15, 1985, p. A22.

81. Kristin Luker, *Abortion and the Politics of Motherhood* (Berkeley: University of California Press, 1984), p. 97.

82. Ibid., p. 92.

83. Ibid., p. 113.

84. David Bryden, "Between Two Constitutions: Feminism and Pornography," *Constitutional Commentary* 2, no. 1 (Winter 1985), p. 181.

85. Ibid., p. 182.

86. Ibid., p. 183. While these elements give the egalitarian flavor of the ordinance, they likely did not survive revision upon Mayor William Hudnut's veto of this version.

87. Ibid., p. 184.

88. Ibid., p. 183.

89. Ibid., p. 185.

90. Ibid.

91. Ibid., p. 157.

92. Ibid., p. 172.

93. Jean Bethke Elshtain, "The New Pornography Wars," *New Republic* (June 25, 1984), p. 16.

94. Bryden, "Between Two Constitutions," p. 171.

95. Ibid.

96. Elshtain, "New Pornography Wars," p. 17.

97. Bryden, "Between Two Constitutions," p. 152.

98. New York *Times,* August 9, 1990, p. B1.

99. Ibid., p. B4.

100. San Francisco *Examiner,* August 12, 1990, p. E5.

101. Ibid.

102. Letter to the Editor, New York *Times,* August 10, 1990, p. A16.

103. Keith Anderson, "Activists Envision Peace Culture," *Christian Science Monitor,* September 8, 1985, pp. C7, 10.

5 The Three Cultures

1. B. Bruce Briggs, *The New Class?* (New Brunswick, N.J.: Transaction Books, 1979).

2. See Mary Douglas and Aaron Wildavsky, *Risk and Culture: An Essay*

on the Selection of Technological and Environmental Dangers (Berkeley: University of California Press, 1982).

3. C. Vann Woodward, "The Fall of the American Adam," *Bulletin of the American Academy of Arts and Sciences* 35, no. 2 (November 1981), pp. 24–34.

6 Media's American Egalitarianism

1. Michael J. Robinson, "Just How Liberal Is the News? 1980 Revisited," *Public Opinion* 6 (February/March 1983), p. 59.

2. Renata Adler, *Reckless Disregard:* Westmoreland v. CBS et al.; Sharon v. *Time* (New York: Knopf, 1988).

3. Martin Linsky, *Impact: How the Press Affects Federal Policymaking* (New York: Norton, 1988).

4. S. Robert Lichter, Stanley Rothman, and Linda S. Lichter, *The Media Elite: America's New Powerbrokers* (Bethesda, Md.: Adler & Adler, 1986).

5. Shanto Iyengar and Donald R. Kinder, *News That Matters: Television and American Opinion,* (Chicago: University of Chicago Press, 1987).

7 Theories of Risk Perception

1. The risk-perception data archives used in this chapter were established in 1981 and 1982 by Kenneth H. Craik, with David Buss and Karl Dake, under National Science Foundation Grant PRA-8020017 to the University of California's Institute of Personality Assessment and Research. See David Buss, Kenneth H. Craik, and Karl Dake, "Perceptions of Decision Procedures for Managing and Regulating Hazards," in F. Homberger, *Safety Evaluation and Regulation* (New York: Karger, 1985), pp. 199–208; and "Contemporary Worldviews and Perception of the Technological System," in Vincent T. Covello, Joshua Menkes, and Jeryl Mumpower, *Risk Evaluation and Management* (New York: Plenum Press, 1986), pp. 93–130. The writing of this chapter was supported in part by the National Institutes of Health under Biomedical Research Support Grant 89–34 to the Survey Research Center at the University of California, Berkeley. Acknowledgment is gratefully made to Dr. Kenneth H. Craik for his permission to use these data, and to Dr. Percy Tannenbaum for the support of the Survey Research Center.

2. Mary Douglas and Aaron Wildavsky, *Risk and Culture: An Essay on the Selection of Technological and Environmental Dangers* (Berkeley: University of California Press, 1982); John Holdren, "The Risk Assessors," *Bulletin of the Atomic Scientists* (1983), p. 39, quotation p. 36.

3. K. R. MacCrimmon and D. A. Wehrung, *Taking Risks: The Management of Uncertainty* (New York: Free Press, 1986); R. G. Mitchell, Jr., *Mountain Experience: The Psychology and Sociology of Adventure* (Chicago: University of Chicago Press, 1983).

4. Ronald Inglehart, *The Silent Revolution: Changing Values and Political*

Styles among Western Publics (Princeton, N.J.: Princeton University Press, 1977).

5. Stephen Cotgrove, *Catastrophe or Cornucopia: The Environment, Politics, and the Future* (Chichester, England: John Wiley & Sons, 1982); Dorothy Nelkin and Michael Pollack, *The Atom Besieged: Antinuclear Movements in France and Germany* (Cambridge, Mass.: Massachusetts Institute of Technology Press, 1981).

6. Mary Douglas, "Cultural Bias," occasional paper 35, Royal Anthropological Institute, London, 1978, republished in *In the Active Voice* (London: Routledge & Kegan Paul, 1982), pp. 183–254; "Passive Voice Theories in Religious Sociology," *Review of Religious Research* 21 (1979), pp. 51–56; *Essays in the Sociology of Perception* (London: Routledge & Kegan Paul, 1982); Douglas and Wildavsky, *Risk and Culture;* Michael Thompson, Richard Ellis, and Aaron Wildavsky, *Cultural Theory* (Boulder, Colo.: Westview Press, 1990).

7. See note 1 above. Intensive assessments of 300 ordinary citizens were conducted, including measures of perceptions of technologies, preferences for societal decision approaches and societal risk policy, confidence in institutions, sociotechnological and political orientations, personal values, environmental dispositions, self-descriptions and personal background, and more.

Two public samples were drawn from cities in the East Bay area of the San Francisco region: Richmond, Oakland, Piedmont, and Alameda. Stratified samples were selected on the basis of an analysis of social trends that provided detailed information regarding the median demographic characteristics of each postal zip code in the sample region. Participants were recruited via telephone directory sampling, letter of invitation, and telephone follow-up. Most—but not all—of the current findings are based on analysis of sample two (134 participants), leaving sample one (166 participants) available for replication of this study.

8. Participants rated how risky, and how beneficial, they judged each of 25 technologies to be: refrigerators, photocopy machines, contraceptives, suspension bridges, nuclear power, electronic games, diagnostic X rays, nuclear weapons, computers, vaccinations, water fluoridation, rooftop solar collectors, lasers, tranquilizers, Polaroid photographs, fossil electric power, motor vehicles, movie special effects, pesticides, opiates, food preservatives, open-heart surgery, commercial aviation, genetic engineering, and windmills. See Baruch Fischhoff, Paul Slovic, Sarah Lichtenstein, Stephen Read, and Barbara Coombs, "How Safe Is Safe Enough? A Psychometric Study of Atittudes toward Technological Risks and Benefits," *Policy Sciences* 9(1978), pp. 127–152.

9. The measure of perceptual accuracy was motivated by Paul Slovic, Baruch Fischhoff, and Sarah Lichtenstein, "Facts and Fears: Understanding Perceived Risk," in R. Schwing and W. Albers, Jr., *Societal Risk Assessment: How Safe Is Safe Enough?* (New York: Plenum Press, 1980), pp. 181–216.

10. Harrison Gough and Alfred Heilbrun, *The Adjective Check List Manual—1983 Edition* (Palo Alto, Calif.: Consulting Psychologists Press, 1983); Harrison Gough, *California Psychological Inventory Administrator's Guide* (Palo Alto, Calif.: Consulting Psychologists Press, 1987).

11. The measure of liberalism–conservatism based on policy preferences follows Edmond Costantini and Kenneth H. Craik, "Personality and Politicians: California Party Leaders, 1960–1976," *Journal of Personality and Social Psychology* 38 (1980), pp. 641–61.

12. Quotations, in order, are from Leonard Furguson, "The Isolation and Measurement of Nationalism," *Journal of Social Psychology* 16 (1942), p. 224: Hans Eysenck, *Sex and Personality* (London: Open Books, 1976), p. 153; Gough, *California Psychological Inventory;* David Buss, Kenneth H. Craik, and Karl Dake, "The IPAR Risk Perception Data Archives: Assessment II Instruments," unpublished document, Institute of Personality Assessment and Research, University of California at Berkeley, 1982.

13. Quotations, in order, are from Eysenck, *Sex and Personality,* p. 155; and Furguson, "Isolation and Measurement of Nationalism," p. 224.

14. Quotations concerning a tax shift and the elimination of poverty are from Costantini and Craik, "Personality and Politicians"; the balance are from Buss, Craik, and Dake, "IPAR: Assessment II Instruments."

15. We report correlations throughout this chapter—not means nor mean differences. For sample two (134 participants), a correlation must be greater than 0.15 or less than −0.15 to be statistically significant. Nothing about average scores or group comparisons is implied.

16. Gordon Allport, *Pattern and Growth in Personality* (New York: Henry Holt, 1961); see also Allport's *Personality: A Psychological Interpretation* (New York: Henry Holt, 1937).

17. Richard Bord and Robert O'Conner, "Risk Communication, Knowledge, and Attitudes: Explaining Reactions to a Technology Perceived as Risky," *Risk Analysis* 10 (1991), 499–506.

18. Thomas Dietz and Robert Rycroft, *The Risk Professionals* (New York: Russell Sage Foundation, 1987), quotation p. 47.

19. Paul Sabatier and S. Hunter, "The Incorporation of Causal Perceptions into Models of Elite Belief Systems," *Western Political Quarterly* 42(1989), quotation p. 253.

20. Gerald Gardner, Adrian Tiemann, Leroy Gould, Donald Deluca, Leonard Doob, and Jan Stolwijk, "Risk and Benefit Perceptions, Acceptability Judgments, and Self-reported Actions toward Nuclear Power," *Journal of Social Psychology* 116(1982), quotations pp. 194–95.

21. Stanley Rothman and S. Robert Lichter, "Elite Ideology and Risk Perception in Nuclear Energy Policy," *American Political Science Review* 81(1987), quotation p. 395.

22. Chauncy Starr, "Social Benefit versus Technological Risk: What Is Our Society Willing to Pay for Safety?" *Science* 165(1969), pp. 1232–38.

23. National Research Council, Committee on Risk Perception and Communication, *Improving Risk Communication* (Washington, D.C.: National Academy Press, 1989).

8   The Turtle Theory

1. For fun as well as enlightenment, see the *New Republic*'s "Quadrennial Recriminations" issue (December 5, 1988).

2. See Sidney Verba and Gary R. Orren, *Equality in America: The View from the Top* (Cambridge, Mass.: Harvard University Press, 1985); whereas 50 percent of Democratic activists believed that the system—not the individual— causes poverty, only 12 percent of Republican activists agreed.

3. See my "Where Bias and Influence Meet," *Public Interest,* no. 91 (Spring 1988), pp. 94–98, a review of Shanto Iyengar and Donald R. Kinder, *News That Matters: Television and American Opinion* (Chicago: University of Chicago Press, 1987). The review is part of Chapter 6 of the present volume.

4. Elmer E. Schattschneider, *The Semisovereign People: A Realist's View of Democracy in America* (Hinsdale, Ill.: Dryden Press, 1975).

5. Byron E. Shafer, "The Notion of an Electoral Order: The Structure of Electoral Politics at the Accession of George Bush," in Byron F. Shafer, ed., *The End of Realignment?* (Madison: University of Wisconsin Press, forthcoming), ch. 3.

6. Seymour Martin Lipset, "A Reaffirming Election: 1988," *International Journal of Public Opinion Research* 1, no. 1 (Winter 1989), pp. 25–44.

7. Paul M. Sniderman, Michael G. Hagen, Philip E. Tetlock, and Henry E. Brady, "Reasoning Chains: Causal Models of Policy Reasoning in Mass Publics," *British Journal of Political Science* 16(1986), pp. 405–30.

8. Evans Witt, "What the Republicans Have Learned about Women," *Public Opinion* 4 (October/November 1985), p. 49.

9. Stuart E. Eizenstat, quoted in the Washington *Post,* September 12, 1989, p. A21.

10. Washington *Post,* April 8, 1990, p. A6.

11. Warren E. Miller and M. Kent Jennings, with Barbara Farah, *Parties in Transition: A Longitudinal Study of Party Elites and Party Supporters* (New York: Russell Sage Foundation, 1986).

10   *The New American Dilemma*

1. Jennifer L. Hochschild, *The New American Dilemma: Liberal Democracy and School Desegration* (New Haven, Conn.: Yale University Press, 1984).

2. Ibid., p. xi.

3. Ibid., p.2.

4. Ibid.

5. Ibid., p. 202.

6. Ibid., p. 203.

7. Ibid., p. 2.

8. Charles E. Lindblom, "The Science of 'Muddling Through,' " *Public Administration Review* 19 (Spring 1959), p. 79; and D. Braybrooke and C. Lindblom, *A Strategy of Decision: Policy Evaluation as a Social Process* (Glencoe, Ill.: Free Press, 1963).

9. Charles E. Lindblom, *The Intelligence of Democracy* (Glencoe, Ill.: Free Press, 1965).

10. See comments to this effect in Aaron Wildavsky, *The Politics of the Budgetary Process,* 2nd ed. (Glenview, Ill.: Scott, Foresman, 1974), pp. xii–xiv.

11. See the preface to the second edition of R. Dahl and C. Lindblom, *Politics, Economics, and Welfare* (Chicago: University of Chicago Press, 1976).

12. In addition to Lindblom, " 'Muddling Through' " and Braybrooke and Lindblom, *Strategy of Decision* and Hochschild, *New American Dilemma,* see Charles E. Lindblom, "Still Muddling, Not Yet Through," *Public Administration Review* 39 (November/December 1979), p. 517. That the debate over pluralism is also essentially a difference over equality may be seen, as well, in Nelson Polsby, *Community Power and Political Theory: A Further Look at Problems of Evidence and Inference* (New Haven, Conn. Yale University Press, 1980).

13. Mary Douglas and Aaron Wildavsky, *Risk and Culture: An Essay on the Selection of Technological and Environmental Dangers* (Berkeley: University of California Press, 1982).

14. Peter Huber, "Exorcists vs. Gatekeepers in Risk Regulation," *Regulation* 7 (November/December 1983), p. 23: and Huber, "The Old–New Division in Risk Regulation," *Virginia Law Review* 69 (1983), p. 1025. See David W. Pearce, "The Preconditions for Achieving Consensus in the Context of Technological Risk," in M. Dierkes, S. Edwards, and R. Coppock, eds., *Technological Risk: Its Perception and Handling in the European Community* (Weston, Mass.: Delgeschlager, 1980); Aaron Wildavsky, "Trial without Error: Anticipation versus Resilience as Strategies for Risk Reduction," in M. Maxey and R. Kuhn, eds., *Regulatory Reform: New Vision or Old Curse?* (New York: Praeger, 1985), pp. 200–21; Robert E. Goodin, "No Moral Nukes," *Ethics* 90 (1980), p. 417.

15. A plausible inference from the cases in Nelson Polsby, *Political Innovation in America: The Politics of Policy Initiation* (New Haven, Conn.: Yale University Press, 1984), is that, over the medium run, slow-moving innovations appear to become more legitimate. A partial parallel is provided by the contrast between the lengthy processes in which environmental legislation is spawned in Sweden and other European countries compared to the spate of legislation in the United States, and the reversal so far as implementation is concerned. See the citations in Aaron Wildavsky, "Doing More and Using Less: Utiliza-

tion of Research as a Result of Regime," a paper delivered to the Joint Science Center Berlin/Stanford University research project and conference on cross-national policy research; conference held in Berlin in December 1983; published in Meinolf Dierkes, Hans Weiler, and Ariane Berthoin Antal, eds., *Comparative Policy Research: Learning from Experience* (Aldershot, England: Gower, 1986), pp. 56–93.

16. Hochschild, *New American Dilemma,* pp. 155–56.

17. J. Thompson and A. Tuden, "Strategies, Structures, and Processes of Organizational Decision," in J. Thompson, ed., *Comparative Studies in Administration* (Pittsburgh, Pa.: University of Pittsburgh Press, 1959), pp. 195–216.

18. Arthur L. Stinchombe and D. Garth Taylor, "On Democracy and School Integration," in W. Stephan and J. Feagin, ed., *School Desegregation: Past, Present, and Future* (New York: Plenum, 1980), pp. 157–86.

19. Ibid., p. 177.

20. Hochschild, *New American Dilemma,* p. 203.

21. See Aaron Wildavsky, "The 'Reverse Sequence' in Civil Liberties," *Public Interest* 78 (1985), p. 32. The article appears in the present volume as Chapter 9.

22. John Ogbu, *The Next Generation: An Ethnography of Education in an Urban Neighborhood* (New York: Academic Press, 1974); "Racial Stratification and Education: The Case of Stockton, California," *ICRD Bulletin* 12 (1977), p. 1; and "Schooling in the Inner city," *Sociology* 21 (1983), pp. 75–79. See also J. Hanna, *Disruptive School Behavior: Class, Race, and Culture* (New York: Holmes and Meier, 1988); D. Holland and M. Eisenhart, *Women's Peer Groups and Choice of Careers* (New York: Praeger Publishers, 1982); John Ogbu, "Investment in Human Capital: Education and Development in Stockton, California, and Gwembe, Zambia," Kroeber Anthropological Papers nos. 63 and 64, 1984; L. Weis, *Between Two Worlds: Black Students in an Urban Community College* (New York: Routledge, Chapman, & Hall, 1985). There is a crying need for ethnographic investigations of contemporary American life. Saying you study, as part of a self-report, is not nearly so reliable as being observed to study by a trained observer who has come to know you and your family. (Much the same is true, of course, of faculty time studies.) The excuses for absences, for instance, are likely to change radically from the approved reasons in the student handbook to more personally relevant reasons when speaking to a knowledgeable and unthreatening observer. It may well be that the much-discussed decline in test scores among whites would yield to a more refined "time and concentration" study.

23. Harry Eckstein, "Civil Inclusion and Its Discontents," unpublished, n.d.

24. Mary Metz, *Classrooms and Corridors: The Crisis of Authority in Desegregated Secondary Schools* (Berkeley: University of California Press, 1978).

25. John Ogbu, "Understanding Community Forces Affecting Minority Students' Academic Effort," paper prepared for the Achievement Council of California, May 1984, and adapted from ch. 1 of *Crossing Cultural Boundaries: Resolving the Paradox of High Educational Aspirations and Low School Performance*, in preparation. Richard Rodriquez writes beautifully of this dilemma for Mexican Americans in his *Hunger of Memory* (Boston: D. R. Godiner 1982).

26. The Oakland *Tribune*, April 7, 1985, and succeeding days, ran a series on such schools.

11   The Bork Nomination

1. Bruce A. Ackerman, "Transformative Appointments," *Harvard Law Review* 101 (April 1988), pp. 1164–84.

2. Michael Pertschuk and Wendy Schaetzel, *The People Rising: The Campaign against the Bork Nomination* (New York: Thunder's Mouth Press, 1989).

3. Ethan Bronner, *Battle for Justice: How the Bork Nomination Shook America* (New York: Norton, 1990).

4. Robert H. Bork, *The Tempting of America: The Political Seduction of the Law* (New York: Free Press, 1989).

12   Groucho's Law

1. "Available data do not support the concept that low-level exposure to asbestos is a health hazard in buildings and schools. The concentration of asbestos fibers in the air, type of asbestos, and size of fibers must be considered in evaluation of potential health risks" (p. 294). See B. T. Mossman, J. Bignon, M. Corn, A. Seaton, and J. B. L. Gee, "Asbestos: Scientific Developments and Implications for Public Policy," *Science* 247 (January 19, 1990), pp. 294–301.

2. J. Lawrence Kulp, "Acid Rain: Causes, Effects, and Control," *Regulation* (Winter 1990), pp. 41–50.

3. "In fact, the CDC [Centers for Disease Control] said it found that 'the pattern of risk among subgroups of Vietnam veterans seemed to be the opposite of the pattern of use of Agent Orange: Navy veterans who served on ocean-going vessels off the coast of Vietnam tended to be at higher risk than Vietnam veterans based on land,' and those who served where Agent Orange was used the most 'tended to be at somewhat lower risk than Vietnam veterans who served in other regions.' " Kenneth H. Bacon, "Cancer Tied to Service in Vietnam," *Wall Street Journal*, March 30, 1990, p. B1.

4. Ellen Robinson-Haynes, "Carcinogens Found in Every Bite," *PD* (February 20, 1990).

5. Bruce Ames, Renae Magaw, and Lois Swirsky Gold, "Ranking Possible Carcinogenic Hazards," *Science* 236 (1987), pp. 271–80; and Ames, "Red

Herrings Don't Cause Cancer,'' San Francisco *Chronicle,* October 3, 1986, p. 20 in ''This World'' section.

6. Alexander Malchick, writing in the San Francisco *Examiner,* July 8, 1990, p. D-1.

7. Ibid., p. A-17.

8. Ibid.

9. Ibid.

10. ''Company Fails Half Taking Test,'' New York *Times,* date n.a.

11. ''The News in Black and White,'' *Media Monitor* 4, no. 2 (February 1990), p. 6. (Published by the Center for Media and Public Affairs, Washington, D.C.)

Index

Ackerman, Bruce, 182, 195
Adams, Laurie, 66
Adler, Renata, 119–20
Agnew, Spiro, 122
Alinsky, Saul, xix–xx
America: capitalism, success of, 214–16; foreign policy, success of, 214, 219–20; doom and gloom in, 213–26
American Civil Liberties Union: 68; initial objectives, 170–71, 177; future of, 177–79; transformation to egalitarianism, 168–69 and consequences of transformation, 174–76
"the American Creed," 9–10
American exceptionalism: 193, 212, 236; background of, 35–41; cultural alliances in, 27, 31–41; demise of, 236–37; and egalitarianism, 30–47; and hierarchy, 31–34, 46–47; and individualism, 30–35, 38–41, 45–47; reversed, 97
American individualism: federalism in, 35, 40, 46; as hybrid culture, 32–35; mass parties in, 35, 40, 46; separation of powers in, 35, 40, 46
Ames, Bruce, 75, 217
animal rights movement, 70–74; see

also egalitarianism, in rights movement

Babbitt, Bruce, 77
Banfield, Edward, xviii
Banning, Lance, 36–37
Bell, Daniel, 39–40
blacks: and education, xxxii, 181–92; desegregation, 181–92; incrementalism in desegregation, 184–88; minority status, xii, xiv; in relation to Jews, xx–xxii
Bord, Richard, 146
Bork nomination: egalitarian influence, 193–212; media influence, 203–5
Bork, Robert, xxx, 193–212
Brennan, William, 200
Bronner, Ethan, 198, 206
Bush, Barbara, 88–89
Bush, George, xxx, 44, 152, 156
Buss, David, 138

Carter, Jimmy, 42–43, 151, 155, 165
Catholic bishops (church): as hierarchical, 229–31; as egalitarian, 227–32
Chomsky, Noam, 220–21

Civil Rights Act, xxiv
Clay, Henry, 36
Cohen, Bernard, 128
Conover, Pamela, 14
Cooney, Patrick (Bishop), 84
corporate capitalism, 31
corporate greed, xxix
Craik, Kenneth H., 138
cultural biases: 135; defined, 136; as
  predictors of perceptions, 136–38,
  145–50
cultural change: in alliances of political cultures, xxx–xxxi; in United
  States, xxx
cultural context: of American exceptionalism, 29–47; in preference formation, 12–26
cultural theory: 12, 30–32; application of, 3–5, 12–26; as predictive
  tool, 15–26; as predictor of risk
  perception, 137–38, 140–50; social
  relations, defined, 135
cultures: defined, 3
Cummin, John S. (Bishop), 227
Cuomo, Anthony, 65
Cuomo, Mario, 65

Dahl, Robert, 17, 40
Dake, Karl, 21, 138
Darwin, Charles, 133
Delli Carpini, Michael X., xxxiii
Dellums, Ronald, xvi
Democratic party: and egalitarian-
  ism, xxviii–xxxiv, 45–46, 49–50,
  53, 58–61; 153, 155, 159–61, 163–
  66; as liberal, xxvii; in local elec-
  tions, 157–60; in presidential elec-
  tions, 151–57; transformation of,
  xxxiv; women, role of, 53–58
Dietz, Thomas, 147
Dingman, Maurice (Bishop), 84
Dole, Robert, 156
Donahue, William A., 169–70, 175
doom and gloom: in perceptions of:

acid rain, 217; America, 213–26;
  drug abuse, 224–26; education,
  218, 221; environment, 217–18;
  global warming, 218; productivity,
  216
Douglas, Mary, 4, 20
Dukakis, Michael, 151–57, 162–63
Dworkin, Andrea, 93–84

Eckstein, Harry, 191
egalitarianism: in alliance with individualism, xxx; in altering institutions, xxxii, 67–69, 73, 105–6, 236,
  238; and authority, 6, 11–12, 16,
  19, 103–4, 106; and blame, 16–17,
  109, 117–21; and Catholic bishops,
  44; and collectivism, 8; as critical
  culture, 102, 106, 110, 121; and defense policy, 24–26; and diminution of differences, xxviii–xxix, 19,
  22, 102, 117, 203; and economic
  growth, 18, 107, and envy, 15; and
  equality, 6, 17; and fairness, 18,
  109–10; and government, 8, 10, 38,
  106; and governing, xxxi, xxxv, 9,
  41, 104, 107, 112; danger, perceptions of, 20–23, 67; and leadership,
  19; nature, perceptions of, 22, 67,
  136–37; and participation, 19–20,
  238, and power, 7; and regulation,
  108; and resource scarcity, 38; and
  religious institutions, 83–86; and
  rights movements, 41–42, 63–64,
  102, 235, 237; splits in, 238–39;
  and World Council of Churches,
  43–44; *see also* egalitarianism, rise
  of, and equality of condition
egalitarianism, rise of: 32, 50, 63–97;
  and academic standards, 233–41;
  consequences of, xxx–xxxv, 10–
  11, 23–27, 60–61, 111–13; influence
  in presidential elections, 151–54
Eisenhower, Dwight, xxii, 43, 45, 49,
  60

Eizenstat, Stuart E., 165
environmentalism, 74–81
Equal Rights Amendment, 61
equality: meanings differ, xviii, 107, 232
equality before the law, 171, 173, 177, 188, 232
equality of condition (result, outcome), xix, xxx, 6–7, 17, 24–25, 27, 32, 35, 38–39, 41–42, 45–46, 50, 60–61, 103–104, 117, 126, 171–73, 175–79, 182–83, 187–88, 193, 195, 201, 204, 230, 232, 236–37, 239–40; see also egalitarianism
equality of opportunity, xix, xxx, 6–7, 17–18, 27, 32–35, 38–39, 41–42, 46, 61, 103, 117, 171–75, 176, 182–83, 186, 188, 193, 204, 232, 236–37; see also individualism
"the establishment", xxix, 33, 103, 111, 118, 176, 238

Falwell, Jerry, 89
Farah, Barbara G., 57
fatalism: and authority, 11; and blame, 16; and inequality, 17; and leadership, 19; and manipulation, 7; and participation, 19–20; and resource scarcity, 18
Feinstein, Diane, 165
Feldman, Stanley, 14
feminism: 63; and abortion, 89–91; and gender equality, 86–89, and pornography, 91–94
Ferraro, Geraldine, 156
Fife, John, 85–86
Ford, Gerald, 42
Forrester, Jay, xviii
Frank, Barney, 165
Freeman, Alan, 183
Freeman, Jo, 58

Gardner, Gerald, 148
Goldsmith, Judy, 89

Goldwater, Barry, 124
Gouge, William M., 38
Groucho's law, 222–26

Halevy, David, 119–20
Hall, Ridgway, 81
Hamilton, Alexander, 36–37
Harries, Owen, 24
Hart, Gary, 43
Hartz, Louis, 30
Hayek, Frederich von, 215
Haywood, Carl, 80
Heidepriem, Nikki, 196
hierarchy: and authority, 6, 11, 117; and blame, 16; danger, perceptions of, 20–21; and defense policy, 25; and economic growth, 18; and envy, 15–16, 103; as exclusive, 12; and fairness, 17–18, 110; and governing, 107, 112; and inequality, 6, 15, 17, 103; as inclusive, 12; and leadership, 18–19; as maintaining differences, xxix; nature, perceptions of, 22, 137; and regulation, 14, 108, 117; and resource scarcity, 18; United States, weakness in, xxix
Hochschild, Jennifer L., 181–91
Holdren, John, 134
Hood, Thomas, 78
Hoover, J. Edgar, 176
Humphrey, Hubert H., 23, 45, 49, 59, 159
Hunter, S., 147
Huntington, Samuel, 9–10

individualism: xxix; alliance with egalitarianism, xxx; and authority, 6–7, 9, 11, 117; and blame, 16–17, 103; dangers, perceptions of, 20–21, 103; and defense policy, 25; and economic growth, 18; and envy, 15; and fairness, 17–18, 109–10; and governing, 112; and gov-

ernment, 107; and inequality, 17; and leadership, 19, 103; nature, perceptions of, 22, 137; and participation, 20; and power, 7; and regulation, 108, 117; and resource scarcity, 18
Iyengar, Shento, 127–32

Jackson, Andrew, xxx, 35–36, 38–39, 41, 46
Jackson, Henry, 23, 45, 59, 159
Jackson, Jesse, 162, 165–66, 221
Jefferson, Thomas, 36–37, 41, 46
Jennings, M. Kent, 50–51, 53, 57, 165
Jews: oppressed, xiv; oppressed, decertification as, xx–xxii
Johnson, Lyndon, 59, 124, 151
Joseph, Lawrence, 126–27

Kalt, Joseph, 21
Kennedy, Anthony M., 210
Kennedy, Edward, 194, 201
Kennedy, John F., xxviii, 43, 59
Kennedy, Kerry, 65
Kennedy, Robert, 65
Kinder, Donald R., 127–32
Koch, Ed, 221
Kristol, Irving, 101

Ladd, Anthony, 78
Lange, Oscar, 215
left/right distinction, xxix, 3, 8, 35–36, 116–17
Lewis, Neil A., 233–34
liberal/conservative distinction, xxviii–xxix, 3, 8, 13–14, 116–117, 200–201
Lichter, Linda S., 123–26
Lichter, S. Robert, 123–26, 148
Lincoln, Abraham, xxviii, 41
Lindblom, Charles E., 5, 45, 184
Linsky, Martin, 121–22
Lippman, Walter, 128
Luker, Kristin, 90

MacKinnon, Catherine, 93
Malchick, Alexander, 219
Marshall, Thurgood, 194
Matthews, Christopher, 219
McClosky, Herbert, 52
McClure, James, 80
media bias, xxxiii, 42, 65, 75, 84–85, 115–132, 237; measuring, 123–27; influence of, 127–32
Metz, Mary, 191
Metzger, Bruce (Reverend), 87
Miller, Warren E., 50–51, 58, 165
minorities: certification as oppressed, xiv–xviii; decertification as oppressed, xx–xxii; elites search for oppressed, xii–xiv, xvi–xix, xxii–xxv; oppressed, xii–xxvi; *see also* "oppressed, search for"
minorityness: making of, xix–xx; as state of mind, xxiii
Mondale, Walter, 118, 151–52, 154
Monroe, James, 46
Morse, Rob, 220
Myrdal, Gunnar, 187–88

Nader, Ralph, 197, 207
Niebuhr, H. Richard, 228
Nixon, Richard, 151

O'Conner, Robert, 146
Ogbu, John, 181, 191–92
oppressed, search for, 65–66, 111, 160–61, 232
Oppression Gap, Growth of (GOG), xiii–xiv, xxii–xxv

Pertschuk, Michael, 197, 201, 206–7
Polanyi, Michael, xvi
political cultures: alliances (coalitions), 6, 11, 19, 26–27, 30–35, 38–41, 46–47, 103, 108–9, 236–37; alliances, America and Europe compared, 31–35, 108; conflict among, 6, 10, 12, 16, 31–32, 34, 41–47,

102; *see also,* egalitarianism, fatalism, hierarchy, individualism
political parties: and change, 44–46;
conflict within, 50–62; transformation of, 49, 53, 57, 59–62, 104–6
Polsby, Nelson, 164
Popper, Karl, 184
poverty: and Catholic bishops, 227–
32; poverty programs, xxiv; preferential option for the poor, 227–32
Powell, Lewis, 193
preferences: as aids to calculation,
13–14; biases, role of, 5–14; and
cultural biases, 4; formation of, 3–
13; and social relations, 4
presidential elections: absence of issues, 152–54; media bias in, 154–
57; media influence in, 154–57;
negative campaigning in, 152–54

Quayle, Dan, 156

Reagan, Ronald, 44, 53, 64, 118, 152–
55, 193, 204
regulation, of land use, 81–83; *see
also* egalitarianism, hierarchy, individualism
Reisman, David, 220
Republican party: alliances in, 8;
conservatism in, 44–46; hierarchy
in, xxviii, xxxiv, 49, 53; individualism in, xxviii, xxxiv, 49, 53; transformation in, xxxiv; women, role
of, 57
revolt of the turtles, 160–63
risk: perceptions of, 20–23; perceptions, rival theories of: cultural
theory, 135–39, 142—43; economic theory, 135; knowledge theory, 20, 134, 138–39; personality
theory, 134, 139, 141—42; political
theory, 135, 139, 142
Robertson, Pat, 165
Robinson, Michael, 116

Robinson-Haynes, Ellen, 217
Rockefeller, Nelson, 49
Rogers, Darrell, 97
Roosevelt, Eleanor, 153
Roosevelt, Franklin D., xxviii, 59
Rosen, S. Elly, xxii
Rothman, Stanley, 123–26, 148
Rycroft, Robert, 147

Sabatier, Paul, 147
Salter, Stephanie, 220
Savage, James, 37
Schaetzel, Wendy, 197, 201, 206–7
Schattschneider, Elmer, 158
Scheuplein, Robert, 217
Schwarz, Michiel, 4
Sedgwick Jr., Theodore, 39
Shafer, Byron, 159
Shawn, William, xvii
Smith, Adam, 108
Sniderman, Paul, 13, 162, 181
social democracy, 32–22, 41
Solow, Andrew, 75
Souter, David H., xxx
Sperling, Susan, 72–74, 236
Starr, Chauncy, 149
state capitalism, 32–33
Stinchcombe, Arthur L., 189
Stover, Gerry, 75

Taney, Roger, 39
Taylor, D. Garth, 189
Thompson, J., 33, 188–89
Thompson, Michael, 4
Thompson-Tuden matrix, 33, 188–89
totalitarianism, 33
Trilling, Lionel, 101
Truman, Harry, xxviii, 49, 59, 159
Tuden, A., 33, 188–89
Tyler, John, 46

Vance, Cyrus, 122
Van Liere, Kent, 78

Walker, Alice, 88
Wallis, Jim, 85
Weakland, Rembert (Archbishop), 85
Weber, Max, 107
Weinberger, Caspar, 24
Wertheimer, Fred, 208
Williams, Bruce A., xxxiii
Woodward, C. Vann, 110–11
ways of life: *See* cultures

World Council of Churches, 68, 83–84
worry syndrome, of Americans, 223–24

Yathay, Pin, 238

Zupan, Mark, 21